THE FLAG HERITAGE FOUNDATION MONOGRAPH AND TRANSLATION SERIES
PUBLICATION No. 9

SYMBOLS IN SERVICE TO THE STATE

FLAGS AND OTHER SYMBOLS IN

SOVIET CIVIL RELIGION

BY ANNE M. PLATOFF, PhD FF

An adaptation of the doctoral thesis in history submitted as part of the requirements for the PhD degree at the University of Leicester (UK), 2021.

DANVERS, MASSACHUSETTS

2021

THE FLAG HERITAGE FOUNDATION MONOGRAPH AND TRANSLATION SERIES

The Flag Heritage Foundation was established in 1971 in order, among other purposes, "to collect, organize, and disseminate information concerning all aspects of flags and related symbols" and "to promote wide public knowledge of the rich history of flags which fosters international understanding and respect for national heritage." It is a registered charity in the Commonwealth of Massachusetts.

The Flag Heritage Foundation Monograph and Translation Series was established in 2009 to publish monographs on flags and related subjects, and to translate and publish in English works previously appearing only in languages inaccessible to many scholars. This is the ninth publication in the Series.

Price: US $20 (plus shipping)

Non-profit organizations, libraries, and vexillological and heraldic organizations
may obtain copies *gratis* or at a reduced rate – inquire of the Foundation.

Table of Contents

In Memoriam – David F. Phillips (1944-2020)

The Flag Heritage Foundation mourns the passing of Series Editor David F. Phillips. David Frank Phillips II (his full name, which he rarely used) was born September 15, 1944. He passed away on March 26, 2020.

David was a longtime member of the Board of Trustees. In this role he was a constant initiator. He was always full of proposals to pursue book projects, to make the most of our collections, to find the best professionals to support our work, and in general to lead the Foundation forward. He was equally adept as an editor, as a researcher, and as a writer. His sense of organization was consonant with his background in law and librarianship. He worked very smoothly with the other Trustees, bringing project proposals that were so fully developed that unanimous endorsement was always a formality. Although his first love was heraldry, he drew respect as a scholar in vexillology as well. All his work was to a very high standard. One could see David as a formidable combination of scholar, editor, and administrator.

David's own publications include, as author, "Emblems of the Indian States" (2011) and "The Double Eagle" (2014), and as editor and lead contributor, "Japanese Heraldry and Heraldic Flags" (2018). All three appear in this series and are available on Amazon. David was a frequent contributor to the British journal *The Heraldic Craftsman* and was one of only two writers granted craft membership in the Society of Heraldic Arts, in England. He also published outside the fields of heraldry and vexillology.

To learn more about David, please see the full obituary on the FHF website at https://www.flagheritagefoundation.org/news/david-phillips-1944-2020.

Dedications and Acknowledgements

Dedications

Soviet children were taught about the 'Lenin path' – the lifelong journey that they would undertake to learn the precepts of Marxism-Leninism and contribute their labour to building a socialist society. Likewise, scholars embark on a 'learning path' through which they develop the skills they need to contribute to our body of knowledge. This book is dedicated to the three primary guides who pointed out the path, escorted me along the way, and helped me reach my destination.

To Dr. Whitney Smith

Whitney founded the field of vexillology, the systematic study of flags. When he called me in 1985 and invited me to spend a week in the archives with him to research the flags of my home state, I had no idea I was embarking on a decades-long journey. He encouraged me to conduct research, to present at conferences, and to publish my work. More importantly, he demonstrated that my fascination with flags could be channelled into scholarly work in the fields of vexillology and history.

To Dr. Scot Guenter

Of all the presentations that I viewed at my first flag conference in 1985, Scot's is the one that has stayed with me to this day. He demonstrated how one object, such as a flag flown over the US Capitol building, could tell us something about our society and ourselves. Scot's scholarship exposed me to new ways of examining the phenomenon of flags and introduced me to the concept of civil religion. His friendship and encouragement kept me moving forward and reminded me to 'Keep studying those flags!'

To Dr. Zoe Knox

The journey to the PhD is long and the path is sometimes difficult to follow. Having an experienced guide really makes a difference. I am extremely grateful that Zoe was willing to mentor a student whose interests, I am sure, seemed a bit esoteric. Her willingness to accept the challenge, her sage advice along the way, and her respectful honesty when I needed to be guided back to the proper path really made a difference. She helped me adapt to and flourish in a new system of higher education and provided the type of personalised instruction that I never received through the formal coursework of my other graduate degrees.

Acknowledgements

Throughout the years of my PhD journey, I was fortunate to have the support and encouragement from my family, friends, and colleagues. My appreciation is extended to all of them, but some deserve special mention here.

University of California, Santa Barbara (UCSB) Slavic Program:

Special thanks to the faculty of UCSB's Slavic Program who loaned me research materials and suggested topics to investigate – Larry McLellan, Katia McClain, Sara Pankenier-Weld, Sven Spieker. I am especially grateful to Larry for the many years that he has allowed me to sit in on his Russian-language classes and for working with me to refine my translations.

UCSB Library:

Thank you to the staff of the Interlibrary Loan Unit, the Librarians Association of the University of California (Santa Barbara Chapter), and to all my Library colleagues who have offered encouragement along the way. I am especially appreciative of the colleagues who gave assistance and feedback on research and writing, or who allowed flexibility in my work schedule in support of my PhD work – Tom Brittnacher, Richard Caldwell, Jane Faulkner, Chuck Huber, Lorna Lueck, Rebecca Metzger, Chizu Morihara, Eunice Schroeder.

University of Leicester:

I would also like to thank Dr. Andrew Johnstone, my second supervisor, for his guidance and advice throughout the years of this project. Thanks also to the faculty and staff of the Doctoral College and the School of History, Politics and International Relations for the support I received during my studies.

Vexillological Community

The community of flag scholars is small and at times seems more like a family than an academic cohort. I am indebted to all the vexillologists from around the world who have accepted my work and encouraged me along the way. Special thanks to Željko Heimer for inspiring me to pursue new options to complete my PhD. Over the years I have presented my work at numerous meetings of the North American Vexillological Association (NAVA), the International Congresses of Vexillology (ICVs), and at a meeting of the Flag Institute in the UK. The questions from the audience and the feedback I received on my work have been an asset for my continued growth as a vexillologist and historian. I am especially grateful to the leadership and membership of the North American Vexillological Association throughout the years. The recognitions that I have received from NAVA and from the *Fédération internationale des associations vexillologiques* (*FIAV*), often based upon NAVA's recommendation, have demonstrated to me that my work is valued. I am especially grateful to NAVA for two grants which helped fund the research for my PhD thesis: the Scot M. Guenter Dissertation Grant (2017-2019) and the Devereaux D. Cannon, Jr. Grant for Research in Vexillology (2016-2017).

Imagery

Many thanks to the following individuals and institutions for assistance with imagery:

- Lawrence Kaplan for images from his collection of banknotes;

- David Phillips for his collection of postal covers;

- Nicholas A. Artimovich, II for sharing images of his Soviet postage stamps;

- Wende Museum of the Cold War (Culver City, California) for allowing me to spend a day examining artefacts from their collections;

- Ken Martinez for photographing the Soviet Banner of Victory in the Central Museum of the Armed Forces (Moscow);

- Tom Brittnacher for assisting me with maps.

Formatting Notes

This book is an adaptation of a thesis submitted for a PhD from a British University. In the narrative text British spellings have been retained, and the author has used the British system for quotation marks – single quotes (' ') for the initial quotation and double quotes (" ") for quotations within a quotation. Likewise, the author has used the British style for punctuation within a quotation. For questions of style not covered above, the book generally uses the *Chicago Manual of Style*.

Image (figure) numbering follows the order in which the images occur in the main text. For discussions of the colour images, see the referenced page in the text. A full image list at the end of the book includes source information for all images.

Transliteration Note

This book uses the Library of Congress (LC) transliteration scheme to convert the Russian Cyrillic to the Latin alphabet. However, when a variant spelling occurs in a quotation or the publication information for cited sources, the original transliteration has been preserved. For letters where the LC system uses ligatures to show where letter combinations stand for one Cyrillic letter the transliteration in this work has omitted the ligature and capitalised only the initial letter (e.g. Chekhov). The LC transliteration systems differ for each language. All transliteration of Ukrainian and Belarusian use the related LC tables including diacritics. For access to the transliteration tables for various languages, see https://www.loc.gov/catdir/cpso/roman.html. Transliterated words are presented in italics in the main text but are only italicised in endnotes and the bibliography where appropriate for the citation style.

Translation Note

Unless otherwise noted all translations are the author's own.

Abbreviations, Initialisms, and Contractions

BSE	*Bol'shaia sovetskaia entsiklopediia*
	Great Soviet Encyclopaedia
CPSU	Communist Party of the Soviet Union
GSE	Great Soviet Encyclopedia
GULAG	*Glavnoe upravlenie lagerei*
	Main Administration of Camps
GUM	*Gosudarstvennyi universal'nyi magazin*
	State Department Store
kolkhoz	*kollektivnoe khoziastvo*
	collective enterprise, used to mean collective farm
Komsomol	*Kommunisticheskii soiuz molodezhi*
	Young Communist League
KPSS	*Kommunisticheskaia Partiia Sovetskogo Soiuza*
	Communist Party of the Soviet Union
MASSR / MASSR	*Moldavskaia Avtonomnaia Sovetskaia Sotsialisticheskaia Respublika*
	Moldavian Autonomous Soviet Socialist Republic
MSSR / MSSR	*Moldavskaia Sovetskaia Sotsialisticheskaia Respublika*
	Moldavian Soviet Socialist Republic
RRMC	Republic's Revolutionary Military Council
RSFSR / RSFSR	*Rossiiskaia Sovetskaia Federativnaia Sotsialisticheskaia Respublika*
	Russian Soviet Federative Socialist Republic
RVSR	*Revoliutsionnyi Voennyi Sovet Respubliki*
	Republic's Revolutionary Military Council (RRMC)
SSR / SSR	*Sovetskaia Sotsialisticheskaia Respublika*
	Soviet Socialist Republic
SSSR	*Soiuz Sovetskikh Sotsialisticheskikh Respublik*
	Union of Soviet Socialist Republics (USSR)
UPA	*Ukraïns'ka povstans'ka armiia*
	Ukrainian Insurgent Army
USSR	Union of Soviet Socialist Republics
VLKSM	*Vsesoiuznyi leninskii kommunisticheskii soiuz molodezhi*
	All-Union Leninist Young Communist League
UN	United Nations

Chapter 1
Icons of Identity: Civil Religion and Symbols

A civil religion is a set of beliefs and attitudes that explain the meaning and purpose of any given political society in terms of its relationship to a transcendent, spiritual reality, that are held by the people generally of that society, and that are expressed in public rituals, myths, and symbols.[1]

– Ellis West

Traditionally, the opening ceremony of any Olympic games begins with a 'Parade of Nations', during which participants from each country enter the stadium following a member of their delegations who has been given the honour of carrying their national flag. Those flags are often the most easily recognisable symbols of the countries that they represent. In the modern era flags serve as the primary icons of nationhood and national identity. From an early age, citizens learn to associate a piece of cloth bearing a specific design with the country in which they live. Flags are respected (or sometimes disrespected) according to set traditions, practices, protocols, or laws in each society. It seems that in the context of patriotic culture the concepts of 'flag' and 'country' are so deeply connected that, more than any other national symbol, the flag serves as a sacred totem for its nation. When someone shows disrespect to, or *desecrates*, a national flag, citizens with a strong emotional attachment to their national banner often interpret it as an insult and affront to the entire country. How is it that a piece of cloth has become so central to the idea of statehood? What historical, political, and sociological processes led to this connection, and how does it relate to an individual's sense of national identity? These questions are core to the field of vexillology, the scholarly study of flags. While this study will address multiple forms of symbols used in the Soviet Union, it was inspired by the author's lifelong interest in flags and is intended as an exercise in academic historical vexillology.

Although flags have been used for centuries,[2] the current term for this field of study appeared in print for the first time in an article written by Whitney Smith in 1959.[3] The word combines the Latin *vexillum* (flag) with the Greco-English suffix *logy* to create a new term defined as 'the study of flags'. Smith offered variant definitions in his many books and articles. In *The Bibliography of Flags of Foreign Nations* (1965) it was described as 'the study of flags and their history', while in *The Flag Book of the United States* (1970) he called vexillology 'the analysis of flags and their usage in different countries'.[4] Five years later, in *Flags Through the Ages and Across the World* (1975), Smith defined vexillology as 'the scientific study of the history, symbolism, and usage of flags or, by extension, any interest in flags in general'.[5] Use of the word 'scientific' in this context stresses that the study of flags should be scholarly, systematic, and methodical. In *Flags and Arms Across the World* (1980) he described it as 'the study of flag history and symbolism'.[6] All definitions suggest that the field of flag studies is multidisciplinary and rooted in both the social sciences and humanities. Vexillology has evolved to be multifaceted and extends beyond flags to study a wide range of symbols. This is because national flags are just one type of political symbol used in modern states. They exist as part of a gallery of national symbols that are used in the cultures of patriotism in each country. Modern nations typically have at least three official (*de jure*) national symbols – a flag, a coat of arms (or emblem), and an anthem. Within these, visual elements or symbolic concepts may be repeated in multiple symbols and are sometimes used separately. In addition, in most countries there are *de facto* symbols that also serve as national symbols.

A political scientist by training, Whitney Smith produced one of the first PhD theses dedicated to the newly formed field in 1968. He not only demonstrated that flags are worthy objects for scholarly study, but also suggested a path forward in the development of the study of political symbols.[7] Smith clearly envisioned vexillology as multidisciplinary, drawing from a variety of other scholarly disciplines including history, sociology, communication, and more. As a consulting vexillologist and publisher he became recognised as the world's leading flag scholar and encouraged others to contribute to the development of the field. Since the publication of Smith's seminal thesis, other flag scholars have followed suit producing PhD theses on vexillological topics in a variety of fields. A notable example was Scot M. Guenter's definitive study of the American flag as a key element in American civil religion.[8] An American Studies scholar and social historian, Guenter has also explored the civil religious aspect of flags and other symbols across multiple cultures in his later works. The prominent British flag scholar, William Crampton, wrote his PhD thesis in government on the role of flags and other non-verbal symbols in the formation and maintenance of national identity.[9] Further advancing the field, Croatian sociologist Željko Heimer explored the nature of vexillology as a social science in his thesis focusing on military flags and identity in his country.[10] These theses, among others, have all demonstrated that flags and national symbols are a valid topic for academic study in a wide range of academic disciplines.

While both Smith and Crampton touched upon the national symbols of the USSR in their theses, neither fully analysed the role of those symbols in that society. Smith focused on how the Soviet usage of symbols appeared to be a digression from Marxist theory, because they were essentially emulating how the aristocracy used symbols as emblems of their power. In Smith's analysis, this was necessary because symbols have become an essential tool for the administration of any modern state. Crampton also looked at the origins of the Soviet symbol system, focusing on the use of revolutionary symbols as communicants of change. Neither thesis, though, discussed the pattern of symbol usage in the USSR in the latter Soviet period, their role in civil religious practice in the country, or how citizens encountered the symbols. This work aims to fill that void and contribute to the in-depth historical analyses of political symbolism as it investigates the role of flags and other symbols in the civil religion of the Soviet Union. An analysis of these symbols will highlight the messages that those in power communicated to their citizens, how national symbols were used to convey ideology, and the critical role of symbols in civil religion.[11]

Like previous works by vexillologists, this study is intended as a further demonstration of the relevance of flag studies to the analysis of the culture of patriotism in modern nation states. While it will examine the full range of symbols used in the Soviet Union, a focus on flags is justified as in many cultures this is the national symbol most frequently encountered. The intent of the book is to look at Soviet national symbols and civil religious practice from the perspective of the average citizen. What were they taught about Soviet symbols and how did they encounter them in their daily lives? While it may never be possible to really know what people thought about the symbols, examining the rhetoric associated with various representations of Soviet identity should at least give an indication of how citizens were taught to interpret them.

One might ask why it is important to study symbol usage in a now defunct country. This is a fair question, but it neglects to consider the importance of the entire field of history in the body of knowledge. History teaches us about the nature of human society, about the patterns of behaviour that flow through those societies over time, and about how the relationships between those who govern and those who are governed evolve and progress. Perhaps this last aspect is the most interesting lesson that we can learn from the history of Soviet political symbolism. The power structure of the USSR was such, that the use of symbols in that country could be perceived as an almost direct communication from the Kremlin to the citizenry. While it is often easier to focus on those in power, it is important to view that relationship from the perspective of the people themselves. How did the average Soviet citizen encounter the symbols of their country in daily life and what messages were conveyed to them from those in power through those symbols? That is the focus of this study. It is also interesting to note an important difference between standard religions and civil religion. Like many established religions, the underlying philosophy of Soviet civil religion was successfully exported and instilled in countries around the world. This makes the Soviet Union an enlightening case study because their efforts to export Marxism-Leninism also resulted in the dispersal of civil religious symbolism. However, while religions grow and evolve over time, they rarely collapse in the way that communism seemed to do when the Soviet Union broke up. This is because civil religions can be closely tied to specific political systems or regimes. Therefore, as belief systems they are more vulnerable to the political ebbs and flows of societies, especially when those societies undergo extreme changes in orientation.

Methodology

As a historical assessment of the use of national symbols, this study is multidisciplinary and draws upon the literature of a variety of fields including history, political science, sociology, anthropology, communication, education, and religious studies. While the field of heraldry has a long tradition as an auxiliary field of history, vexillology has benefited from the trend of interdisciplinary studies that blossomed in the latter half of the twentieth century. Although primarily focused on national symbols in the historical context of the Soviet Union, this research requires a broader perspective through which to examine symbols as social constructs. For this reason, it will examine emblems and imagery as they were used in the civil religion of the Soviet Union and provide an analysis of how various symbols were used in the patriotic culture of the country. Civil religion offers a useful lens through which to understand how symbols were used in the USSR, as the psychological, social, and emotional relationship that people have with their homelands can sometimes be analogous to a religious experience.[12]

From the fields of political science and sociology, the book will touch on identity studies, particularly the processes through which citizens form their own sense of national identity and develop a personal connection to their country. When studying the development of national identity in children, especially amongst the youngest citizens, social scientists have used children's recognition of, and opinions about, flags and political imagery as indicators. A review of their results, as well as a discussion of Soviet pedagogy, will demonstrate that there was a deliberate use of symbols in the enculturation process through which children in the USSR were taught the values of their country. Two key concepts explored in this work – civil religion and banal nationalism – are widely cited in the literature of identity studies, as they offer useful perspectives from which to view the phenomenon of national identity. These concepts provide a lens through which to study the role of symbols in the process of identity formation and how prolonged exposure to patriotic imagery reinforces political enculturation throughout the lifetime of the average citizen. These are key issues in any study of national symbols.

One other aspect of methodology, which is both interdisciplinary and connected to the concepts of civil religion and banal nationalism, is the idea of symbols as a means of communication. Messages conveyed by national symbols are a form of information transmission from those in power to the citizenry. Throughout the history of the USSR, this communication was often conveyed through secondary agents such as formal publishing, officially sanctioned artwork, and state programmes of propaganda and agitation. Thomas A. Sebeok, a leading theorist in the field of semiotics and linguistics, offered the following definitions relevant to this study:

Sign	something that stands for something else[13]
Symbol	sign form that stands arbitrarily or conventionally for its referent[14]
Icon	sign form which stimulates its referent in some way[15]
Signal	sign that naturally or conventionally (artificially) triggers some reaction on the part of a receiver[16]

Therefore, in Sebeok's taxonomy, symbols, icons, and signals are all types of signs. However, in the literature about civil religion and national symbols the word 'symbol' is used more generically and clearly incorporates all four of the ideas conveyed by these definitions. In examining national symbols, the key is to remember the functions they serve as tools of communication: how they represent ideals of the state and serve as a representation of the nation, the way that they stimulate the observer, and the reaction that is triggered when a citizen views the symbols of their country.

Another useful theoretical model would be to address the topic through the viewpoint of art history, as scholars in this area regularly study how images are interpreted. An example can be found in Erwin Panofsky's classic 1955 essay 'Iconography and Iconology'. In this approach the focus is on interpretation from the perspective of the viewer, as much as it is on the intent of the creator. Panofsky proposed three levels or layers of interpretation, each of which contributes to the conveyance of meaning from creator to viewer. The most basic level, which he described as 'a pre-iconographical description of the work of art', focuses on the '*primary or natural subject matter*, subdivided into *factual* and *expressional*'. This level of interpretation relies on the viewer's '*practical experience* (familiarity with *objects* and *events*)'. In other words, the viewer perceives an image (and the artistic motif therein) and processes what forms they are seeing and the expressional qualities of the scene.[17] The next level of interpretation, which Panofsky described as 'iconography', is concerned with the '*secondary or conventional subject matter*'. Interpretation at this level relies on the viewer's '*knowledge of literary sources* (familiarity with specific *themes* and *concepts*)'.[18] In this layer of meaning, the viewer first recognises the primary or natural subject matter and then correlates it to their own cultural knowledge to draw meaning from the image. In this sense, Panofsky's iconography relates to Sebeok's broader definition of *sign*.[19] Finally, Panofsky called his third level 'iconology' – the process through which the viewer synthesises their interpretation in order to find '*intrinsic meaning* or *content*, constituting the world of *"symbolical" values*'.[20] This is the deepest form of interpretation, as it relies on 'synthetic intuition (familiarity with the *essential tendencies of the human mind*)'. Panofsky explained that interpretation at this level draws upon the 'history of *cultural symptoms* or *"symbols"* in general (insight into the manner in which, under varying historical conditions, *essential tendencies of the human mind* were expressed by specific *themes* and *concepts*)'.[21]

6

When thinking about national symbols as a form of communication, it seems obvious that in order for the underlying message to be understood by the recipient, they must be able to process the imagery at an iconographical level, and ideally at the iconological level. As will be demonstrated in Chapter 3 of this book, the cultural background necessary for the former is taught as part of a society's educational system in childhood, while the latter is attained as the viewer becomes more sophisticated in their understanding of societal norms and values. Understanding how people perceive and understand symbols is important, as it helps to bring clarity to how images are perceived, processed, and interpreted when people encounter them in their environments. Using Panofsky's model, it would have been interesting to compare the interpretations of a visitor to the Soviet Union with those of a citizen, when viewing the symbols of the USSR. A tourist would have recognised the significance of the state flag and arms as national symbols but lacked the cultural background to interpret the symbols as intended. The visitor's own cultural background would have caused them to interpret these symbols not only as foreign, but perhaps as something ominous if they had been socialised to perceive communism as a threat. In contrast, we can assume that a citizen of the Soviet Union or another socialist state who saw the combined hammer and sickle emblem not only recognised the tools themselves, but also applied their cultural knowledge to remember what those tools represented, and then synthesised meaning through the process. This section has introduced just a few examples of the various approaches that can be used to study national symbols. Throughout the book, theoretical models will be presented and applied to explore the role of flags and symbols in the civil religion of the Soviet Union.

Periodisation

The history of the Soviet Union is often presented by emphasising the developmental stages of the country, starting with the Bolshevik Revolution of 1917 and concluding with the breakup of the USSR in 1991. The early period, from the October Revolution through the formation of the Soviet Union in December 1922, was a period of upheaval during which the Bolsheviks seized and consolidated power, counter-revolutionary elements were suppressed, Soviet ideology was propagated and traditional religions were repressed, and the very foundations of the society were rebuilt. In the next period new economic policies were put in place, Vladimir Il'ich Lenin died and was succeeded by Iosef Vissarionovich Stalin, five-year plans were initiated to promote economic and technological development, and the period of 'High Stalinism' was characterised by repression of real, or perceived, challenges to the status quo. Next came a period characterised by large-scale destruction, societal trauma, and the ultimate victory of Soviet forces during the Great Patriotic War (World War II), the laborious efforts to rebuild the country, and the initial years of the Cold War which pitted the Soviet Union against its former western allies. Following the death of Stalin in 1953, the nature of Soviet leadership changed. The Khrushchev era (1953-1964) was marked by a period in which reforms were enacted to try to counter the excesses of Stalinism. The Brezhnev years (1964-1982) later became characterised as 'the era of stagnation' due to the decline in economic growth in the country. However, it was also a period in which the standard of living increased and Party leaders perceived Soviet society as having reached maturity. The 1980s saw three different leaders, the reforms of the Gorbachev era, and climaxed with the eventual breakup of the Soviet Union in 1991.[22]

Soviet sources usually defined the era of *mature*, or *developed*, socialism in the USSR as the period from the 1960s forward. In the philosophy of Marxism-Leninism, *socialism* was just the first stage of *communism*. As the Soviet Union advanced in its development, the society was believed to be progressing toward the ultimate goal – attainment of *communism*, in this sense explained as 'a stage or phase in the development of this postcapitalist formation that is more advanced than socialism'.[23] In 1936, Stalin declared that the USSR had achieved socialism and was well on its way to reaching communism. His successor, Nikita Sergeevich Khrushchev, suggested that communism would be achieved in the 1970s. However, Khrushchev's successor, Leonid Il'ich Brezhnev, recognised that it would be necessary to extend the period of 'building socialism' while still emphasising the many advances that had been made in the country since the Bolshevik Revolution. Therefore, the General Secretary introduced the phrase 'developed socialist society' in his report to XXIV Congress of the Communist Party of the Soviet Union (CPSU)[24] in April 1971. Brezhnev backdated the origin for the idea of 'developed socialism' to 1918, crediting Lenin with the concept. In the speech, the General Secretary noted:

> An immeasurably higher level has been achieved in the national economy, in socialist social relations and in the culture and consciousness of the broad masses. The developed socialist society that V. I. Lenin spoke of in 1918 as the future of our country has been built by the selfless labor of Soviet people. This has made it possible for us to take up the practical accomplishment of the great tasks posed by the Party Program and by the Party's most recent Congresses – the creation of the material and technical base of communism.[25]

The *Great Soviet Encyclopedia* (*GSE*) explained that 'The main tendency in the development of the social structure of mature socialism is the gradual transition from class differentiation to social uniformity'.[26] Furthermore, it stressed that this stage of development was characterised by 'the dominance of Marxist-Leninist ideology and a high educational level and cultural level'.[27] Ideologically, this period of Soviet history is significant because it emphasised that the country had reached an important milestone in the development of a socialist society. In theory, *social uniformity* was meant not just to apply across classes, but also across ethnic groups so that the many peoples of the Soviet Union would perceive themselves as part of one group – the *Soviet people*.

For this study, the period of *mature socialism* is of special interest, not because of the level of economic development in the country, but because it was a relatively stable time in the country's history. It is during periods of stability that a more *normalised* form of civil religion emerges. This was the period when the society had moved beyond stressors such as the civil war, the excesses of Stalinism, and the trauma of World War II. When countries are facing challenges to their stability, the culture of patriotism takes on different characteristics. During times when a state is focused on an external threat, one might expect to see an increase in patriotic behaviour and the nature of that patriotism will likely be more intense than that seen during periods of stability.[28] This was certainly true in the Soviet Union during World War II, when resurgent Russian nationalism was effectively harnessed as a model for *Soviet* patriotism in the defence of the homeland. An example of a more *normalised* form could be found in how athletic talent was carefully cultivated so that sporting prowess, rather than military might, could serve as an international representation of the power and success of the USSR. Therefore, to get a glimpse at a *normalised* form of Soviet civil religion, the purported 'social uniformity' that the *GSE* cited as a characteristic of *mature socialism* makes this a particularly useful period for which to analyse the use of Soviet symbols. For this reason, this study will focus on the last three decades of the Soviet era when analysing source materials for the portrayal and interpretation of the symbols of the USSR.

Civil Religion: Definitions and Evolution

Before beginning a study of civil religion, it is useful to review the evolution of the concept. In his 1762 book, *On the Social Contract*, Swiss philosopher Jean-Jacques Rousseau examined the historical relationships between rulers, their people, and religion. Drawing upon examples from the classical era through the development of the Christian states Rousseau observed that, 'Considered in relation to society, which is either general or particular, religion can also be divided into two types, namely the religion of man and that of the citizen'. Rousseau described the first type as the religion of the Gospel, while the latter was specific to a single country. According to Rousseau the second type of religion, which he labelled 'civil religion', was what unified a people and differentiated them from citizens of other countries who might share the same faith. He cited the ways civil religion could unite the citizenry and how 'by making the homeland the object of the citizens' prayers, it teaches them that to serve the State is to serve its tutelary God'. According to Rousseau, a country's sovereign should establish a simple set of dogmas that would function as 'sentiments of sociability without which it is impossible to be a good citizen or a faithful subject'.[29]

In the centuries that followed Rousseau's writing, much changed in the geopolitical landscape. Near the end of the eighteenth century, the American and French revolutions ushered in a new era of nation states in which the people, and not a sovereign, determined the nature of civil society and national character. In its first century, the United States of America survived both a war to ensure its continued independence from Great Britain and a bloody civil war which threatened to tear the nation in two. These experiences influenced the American national character in such a way that, by the mid-twentieth century, there existed in the United States a unique culture that American sociologist Robert N. Bellah recognised as a form of Rousseau's concept of 'civil religion'. In the United States Bellah detected:

> … certain common elements of religious orientation that the great majority of Americans
> share. These have played a crucial role in the development of American institutions and still
> provide a religious dimension for the whole fabric of American life, including the political
> sphere. This public religious dimension is expressed in a set of beliefs, symbols, and rituals
> that I am calling the American civil religion.[30]

Bellah cited numerous examples of American political leaders invoking God's favour on the American state, but also noted that while undoubtedly there was a Christian background behind the character of American civil religion, there was also a secular aspect. He noted that civil religion in America had 'its own prophets and its own martyrs, its own sacred events and sacred places, [and] its own solemn rituals and symbols'.[31] Bellah's 1967 article not only ignited a lively debate among scholars in the US over the existence or non-existence of American civil religion, but it also prompted a renewed discussion of Rousseau's idea of civil religion within the context of modern nation states. The American example, unlike that suggested by Rousseau, had developed organically within American culture rather than as a deliberate strategy set forth by a sovereign. Following Bellah's reasoning, the secular nature of American civil religion is also a divergence from Rousseau's concept of how civil religion would be tied to a single religious tradition in each society.

In an edited volume from 1974, wherein American scholars discussed the nature of Bellah's concept of American civil religion, religious studies scholars Russell E. Richey and Donald G. Jones proposed five definitions of the term, based upon the debate in progress. The first defined civil religion as '*folk religion*'. Richey and Jones suggested that, 'by examining the actual life, ideas, values, ceremonies, and loyalties of the people, conclusions are drawn as to the existence and status of civil religion'. Further, they contended that:

> … civil religion in this sense emerges out of the ethos and history of the society and inevitably becomes an idolatrous faith competing with particularistic religions rooted in a reality and traditions transcending the common life of a people.[32]

Their second type of civil religion was the '*transcendent universal religion of the nation*'. For Richey and Jones, 'this civil religion stands in judgment over the folkways of the people'. They equated their third definition with '*religious nationalism*' or 'the religion of patriotism'. In this definition, the nation is 'not the church of national religion', but rather 'the object of adoration and glorification'. Richey and Jones noted that 'the nation takes on a sovereign and self-transcendent character'. Their fourth and fifth meanings were more specific to the American variety of civil religion in that they were identified as 'the *democratic faith*' and '*Protestant civic piety*'.[33] Building upon the new literature on the topic, political scientist Ellis M. West then proposed a neutral definition of the term in 1980:

> A civil religion is a set of beliefs and attitudes that explain the meaning and purpose of any given political society in terms of its relationship to a transcendent, spiritual reality, that are held by the people generally of that society, and that are expressed in public rituals, myths, and symbols.[34]

Furthermore, West suggested that,

> As such, civil religion is both a type or aspect of political culture and 'a special case of the religious symbol system, designed to perform a differentiated function which is the unique province of neither church nor state.'[35]

For scholars of civil religion, these new definitions can provide a valuable model for the study of similar phenomena in other countries. As this template is applied to the study of different societies, it will enable scholars to recognise patterns inherent to national cultures of patriotism and will identify ways in which civil religions vary between cultures.

An excellent model for writing about specific symbols through the lens of civil religion is Peter Gardella's book, *American Civil Religion: What Americans Hold Sacred*. Gardella discussed a variety of American symbols, both official and unofficial, analysing each as elements of American civil religion. Additional examples can be found in the works of Scot Guenter, who expanded his scope of civil religious study beyond the field of American studies. Guenter has examined the phenomenon of national symbols in diverse locations such as Micronesia and Singapore. His study of patriotic culture related to Singapore's national day provides valuable insight into the importance of trying to understand civil religion as it is experienced by the citizen participant. Guenter's description of his emotional reaction as a participant in the rituals associated with the National Day Parade extravaganza are illustrative of the power of civil religious ritual culture, even on foreign observers.[36]

It is important to recognise that the concept of civil religion is not without its critics. As evident by the debate in the United States, many critics have focused on the use of the word 'religion' in their criticism, citing that civil religion does not meet the definition of an established religion. This viewpoint, though, fails to recognise that the concept of religion, when viewed across cultures and disciplines, encompasses much more than traditional theistic religions. Emilio Gentile, a leading scholar in the study of fascism and totalitarianism as 'political religion', addressed this criticism by defining a religion as:

> ...a system of beliefs, myths and symbols which interpret and define the meaning and the goal of human existence, making the destiny of an individual and of the community dependant on their subordination to a supreme entity. This definition is related to an interpretation of religion as a phenomenon that expresses the dimension of the sacred as a human experience and, consequently, does not necessarily coincide with the dimension of the divine.[37]

According to Gentile, the key is to understand that political religions do not merely use religious analogies in their ideologies, but instead serve to fulfil the spiritual needs of their followers. Essentially, political religions seek to politicise the people's faith and use it for ideological purposes. It is also important to note that Gentile distinguished between *political religion* and *civil religion*. He explained that 'the concept of political religion does not refer solely to the institution of a system of beliefs, rites or symbols', in the way that civil religion is generally defined.[38] It is a broader term that encompasses the full breadth of authoritarianism and totalitarianism. While recognising that there is a lack of scholarly consensus about what exactly constitutes a *political religion*, the narrower concept of *civil religion* as it focuses on the three key elements of myth, ritual, and symbols, is a much better framework within which to analyse the use of symbols in the Soviet Union. This concept has enjoyed more acceptance across disciplines and has also been accepted for cross-cultural studies and comparisons. For this reason, *civil religion* will be used as the theoretical framework employed in this study.[39]

By the time that Bellah was prompting a discussion of civil religion in America, the developed world had polarised into two alliances led by the superpowers that emerged out of World War II. On one end of the spectrum was the United States of America, a multi-ethnic state formed from a mixture of Christian ethics and Enlightenment ideals, which championed itself as the 'leader of the free world'. On the other extreme was another multi-ethnic state – the Union of Soviet Socialist Republics. During the Cold War, these two countries were engaged in a conflict that manifested itself in many forms of competition including political posturing, a technology and arms race, and numerous proxy wars in which each country supported ideological surrogates in regional conflicts. As the discussion of civil religion developed, western scholars began to recognise that characteristics of civil religion were evident not only in the 'God-fearing' United States, but also in the 'godless' Soviet Union. These studies of Soviet civil religion typically focused on several themes: the analysis of Marxism-Leninism as a religion or civil religion, the ritual practice of Soviet civil religion, the 'Lenin cult', and the use of symbols. This book will complement existing works on Soviet civil religion in that the focus is on the messages that the regime conveyed to the citizens through symbols. It is important to remember that the purpose of Soviet civil religion was not just to instil a sense of patriotism or to prescribe a uniform standard of patriotic culture for the citizens of the USSR. More importantly, it was meant to create a unified sense of *Sovietness* among people from many different ethnic, linguistic, and religious groups distributed across a vast territory.

Some western historians have focused on why the Soviet Union broke apart, rather than why it stayed together for as long as it did.[40] It is tempting to conclude that once Gorbachev allowed citizens to openly criticise the state, this allowed long-suppressed nationalist movements to flourish leading to the eventual breakup of the Soviet Union. However, this type of reasoning overlooks the many economic and social factors that were inherent to the dissolution of the USSR. While nationalism was certainly a factor, especially in the Baltic republics and western Ukraine, in other former Soviet republics people have remembered the Soviet past more favourably. The legacies of Soviet civil religion illustrate that, at least in some regions of the former Soviet Union, there is a sense of nostalgia for the Soviet era. A thorough examination of the legacies of Soviet identity and civil religion is worthy of a dedicated study but is not possible within the scope of this publication. It is fascinating that, nearly three decades after the breakup of the Soviet Union, the symbolic legacy of Soviet civil religion has endured. This is a testament to the importance of symbols in the political culture of the USSR, and the role that those symbols played in people's sense of identity. Furthermore, it will be shown how this study of symbols in the Soviet Union can help us to better understand the role of symbols in modern political culture. As West suggested in his definition of civil religion, it was through the combined use of national myths, patriotic rituals, and symbols that identities were created and reinforced.[41] National symbols were an essential part of the process.

Soviet history offers a unique context to study the importance of symbols within the phenomenon of civil religion. While the civil religions of many countries developed incrementally over time, the civil religion of the Soviet Union was forged in a relatively short period. Many aspects of Soviet civil religion were specifically designed to replace elements of Russian Orthodoxy; others were unique to the practice of Marxism-Leninism in the USSR. In addition, the symbols of Soviet civil religion were much more widely present in the material culture of the country than in other nations. In their everyday life, Soviet citizens constantly encountered political symbols – in their homes, in their workplaces, and in many other places they visited. The symbols were meant to serve as a constant reminder of their identity as Soviet citizens, their place in that society, their obligations to the Soviet Motherland, as well as the goals and ambitions of the Soviet state. As in many countries, the primary purpose of civil religion in the USSR was to create a sense of Soviet identity among a population comprised of many different ethnic and linguistic groups. Much of the country's culture of patriotism focused on unifying the people and giving them a common purpose – the building of communism. Finally, the example of Soviet civil religion is especially interesting, not because it provided a sense of unity during the decades of Soviet rule, but because in the end it failed to provide a cohesive sense of comradeship when the people in different Soviet republics were finally allowed to express their aspirations for independence. Additionally, it is particularly interesting to see how the legacies of Soviet civil religion are still evident in some countries of the former Soviet Union. In this way, this discussion will contribute to the scholarship in the field by providing a new perspective on the use of symbols in Soviet civil religion. In examining the legacies of Soviet symbolism, this work will provide valuable insights into the current politics of the fifteen countries that were once part of the Union of Soviet Socialist Republics. This type of analysis will provide a valuable example of the relevance of historical study to an understanding of national symbols in modern nation states.

Chapter 2
Communicating Soviet Values: The Role of Symbols

The state coat of arms of the USSR symbolizes the basis of the entire people's state – a union of workers and peasants, the voluntary association of Union republics with equal rights in a single Union state, and the equality of socialist nations. It also expresses the idea of the international solidarity of the peoples of the USSR with the working people of the world.[42]

– *Great Soviet Encyclopedia* (1973 ed.)

It is worth reviewing the geographical features and ethnic diversity of the Soviet Union, as this will provide the context for the primary messages of the national symbol system. The USSR was the world's largest country that, at its peak, spanned an area of 22,402,200 square kilometres (8,649,500 square miles) across 11 time zones in north-eastern Europe and northern Asia. Borders of the country measured more than 60,000 kilometres (37,282 miles) and were adjacent to 12 countries, 12 seas, as well as the Arctic, Atlantic, and Pacific oceans. The population (which numbered 285,743,000 in 1989) was far from homogeneous. A Soviet secondary school geography textbook published in 1976 noted that:

> According to the nationwide census of 1970, there were 91 peoples in the USSR numbering over 10,000, and many smaller nationalities and ethnic groups listed as 'other nationalities'.

> The numerous peoples of our country speak different languages and have marked cultural distinctions, but their common historical heritage stretching back over several centuries and their close economic and cultural links brought these peoples closer and closer together.[43]

Lenin contended that the best way to deal with the 'nationalities question', as the Bolsheviks called it, was to ensure the equality of all the peoples within a state controlled by the proletariat. In an essay published in 1924, he wrote: 'True democracy, headed by the working class, holds aloft the banner of complete equality of nations and of unity of the workers of all nations in their class struggle.'[44] He suggested that, by ensuring that the rights of different nationalities were respected within a voluntary union, a multinational socialist state would succeed where others had not. Lenin insisted that 'The class solidarity of the workers of the different nations is strengthened by the substitution of voluntary ties for compulsory, feudalist and militarist ties.'[45] His ideas about the power of socialist unity were fundamental to Soviet doctrine on nationalities policy. Lenin's works emphasised building a sense of internationalism among the population, reminding the people that nationalist ideas benefited the bourgeoisie, and promoting the solidarity of the working people of all nationalities. The Soviet regime followed suit, and the underlining theories of Lenin served as a foundation for the way the Soviet Union was organised and presented itself in its constitution. In 1913, Lenin wrote:

> The workers will not allow themselves to be disunited by sugary speeches about national culture, or 'national-cultural autonomy'. The workers of all nations together, concertedly, uphold full freedom and complete equality of rights in organisations common to all – and that is the guarantee of genuine culture.

> The workers of the whole world are building up their own internationalist culture, which the champions of freedom and the enemies of oppression have for long been preparing. To the old world, the world of national oppression, national bickering, and national isolation the

workers counterpose a new world, a world of the unity of the working people of all nations, a world in which there is no place for any privileges or for the slightest degree of oppression of man by man.[46]

Therefore, Soviet civil religion was designed for the arduous task of uniting the many peoples of the USSR into a cohesive group and instilling in them a shared set of values. The objective was to create a new multinational community – the Soviet people (*sovetskii narod*).

It is important to acknowledge several points about Soviet nationalities policy. First, governmental policies changed and evolved over time based upon the needs of the state. More importantly, there was often a disconnect between Soviet propaganda about the treatment of different ethnic groups and governmental policies as they were implemented. Works published in the USSR frequently cited the writings of Lenin, such as the preceding quotation, as a way to link updated Soviet rhetoric back to the founding philosophy of Marxism-Leninism. While interpretations of specific concepts changed over time, linkages to Lenin's works were meant to convey the idea of continuity to the readers and were used to legitimise updated Party doctrine.

An entry in the *Great Soviet Encyclopedia* (*Bol'shaia sovetskaia entsiklopediia*) emphasised the Party's assertion that the people of the USSR had transcended their ethnic identities to form a new society characterised by internationalism and the common goal of building communism:

> **SOVIET PEOPLE**, a new historical, social, and international community of people possessing a common territory and economic system, a socialist culture, a state based on a union of the entire population, and a common goal – the building of communism. Such a community appeared in the USSR as a result of socialist transformations and the growing together of working classes and other social strata, of all nations and nationalities.[47]

Throughout Soviet publications the 'common goal of building communism' was a recurrent theme, portrayed both textually and visually. The next paragraph in the entry described Lenin's vision of a society in which the working people of many national groups would join together to form the basis of a new type of multinational state, in which a sense of socialist internationalism would provide a bond of unity for the proletariat. It explained:

> The Soviet people constitute a multinational collective entity of urban and rural workers united by a common socialist system, Marxist-Leninist ideology, the communist ideals of the working class, and the principles of internationalism.[48]

Russian served as the unity language of the country, but ethnic groups were also encouraged to preserve their own languages. While all Soviet citizens were expected to be fluent in Russian, officially it was a point of pride that the many peoples of the USSR had retained their native languages and cultural diversity.[49] Next, the authors explained the role of the Communist Party, and how the party continued the teaching of Lenin and served the citizens of the USSR. Soviet rhetoric explained that, as a result of the Party's success in unifying the proletariat, the many peoples were no longer subjects of the Russian Empire, but rather equal partners in the development of socialism and in the goal of building a communist society:

> The CPSU, which united within its ranks that part of the friendly classes, groups, nations, and nationalities whose level of consciousness is highest, expresses the vital interests of the entire Soviet people and cements the community of Soviet individuals in all areas of life.[50]

It is important to remember that the Communist Party was intended to be the party of the *people*. The 'dictatorship of the proletariat' implied that the working people, and not the bourgeoisie, were guiding the development of the country for the benefit of all Soviet *people* and *peoples*. In Russian, there are two words that equate to the term 'people' in English – *liudi*, which is synonymous to 'persons', and *narod*, which is typically used to mean 'nation' or 'race'. In the Soviet Union, the term *narod* was used in political language to describe both, the working class and all the people of the country. This linguistic choice was deliberate as it signalled not just the idea of a plurality of individuals, but something much deeper – a group unified by a set of shared characteristics. This ideological point was evidenced by multiple definitions of *narod* presented to readers of the *Great Soviet Encyclopedia*. While acknowledging that 'the people' can refer to the entire population of a country, it stressed that:

> In historical materialism, the people, or popular masses, are a social community comprising, at various historical stages, those strata and classes that, owing to their position in society, are capable of actively participating in the progressive development of society; they are the makers of history, the determining force in fundamental social transformations.[51]

The article then explained that at different stages of history the composition of 'the people' has varied, based upon the economic and social structure in the country:

> In social formations based on class antagonism, the people do not include the dominant exploitative groups with their antipopular and reactionary policies. Only under socialism, when the exploitative classes are eliminated, does the concept of the people embrace all social groups.

> Marxism-Leninism elucidates the differences in position of the various classes, strata, and groups of the population and then, taking into account their class interests, determines the composition of the people. At all stages of social development, the majority of the people consists of the working masses, the principal productive force of society.[52]

Finally, the article addressed the definition of a 'people' in terms of an ethnic group or nationality. Soviet readers were expected to understand the nuanced connotations inherent to the use of the word *narod*, and it was intended to evoke a sense of class consciousness as well as the idea of a multinational collective. The article stressed the Party's claim that, 'Under conditions of developed socialist society in the USSR, a new historical community has evolved – the *sovetskii narod*'.[53] In the entry on the Soviet People, the reader was reminded about the role of the proletariat in the development of the national economy. Next, the article emphasised two key points of Party rhetoric: how economic advancement benefited all republics, and therefore how the many Soviet peoples benefited from their membership in the Union:

> The economic and cultural community of Soviet people has developed comprehensively under conditions of mature socialism. The increasing social homogeneity and socio-political unity of Soviet society, as well as the transformation of the dictatorship of the proletariat into a popular state, led to an even greater union and friendship between all classes, social groups, nations, and nationalities of the USSR, whose representatives have gradually acquired more pan-Soviet, international traits. Under mature socialism and the building of communism, the international economic community is expanding, and a higher level has been achieved by the Union's economy—an economic entity including the economies of all the Union republics and developing according to a single state economic plan serving the interests of the country as a whole and of each republic separately.[54]

15

The text also reinforced the key claim that citizens from different ethnic groups in the USSR, while retaining their cultural traits, had grown closer together so that their sense of Soviet identity became dominant. This sense of *Sovietness* was presented as a form of domestic internationalism that would serve as a model for the peoples of all socialist states as they worked together to build communist societies across state borders.

> The most important result of the revolutionary transformation of society has been the birth of a new intellectual and psychological makeup of the Soviet people, who exhibit internationalist traits yet maintain their national distinctiveness. The national community forms an organic whole with a higher, international community, and the representatives of any given nation and nationality of the USSR consider themselves Soviet people first and foremost. This sentiment is reflected by the emergence of the Soviet people's sense of common national pride.[55]

Throughout the article on the *Soviet people* there were many references to the primary theme of Soviet civil religion and propaganda – the idea of union (*soiuz*) and unity (*edinstvo*) on multiple levels. There were, in fact, three levels of union and unity that were portrayed through the symbols of the country: 1) the solidarity of the working class (workers, peasants, and intelligentsia); 2) the assertion of the voluntary union of Soviet republics and friendship of the many peoples of the USSR; and 3) the development of a sense of socialist internationalism amongst Soviet citizens and all the workers of the world. The most fundamental of these types of unity was that of the working class, as this was the core of Marxist-Leninist teachings. Under the leadership of the workers, the Soviet people were described as working toward a common goal – the development of a socialist system with the goal of building a communist society. According to theory, as the unified peoples of the USSR worked to build communism they were to be guided on the path by the teachings of Lenin, the precepts of Marxism-Leninism, and the continuing leadership provided by the Communist Party of the Soviet Union.

With the doctrines of Marxism-Leninism in mind, an additional purpose for Soviet civil religion should also be considered in this discussion. Historically, the many peoples of the Soviet Union came from a variety of religious traditions. While Russian Orthodoxy was the most prominent religion in the Russian Empire, there were also significant populations of Christians from other Orthodox traditions, as well as Catholics and Protestants. In addition, the country had large Jewish, Muslim, and Buddhist minorities as well as small faith communities such as adherents of Shamanic traditions.[56] Most of these populations were geographically concentrated in various parts of the country. For example, Catholics lived mostly in the western border regions, Muslims were primarily found in the Caucuses and in central Asia, and Shamanist peoples were indigenous throughout much of Siberia. During the Soviet era, organised religious practice was discouraged, mocked, disincentivised, and devout adherents thereof were frequently persecuted.[57] However, there was a recognition that the people needed spiritual elements in their lives and a well-developed set of moral teachings. Therefore, the environment was suitable for the creation of a Soviet civil religion to fill the void left by the discouragement of traditional religious practices.

James Thrower and Nina Tumarkin, in their assessments of Marxism as a religion, harkened back to discussions amongst Russian Marxists prior to the Bolshevik revolution. They focused on the work of Anatolii Vasilevich Lunacharskii, who discussed Marx's ideas from what could be considered a religious viewpoint. Lunacharskii's seminal work on the topic was a 2-volume work from 1908 entitled *Religion and Socialism*. In the book, Lunacharskii advocated for a 'cultural revolution' through a process he referred to as 'god-building' (*bogostroitel'stvo*). He suggested that socialism should be viewed as a form of religion in which human beings replace traditional deities. Essentially, he envisioned the potential of socialism for fulfilling the same spiritual needs as established religions, its role in the enlightenment of the people, and its potential to create a new humanistic culture. In this new culture the individual and collective would become one and, through their work to build communism, the citizens would achieve a form of immortality.[58] Lenin, however, did not share that perspective. As a proponent of scientific Marxism, he criticised 'god building' as 'the worst form of self-humiliation'.[59] Despite their differences of opinion, Lunacharskii served as the first Soviet Commissar for Education and was one of the chief architects of the system for educating Soviet citizens. As will be demonstrated in Chapter 3, educational planners incorporated the techniques of the god-builders into the curriculum for Soviet civic education. Ironically, Lunacharskii's position as a member of the planning committee for Lenin's funeral and memorialisation gave him an opportunity to contribute to the cult of Lenin that developed in the Soviet Union, thus Lenin was installed as the embodiment of Marxist-Leninist revolutionary ideals.[60] This concept will be discussed later in the chapter.

In examining the religious aspect of Soviet communism, Thrower asked: 'did Marxism-Leninism, as it developed and became systematised, institutionalised, and established as the state ideology of the Soviet Union, and of countries which looked to the Soviet Union for guidance and inspiration, take on characteristics which can fairly be called "religious"?'[61] Many western scholars believed that it could. Even in the early decades of the Soviet era, western scholars were already discussing the religious aspects of Marxism and Leninism. In his 1942 book *Capitalism, Socialism, and Democracy*, political economist Joseph Schumpeter observed that:

> Marxism *is* a religion. To the believer, it presents, first, a system of ultimate ends that
> embody the meaning of life and are absolute standards by which to judge events and actions;
> and secondly, a guide to those ends which implies a plan of salvation and the indication of
> the evil from which mankind, or a chosen section of mankind, is to be saved.[62]

For Thrower, though, the key was to focus on Marxism-Leninism as a *civil religion*, rather than as a new form of conventional religion. Civil religions differ from traditional faiths in that they focus on creating a bond between citizens and their countries, as well as providing a common culture of patriotism within which citizens acquire a sense of national identity and learn to demonstrate their fealty to the state. Thrower suggested that there were two reasons to draw the conclusion that Marxism-Leninism was, indeed, the civil religion of the Soviet Union:

> The first is that Marxism-Leninism had the basic hallmark of civil religions the world over:
> that is, a myth of origin and legitimation, together with a myth of historic destiny. The
> second reason is that it sought to give expression to its fundamental outlook and values in a
> system of civil rites and rituals which was one of the means (but not the only means) by
> which it sought to socialise the vast and multi ethnic population of the Soviet Union into
> accepting its total view of the world.[63]

Thrower made a compelling case that the culture of patriotism in the USSR did, indeed, constitute a civil religion. As discussed in Chapter 1, other scholars who have studied Soviet civil religion have primarily focused on the 'cult of Lenin'; Soviet civil holidays; the elaborate ritual system that developed in the society; the mythic nature of Lenin and an array of Soviet heroes; and the government's use of propaganda to promote its agenda.[64]

Reflecting upon Ellis West's discussion of civil religion it is important to remember that religions rely upon the existence of a 'sacred cosmos' – 'a set of myths and symbols that explains this world in terms of the other reality that is affirmed in religious attitude'. West later explained that:

> ...a civil religion can be said to exist whenever the people of any given nation believe in a transcendent, spiritual reality, believe that reality to be the source of meaning and order for their nation, and express that belief and meaning in certain public rituals, myths, and symbols.[65]

Soviet civil religion was multifaceted drawing upon the three elements identified by West. While this study will briefly touch upon Soviet rituals and myths, it is the third category – symbols – that are the primary focus of the discussion. The Soviet symbol system was well-developed, a crucial element in Soviet civil religion, and a common sight in Soviet society, as will be further demonstrated.

National Symbols as Communicators of Identity

While it is outside the scope of this study to provide a definitive history of every Soviet symbol, a brief discussion of the preeminent symbols will enhance understanding of the use of symbols in the civil religion of the USSR. In his doctoral dissertation Whitney Smith stressed that the word 'symbol' is 'a generic term for anything which conveys to the human mind a meaning other than that implicit in its own nature; i.e. symbols are the <u>media of communication</u>'.[66] Smith noted that:

> First the form of the symbol is not restricted to graphic representations; it may indeed be a picture or written word, but it may just as well be a sound (spoken word, music), mental impression (image, dream), concrete object (staff, building), action (winking, kneeling), or condition (the arrangement of objects, actions, etc.)[67]

In his discussion of symbols, Smith emphasised that:

> ...it is important to think of the end of symbolism, communication, in its broadest sense of the making common of knowledge between any two communicants; i.e. one individual and another or one individual and a group. This is true whether the two are in direct confrontation or not, and whether or not either one or both are aware of the communication.[68]

It is the communicative purpose of national and political symbols that make them so important in the study of modern states. Smith noted that 'the symbolic word or picture or gesture of a political nature always attempts to create a communication with another, to bring about a community of understanding between people'. Essentially political symbols, particularly national symbols, serve as tools to unify a given population, to create a sense of community, as well as to instil and reinforce a shared set of societal beliefs among the individuals in that community.[69] The word 'national' can be problematic when discussing the Soviet Union. This is because the USSR was, essentially, a state of nations rather than a nation state. For the sake of this discussion, 'national symbol' will be used to describe the primary symbols of the Soviet state rather than symbols representative of any particular people resident in the USSR. The phrase 'state symbol' had a distinctive meaning in Soviet usage, which will be explained later in the discussion.

Sociologist Karen A. Cerulo examined the communicative role of national symbols in helping to create a collective sense of national identity amongst the residents of a country. First, she explained that 'national symbols objectify each nation's identity, making tangible that which might otherwise be impossible to meaningfully apprehend, and bringing a sense of concreteness to the highly abstract.'[70] For example, national anthems connect the citizen with the nation through the combination of meaningful lyrics, a rousing tune, and the ritual of performance. In her book, Cerulo noted that national hymns 'unite citizens every time they are performed, bringing citizens together (albeit mentally in many cases) in patriotic communion'.[71] This concept of national identity is key to understanding the role of symbols in civil religion. Official national symbols are deliberately designed through the government apparatus, formally adopted, and used as a tool to represent the authority of the state. By affixing symbols such as a state seal or national emblem to official documents, the image becomes a representation of approval by a higher power. State symbols such as coats of arms and/or national flags are displayed in government buildings, thus symbolically marking them as seats of power. This idea of state authority is also conveyed in how elements of state symbols are often incorporated into the military symbols of a country, reinforcing the concept of state power through the personnel and hardware of the armed forces. The implication of state symbolism is that national symbols are the domain of the government and that, when they are used directly by the citizenry, it is through the consent and goodwill of the highest authority in the country.

Furthermore, the primary meaning of national symbols is defined by the state and communicated to the citizenry through the educational system and other channels. When used as tools in the political socialisation of children, they help communicate a shared set of values to young citizens. In adult life these same symbols reinforce a common bond among citizens of the state. Cerulo explained how this process works in modern societies:

> National symbols also function to *create bonds* between citizens. This bonding power emerges from the unique, sacred nature of these symbols – one distinct from that of any individual who apprehends the symbol, and one that becomes the object of intense collective reverence. In this way, national symbols exert a moral authority that renders individual interests secondary to the collective attributes the symbols represent. Moreover, the symbols bring individuals out of themselves and into contact and communication with others. They represent a power that binds citizens in a shared consciousness, linking them despite differences in wealth, social standing, power, or age: 'By uttering the same cry, pronouncing the same word, or performing the same gestures in regard to these [symbolic] objects, individuals become and feel themselves to be in unison' (Durkheim 1915: 262).[72]

In citing a major work of sociologist Émile Durkheim – *The Elementary Forms of Religious Life* – Cerulo was emphasising the importance of national symbols in civil religion, as they play a vital role in any culture of patriotism. Like traditional creeds, civil religions harness the communicative power of symbols as totems and messengers of dogma. Durkheim explained this role:

> It is obvious that for any kind of group an emblem is a useful rallying point. Expressing social unity in a material form makes it more tangible to everyone; for this reason the use of emblematic symbols must have quickly spread once the idea took shape. Moreover, this idea must have sprung spontaneously from the conditions of common life, for the emblem is not only a convenient method of clarifying society's awareness of itself, it actually creates this feeling: it is a basic element of this feeling.

Durkheim emphasised how symbols work to take individuals, each with their own consciousness and feelings, and to fuse them into a cohesive group that shares a common identity:

19

> By shouting the same cry, pronouncing the same words, making the same gesture to the same object, they become and feel as one. To be sure, individual representations also have organic consequences that are not unimportant; yet such representations can be conceptualized as distinct from those physical repercussions that accompany or follow them but do not constitute them.[73]

Cerulo also noted the work of Christel Lane, a sociologist whose observations on symbols and rituals in the USSR confirmed Durkheim's theory. Lane's study of Soviet ritual, written in 1981, demonstrated how national symbols were incorporated into a system of rituals as part of a civil religion focused on the primary values of Soviet society and on promoting unity of purpose. Lane explored the ways in which rituals were used in the culture of patriotism in the USSR. She analysed the Soviet ritual system as 'an instrument of cultural management enabling political elites (through their ideological cadres) to gain acceptance for a general system of norms and values congruent with their interpretation of Marxism-Leninism'. However, outside the context of the ritual system, Lane did not expound upon the role of Soviet symbols in a broader social context.[74] While citizens would have learned the myths associated with Marxist-Leninist teachings and participated in various rituals designed to instil in them the values inherent to the faith, it is the third aspect – symbols – that were meant to reinforce those values on an almost daily basis, primarily through visual exposure in the social environment.

Soviet Symbols: Themes, Influences, and Intended Messages

This chapter examines the preeminent symbols of Soviet civil religion, focusing on their communicative roles and the messages conveyed to the populace through their use. In analysing the primary symbol set, it became clear that the prominent theme – union (*soiuz*) and unity (*edinstvo*) – was shown in multiple ways. Unity symbolism was a central element of Soviet visual culture and was communicated through a well-developed programme of agitation and propaganda. In Soviet practice these two concepts were closely linked, with propaganda defined as 'the dissemination of political, philosophical, scientific, artistic, or other views or ideas, with the aim of instilling them in the public consciousness and encouraging mass action'.[75] Soviet propaganda was designed to inspire enthusiasm for, and a sense of purpose in, the ultimate goal of developing socialism and building a communist society. The strategic objective was to enable every citizen, no matter their age or profession, to understand the goal that everyone in the country was working to achieve, to recognise the importance and relevance of their own labour to the accomplishment of that goal, and to take pride in their contributions to society. In contrast, agitation was 'a means of politically influencing the masses [and] a weapon in the struggle between classes and their parties. Agitation is the spreading of a certain idea or slogan that arouses the masses to action'.[76] In distinguishing between the two, the Russian Marxist philosopher G. V. Plekhanov explained in 1892 that 'the propagandist conveys *many* ideas to one or a few persons; an agitator conveys *only one or a few ideas*, but to a *great mass of people*'.[77] In terms of agitation and propaganda, Soviet symbols conveyed Soviet values through a variety of symbolic representations. The multivocality of the preeminent civil religious symbols meant that one symbol, such as the flag or coat of arms, could convey multiple meanings through the combination of different symbolic elements. Those elements, similarly, could serve as distinct symbols on their own and could also have multiple meanings.

To understand the role of Soviet symbols during the era of mature socialism, it is first necessary to review the origins of those symbols. Their lineage from the time of Lenin was meant to imbue them with legitimacy and sacredness in Soviet ideology. In their study of the language and symbols of Russia in 1917, historians Orlando Figes and Boris Kolonitskii stressed the role of symbols in times of social upheaval:

> Like all modern social revolutions, the Russian Revolution was a struggle for state power. Each side of this power struggle was defined by its own symbolic system – flags and songs, political phrases and slogans, pictures and emblems – which served to articulate its ideology and to rally its supporters to 'the cause'. These symbolic systems played a complicated role in the politics of 1917. They did more than just reflect the clash of ideologies. There were times when the symbols were themselves the object of the struggle, times when they defined it, provoked it or contained it, and times when the struggle was entirely fought on a symbolic plain.[78]

The Soviet strategy for the use of symbols in civil religion directly evolved from their use in both the February and October revolutions of 1917, and from how the Bolsheviks harnessed the power of symbols during the civil war.[79] Another significant cultural influence was the role of symbols in Russian Orthodox religious practice. Historian Paul Gabel suggested that:

> Soviet art was carefully positioned to replace church art – and the ikons in the home. The dark interiors of Russian churches sparkled mysteriously with light and color. Candles reflected off vestments, gilded crosses, and draperies. So, too, ikons in the home contrasted with the dull and bare walls of the average peasant's dwelling. The new art of 'Soviet realism' provided replacement color and a new moral message. With vivid hues and large splashes of color, Soviet posters in the new style proudly portrayed Bolshevik leaders and the Red Army in action.[80]

Religious symbols and icons originated in an era when a large portion of the congregation would have been illiterate. At the time of the October Revolution, this would still have been the case across much of the former Russian Empire. Therefore, the Bolsheviks adopted a proven and culturally appropriate strategy of mass communication that relied on a combination of visual elements and verbal communication to spread their message to the masses. Historian James H. Billington observed that icons also influenced the Bolshevik's strategic use of Orthodox memes and symbolism in their strategy of propaganda and agitation:

> Just as the hymns and chants of the church had provided new themes and inspiration for early Russian iconographers, so their rediscovered paintings gave fresh inspiration back to poets and musicians as well as painters in late imperial Russia. Under the former seminarian Stalin, however, the icon lived on not as the inspiration for creative art but as a model for mass indoctrination. The older icons, like the newer experimental paintings, were for the most part locked up in the reserve collections of museums. Pictures of Lenin in the 'red corner' of factories and public places replaced icons of Christ and the Virgin. Photographs of Lenin's successors deployed in a prescribed order on either side of Stalin replaced the old 'prayer row,' in which saints were deployed in fixed order on either side of Christ enthroned. Just as the iconostasis of a cathedral was generally built directly over the grave of a local saint and specially revenced with processions on a religious festival, so these new Soviet saints appeared in ritual form over the mausoleum of the mummified Lenin on the feast days of Bolshevism to review endless processions through Red Square.[81]

In her study of Soviet propaganda art, historian Gloria Calhoun reinforced Billington's observation as she demonstrated how the Bolsheviks appropriated visual archetypes used in Russian Orthodox icons for use in their political posters. Calhoun noted that, 'Symbols can be culturally recycled because, once a cognitive association has been culturally established between a symbol and its meaning, that association also helps organize future perceptions.'[82] Moreover, in the initial post-revolutionary period, the appropriation of existing symbols made it easy for the Bolsheviks to communicate important concepts to the masses while they were working to develop a national system of universal education through which they could socialise the people of the country. In her thesis, Calhoun examined the traditional role of icons in Orthodox belief as 'embodiments of sacred truth', and their utility as a ready source of 'symbolic precedents that visually signified politically important concepts, such as legitimacy, heroism, and utopian transformation'.[83] Cultural recycling gave Soviet propagandists a powerful tool because, as Calhoun noted, 'symbols familiar from religious icons elicited powerful emotions in ordinary Russians, whose cultural frame had for centuries been shaped by Russian Orthodoxy'.[84] The most significant examples of the reuse of Russian Orthodox archetypes for signifying communist authority were the use of red as a sacred colour and how imagery of Lenin was used to convey the legitimacy of the Communist Party.[85]

Preeminent Symbols of Soviet Civil Religion

To gain insight into the role of symbols in Soviet civil religion it is first necessary to review the *simvolika* of the USSR. In Russian the word *simvolika* describes the 'symbolic meaning, attributed to something' *and* the 'combination of any symbols' – so that it encompasses both a collection of related symbols and the meanings attached to those symbols.[86] Within Soviet civil religion there were two distinct categories of *simvolika* used – official state symbols (*gosudarstvennaia simvolika*) and other symbols that held significant meaning in the society. The Soviet Constitution specified three official state symbols – the national flag, the state emblem, and the national hymn. Additionally, the same chapter of the Constitution designated the city of Moscow as the capital of the USSR. In many ways Moscow (typically portrayed through images of Red Square, the Kremlin, or a red star atop a Kremlin tower) served as an additional state symbol. Supplementing the official state symbols, three elements of the national flag design – the hammer and sickle emblem, the red five-pointed star, and the red banner of revolution were prominent in civil religious contexts in the country. Finally, Lenin also served as one of the most important civil religious symbols of the Soviet Union.[87]

The emphasis of this study is on how Soviet citizens learned about the symbols of their country and how those lessons were reinforced throughout their lives. Therefore, the ideal primary sources are those that were designed for, and available to, ordinary people. These include reference works such as the *Bol'shaia sovetskaia entsiklopediia*, children's books, books for general audiences about Soviet symbols, recommendations for educators on how to teach about them, and academic articles written by Soviet scholars. In addition, objects of Soviet material culture are extremely valuable, not just as illustrations in the text, but also as a mode of communication in themselves. Chapter 5, specifically, will address this category of primary source material in detail. This chapter will focus on the preeminent symbols used in Soviet civil religion, the meanings associated with those symbols, and the ways in which they were explained in Soviet sources.

In considering the official state symbols it is vital to start with one symbol that predates the union treaty – the state emblem of the Russian Soviet Federative Socialist Republic (RSFSR). Russian historian Nadezhda Aleksandrovna Soboleva noted that 'The lack of a unifying Bolshevik insignia on seals, special tokens, and membership cards is evidence that prior to the October Revolution, the Bolsheviks had developed nothing that they could later sanction as an insignia of state.'[88] In his essay 'Soviet State Symbolism', Whitney Smith suggested that the first emblem of the RSFSR was adopted out of the practical needs of statehood.[89] Some sort of official seal or emblem was needed for government documents and proclamations, as well as for use on currency and postage stamps. As early as January 1918 work was underway to design an official emblem for the new state to replace the 'democratic' double-headed Russian eagle used by the Provisional Government – the traditional symbol of Russia without the attributes of imperial power (the crown, orb, and sceptre).[90] Many Soviet texts, both for popular audiences and for academics, discussed the work to create the first Soviet arms. Some accounts directly linked Lenin with a significant decision regarding the design. According to the story, Lenin was shown a prototype for the emblem featuring a hammer, a sickle, and a sword. He specifically asked about the use of the sword, noting that while the Soviet people were fighting to defend the revolution and the dictatorship of the proletariat, it would not always be so. Lenin suggested omitting the sword as it seemed too militaristic, explaining:

> Socialism will triumph in all countries – this is indisputable. The brotherhood of the peoples will be proclaimed and realized throughout the entire world, and we will not need the sword, it is not our emblem…[91]

This story illustrates an important theme of Soviet symbolism. First, it links Lenin directly to the development of the symbols of the Russian SFSR. Next, it shows how those early emblems influenced the Soviet coat of arms – the primary symbol of state authority in the USSR. By connecting Lenin to the design process for the Russian SFSR symbols, and those symbols to the Soviet state emblem, the story links the legacy of Lenin to the arms and contributes to the legitimacy and authority of the government represented by the symbol.[92]

An examination of the first symbols of the Russian republic reveals early versions of symbolic elements that were later used in the Soviet Union. These components included the combined hammer and sickle, the rising sun, the wreath of wheat, use of the colour red, and the quote from the last page of the *Manifesto of the Communist Party* (*Communist Manifesto*). Each of these elements will be examined to learn more about their origins and how they were used as *simvolika*.

Figures 2.1-2.2. Early emblems of the Russian Soviet Federative Socialist Republic (RSFSR). *Left:* Seal of the RSFSR (1918-1920). *Right:* Coat of arms of the RFSFR (1920-1956). *See colour on plate C-1.*

The 1924 Constitution of the Soviet Union provided for the adoption of a state emblem and flag. In Russian, the state emblem was usually described using the traditional word for 'coat of arms' (*gerb)*, although the design intentionally deviated from heraldic standards. The Soviet emblem

23

signalled a new style of *socialist* heraldry that had evolved beyond the coats of arms traditionally used to represent the nobility and their domains. In place of an escutcheon (shield), the Soviet arms used the globe of Earth depicted above the rising sun. The globe tilted to show Eurasia with Africa below. In this perspective, the USSR became the focal point over which a gold (or yellow) crossed hammer and sickle emblem appeared. The red star served as a crest, in the position once reserved for the royal crown in the heraldic tradition of the Russian Empire. Instead of the traditional supporters on either side of the shield, the Soviet emblem used a wreath of grain, tightly wrapped in a red ribbon inscribed with the last line from the *Communist Manifesto* in multiple languages. The *Great Soviet Encyclopedia* offered readers this explanation of its meaning:

> The state coat of arms of the USSR symbolizes the basis of the entire people's state – a union of workers and peasants, the voluntary association of Union republics with equal rights in a single Union state, and the equality of socialist nations. It also expresses the idea of the international solidarity of the peoples of the USSR with the working people of the world.[93]

It is important to recognise that the state arms were a graphic representation of state authority. They were found on official buildings, identity documents, diplomas and certificates, badges (both official and souvenir), patriotic items, stamps, postcards, and featured in public decorations for major national holidays. In this way, this specific symbol would have been present on important occasions in the life of an average Soviet citizen, much in the way that state or religious symbols would have been seen in the tsarist era. The depiction of the state emblem on banknotes and coins not only emphasised these items as official currency in the country, but also symbolised the nature of the economic system in the USSR as it was managed by the state. Most importantly, the state emblem incorporated the elements of the official state *simvolika*, making it a valuable starting point for the expression of a shared set of Soviet symbols and values.[94]

The symbolic themes of unity and internationalism in the arms were multifaceted in their depiction. The rays of the sun, symbolising the dawn of the new era of socialism, illuminate the globe with Eurasia and Africa in view. While the Soviet Union was the focal point on the globe, it was highly significant that the continents were portrayed without international boundaries. In Soviet symbology, this emphasised the unique status of the Soviet Union as the first socialist state and its natural role in championing the aspirations of the working people of all countries through the brotherhood of world communism. Unity symbolism was also inherent in the individual elements of the arms as they were frequently used on their own throughout Soviet society.

Figure 2.3. State Emblem (coat of arms) of the USSR: version 4, 1956-1991 (15 republics). *See colour on front cover.*

24

When discussing the meaning of the red five-pointed star atop the arms, Soviet sources described it as a symbol of internationalism, although its origin was military in nature.[95] The red star (*krasnaia zvezda*) derived from the emblem of the Workers' and Peasants' Red Army, established in early January 1918. The design of an insignia to be worn by members of the Red Army was announced on 19 April 1918 in both *Pravda* and *Izvestiia*. As explained in *Pravda*:

> In order to distinguish the grey greatcoat from the 'flour party' from the grey greatcoat of the revolutionary Red Guard, all soldiers of the Red Army will be issued a chest insignia.

> The draught of the symbol is now approved. It is a Mars star with gold trim, midway on the red field are golden images of a plough and a hammer.[96]

The term 'Mars star' refers to Mars, the Roman god of war whose colour was red. In addition, the red alludes to the field of the red banner of revolution, which will be discussed later in this chapter. Finally, it is interesting to note that 'Field of Mars' was a term used in Russian and other languages to describe a military parade ground. The Field of Mars in Saint Petersburg was the site of military reviews in the tsarist period but took on new symbolic significance in the Soviet era as a common burial site for victims of the 1917 revolutions and the Civil War. During the Siege of Leningrad, which lasted for 900 days between 1941 and 1944, the square was used to grow food for the population trapped inside the city. After the war, it became the site of the first eternal flame in the Soviet Union as a monument to those who perished in the Great Patriotic War.

This emblem with the hammer and plough was used until 13 April 1922 when the design of the Red Army badge was changed, replacing the plough with a sickle. This new configuration created a cleaner visual symbol, both aesthetically and symbolically. The simplicity of the sickle made it clearly recognisable, ensuring that the emblematic message was readily apparent. In its new configuration the red star with the combined hammer and sickle served as the primary symbol of the military until the breakup of the Soviet Union. In military usage the red star, sometimes with the implements and sometimes without, was used on insignia, awards, banners, and as a national identifier on military vehicles and aircraft. When formally emblazoned with the hammer and sickle, the red star would have been primarily utilised as a military symbol.[97]

Figures 2.4-2.6. Badges of the Red Army. Variants of this design were used from 1918 until the breakup of the Soviet Union in 1991. ***Left:*** Badge of the Workers' and Peasants' Red Army with the red star, hammer, and plough (ca. 1918-1922). ***Centre:*** Badge of the Workers' and Peasants' Red Army as established by RRMC[98] Order No. 753 (13 April 1922). ***Right:*** Badge of the Workers' and Peasants' Red Army as established by RRMC Order No. 1691(11 July 1922). *See colour on plate C-1.*

While the red five-pointed star had its roots as the emblem of the Soviet military, it became a potent symbol of internationalism and the brotherhood of international socialism. In this context the five points of the star represented the five populated continents, with Eurasia considered to be one continent in Soviet usage. The five-pointed star, either coloured red or shown in gold/yellow against a field of red, became an international symbol of the communist cause and was incorporated into the national flags and/or coats of arms of numerous socialist countries in Eastern Europe, Africa, and Asia. This symbolism would have been apparent not only to citizens of the USSR, but also to residents of any socialist society. Therefore, it became one of the most important symbols of international communism.[99]

One final usage of the red star merits inclusion in this discussion. Following their ascent to power the Bolsheviks embarked on a campaign of iconoclasm intended to remove symbols of the tsarist regime with the aim of creating a new Soviet landscape. As part of this campaign, the large imperial double-headed eagles were removed from the towers of the Moscow Kremlin. In their place, large red stars constructed of copper-plated steel and ruby-red glass were designed for installation on five of the Kremlin towers. Each was proportioned for the tower on which it was placed and illuminated at night. A short booklet about the stars produced in 1980 noted their symbolic value:

> In 1935, five-pointed stars were first installed on the Kremlin towers. They have become the symbol of Soviet Moscow, socialist Moscow, the symbol of peace, light and truth for all of mankind.[100]

The original stars had the hammer and sickle in the centre, comprised of semi-precious stones. However, the stones soon lost their lustre, so new stars made of just metal and ruby-coloured glass replaced the originals in 1937. In photographs and artwork, the Kremlin stars were portrayed as a magnificent representation of Soviet power and national pride. For internal and external audiences, the Kremlin stars served as a symbol of the Soviet Union whether they were shown in broad scenes of Red Square and the Kremlin, in views of a single tower and star, or on their own. The stars were shining examples of Soviet craftsmanship as well as potent symbols of the power resident in the Kremlin below.[101]

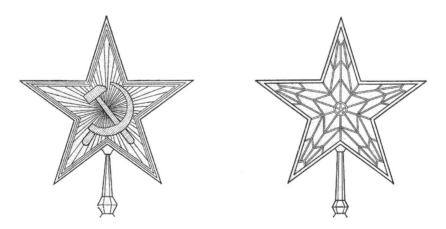

Figures 2.7-2.8. Diagrams of the Kremlin star designed for placement on Saviour Tower (*Spasskaia bashnia*): *Left:* Version installed in 1935. *Right:* The replacement version from 1937.

Symbolically the power and military might of the USSR as represented by the red five-pointed star, at least to an internal audience, was viewed as defensive in nature. The armed forces were portrayed as defending not just the first socialist state, but also the revolutionary struggle of the worldwide proletariat in its efforts to free itself from bourgeois oppression. As Lenin's purported comment about the prototype RSFSR emblem illustrated, communist theory held that as human society naturally progressed the result would be the establishment of a new world order. Therefore, despite the military origins of the red star and its use as a symbol of the Soviet armed forces, the red star's primary meaning in Soviet symbolism was of socialist internationalism.

This important concept in Soviet symbolism was closely tied to another theme that was widely used by the CPSU after World War II. In addition to its role as the champion of the communist cause internationally, the Party portrayed the USSR as a nation committed to world peace. This aspect of internationalism was sometimes illustrated through the depiction of three people – one European, one Asian, and one African (the three-races theme). Of course, the Soviet Union's representation of itself as a champion of world peace is contrary to the western Cold War stereotype of the USSR. In Soviet political philosophy this is, again, explained by the belief that the natural evolution of human society would eventually lead all peoples to join the communist cause. Violence and warfare, in the Soviet worldview, were the result of capitalist and imperialist attempts to hinder this natural evolution in order to preserve the privileged position of the bourgeoisie and its ability to exploit the workers. Other examples of the peace theme typically employed the Russian slogan *Miru mir*, which translates as 'To the world, peace'. Additional visual representations included the use of established symbols of peace such as white doves. The peace theme was common in the celebration of holidays with international significance such as International Workers' Day (1 May) and International Women's Day (8 March). This motif was also prevalent when the Soviet Union hosted international events and visitors.[102]

One little discussed element of the Soviet emblem is the sun, which is shown illuminating the Earth. Its placement and the visual effect created by the upward motion of the rays cause the viewer's focus to be directed toward the globe. Therefore, the observer does not immediately notice the sun in the imagery of the symbol. As previously mentioned, the sun was typically interpreted as symbolising 'the dawn of a new era' – the socialist epoch in which the dictatorship of the proletariat would direct society in the building of communism. In addition, the red star was often used as a source of illumination in Soviet art, shining down on figures depicted in the works. Gloria Calhoun suggested that this use of illumination is an example of cultural recycling of symbols and drew directly from the symbology of Russian Orthodox icons. She noted that in Christian symbolism the sun represented salvation. The red star, on the other hand, was frequently described as the 'Light of Truth'. In her analysis of the early Soviet period Calhoun noted that, 'In the developing Bolshevik master fiction, depicting the red star against the sun reinforced the red star's power and legitimized the star's use as the new symbol of salvation.'[103] She also explained that 'the sun's golden rays illuminate the countryside and in doing so symbolise the physical world's transfiguration'.[104]

Therefore, the two sources of illumination in the Soviet arms – the rising sun and the shining red star at the apex of the emblem – work together to symbolise how the revolution, the Party, the philosophy of Marxism-Leninism, and the common goal of the Soviet people were transforming the country into a new socialist paradise on Earth. One final mention of illumination bears inclusion here, although it is not portrayed in the imagery of the state emblem. In her analysis, Calhoun demonstrated how the use of 'glories' (illuminated regions around human figures) in Soviet political posters appeared to have derived from the use of haloes and illumination in Christian art to show the sacred nature of the person portrayed. While this aspect of symbolic light is outside the scope of this study, it is an excellent example of how religious symbolism was culturally recycled by the Soviets, and how new meanings were assigned to those symbols. For this reason, sources of illumination can also be viewed as a symbol of legitimacy as they imply that the Soviet people and the Communist Party were all working for a higher cause.[105]

In her article about the development of the Soviet symbol set, Soboleva cited conflicting claims for the authorship of the combined hammer and sickle emblem. She explains that, during the February Revolution, images of workers from various trades were common on the banners carried at demonstrations. On these banners the concept of labour was communicated through a variety of symbols including 'anvils, gear wheels, hammers, sickles, and so forth'. Soviet art historian Vladimir Pavlovich Lapshin explained:

> There were banners that reflected what the demonstrators did for a living (cooks carried banners with portraits of a cook, a housemaid, and a butler, while janitors marched with a placard showing a man with a broom).[106]

Thus, the hammer and the sickle were just two of many symbols which represented the working people of Russia during the turbulent times of the 1917 revolutions. It may never be known who was the first to combine these two tools into one symbol to represent the proletariat. Soviet philologist Aleksei Fedorovich Losev suggested:

> All appearances are that this symbol was certainly not created by any one artist, that in general many artists offered up the symbol at the beginning of the Revolution, or, more accurately, that its true author was the entire Soviet reality of the time or, even better, the entire people.[107]

Regardless of the difficulty in tracing the precise origin of the symbol, the meaning was made clear to citizens of the Soviet Union. It was closely tied to the values of the society and to the lessons taught in the educational system throughout the country. Marxism-Leninism explained that the total victory of the working class over the bourgeoisie would be achieved through the unity of those whose labour produced the basis of human survival and social advancement – the workers and the peasants, as well as the intelligentsia.[108]

An article in the *Great Soviet Encyclopedia* clearly identified the symbolism and importance of the hammer and sickle for the people of the Soviet Union:

> The hammer and sickle symbolizes the peaceful labor of Soviet people and the indestructible fraternal alliance of workers and peasants. It shows that all power in the land of the soviets belongs to the working people.
>
> Because of the special importance of the hammer and sickle in Soviet symbolism, its depiction is regulated by various laws, for example, by the Statute on the State Flag of the USSR, confirmed by a decree of the Presidium of the Supreme Soviet of the USSR of Aug. 19, 1955.[109]

The hammer and sickle emblem represented the value of labour and the unity of the working class as the most fundamental basis for Soviet society, essential for building socialism and the shared goal for attaining true communism.[110] In addition to the hammer and sickle emblem, the agricultural wreath illustrated the fruits of labour and the products of Soviet agriculture. Imagery using grain and other agricultural produce as a symbol of abundance was common in Soviet propaganda.[111] Through the representation of the people and their productivity, these symbols

28

were meant to emphasise the effectiveness of the socialist system and illustrate how the people derived benefit from the fruits of their collective labour. This theme extended across a broad range of propaganda media including visual arts, literature, and other forms of government-sponsored communication.

Perhaps the most obvious unity symbol included in the state emblem was the text. The Russian inscription on the ribbon read '*Proletarii vsekh stran, soediniaites'!*' ('Proletarians of all countries, unite!').[112] It is important to recognise that the motto was a symbol of internationalism – both *between* the Union republics and *beyond* the borders of the USSR. Repeated in the official languages of each Soviet republic, the motto symbolised the unity of the many peoples of the Soviet Union and served as a token of the socialist brotherhood of all working people around the world. In appearance the ribbon changed several times – twice when additional republics were added to the USSR, as well as in 1956 when the Karelo-Finnish SSR was renamed and became an autonomous republic within the Russian SFSR. On all versions of the emblem the languages were arranged beginning with the Russian language at bottom and progressing up the ribbon on both sides, alternating left to right across the globe. Emblems used after 1936 had the Russian-language inscription at the base where heraldic mottos are traditionally displayed on a banderole (speech scroll).[113]

Figures 2.9-2.11. Evolutionary stages of the Soviet State Emblem. ***Left to Right:*** Version 1, 1923-1936 (4-7 republics). Version 2, 1936-1946 (11 republics). Version 3, 1946-1956 (16 republics). *See colour on inside front cover.*

The first three designs of the state emblem placed the languages in groupings by order of admission to the Soviet Union, although the listing of republics admitted in the same year varied in the different versions. On the first version (1923-1936) the order of the six languages was Russian, Ukrainian, Georgian, Turko-Tatar, Byelorussian, and Armenian. By 1936 the number of republics had increased to eleven, reflected by the addition of five languages, in this order on the second version: Russian, Ukrainian, Byelorussian, Georgian, Armenian, Azerbaijani, Uzbek, Turkmen, Tajik, Kazakh, and Kirghiz. This version was used from 1936-1946. The state emblem was again altered in 1946, increasing the number to sixteen. On the third version (1923-1936) the order was Russian, Ukrainian, Byelorussian, Azerbaijani, Georgian, Armenian, Turkmen, Uzbek, Tajik, Kazakh, Kirghiz, Karelo-Finnish, Moldavian, Lithuanian, Latvian, and Estonian.[114]

In the final version, used from 1956-1991, the languages were arranged in the order in which the republics were listed in Chapter 8, Article 71 of the 1977 Soviet Constitution: Russian SFSR, Ukrainian SSR, Byelorussian SSR, Uzbek SSR, Kazakh SSR, Georgian SSR, Azerbaijan SSR, Lithuanian SSR, Moldavian SSR, Latvian SSR, Kirghiz SSR, Tajik SSR, Armenian SSR, Turkmen SSR, and Estonian SSR. This arrangement predates the 1977 constitution, placing the republics in order by population (matching statistics from 1940).[115] It matches the data from the 1939 census except that in that year the Kirghiz SSR would have come before the Tajik SSR. After publication of the 1977 constitution the arrangement eventually became known as 'Constitutional order' and was widely used as a standardised sequence for listing the republics. This order was used not just for formal displays of symbols, but also in images where the intent was to represent each of the republics as equals. In all versions of the arms, the Russian language was placed in a position of prominence, emphasising its importance as the unity language across the country and also the role of the Russian people in unifying the many peoples of the country. It is also interesting to note that in all versions used after 1936 the three Slavic languages of the titular nations were listed first. The symbolic elements on the state emblem all served to reinforce the concept of the unity of the Soviet republics and peoples. Additionally, the Soviet state emblem served as a template for each of the emblems of the individual republics of the USSR. In this way, a glimpse at the state arms of a union republic was meant to remind the viewer of that republic's place in the greater whole of the Union of Soviet Socialist Republics (see Appendix).

One of the most important symbols for a modern nation-state is the flag. The Treaty Concerning the Formation of the Union of Soviet Socialist Republics, adopted on 30 December 1922, specified that the new country would have 'its own flag, arms, and state seal', but did not specify the designs of those symbols. When the Presidium of the Central Executive Committee created six commissions to draft different portions of a new constitution, one was delegated the task of designing a flag and coat of arms. The Central Executive Committee of the USSR met from 29 June to 7 July 1923 to draft a new constitution. In the draft prepared at the First Convocation, Second Session, Article 71 read 'The state flag of the Union of Soviet Socialist Republics shall consist of a red or scarlet cloth depicting the State Arms.'[116] However, there is some question about whether or not this flag was widely used. On 12 November 1923 a decree of the government of the USSR described a more simplified flag design:

> The state flag of the Union of Soviet Socialist Republics comprises a red or scarlet cloth,
> with a representation in the upper corner near the staff of a gold sickle and hammer, and
> above them a red five-pointed star, framed with a gold edge. The ratio of width to length:
> 1:2.[117]

It was this form of the flag that was adopted in Chapter 11, Article 71 of the constitution confirmed by the second Congress of Soviets on 31 January 1924.[118]

Figure 2.12. National Flag of the Soviet Union. *See colour on inside back cover.*

On 18 April 1924 the Presidium of the Central Executive Committee issued a decree that further defined the details of the flag:

> A red (or scarlet) rectangular flag, with a proportion of length to width of 2:1. A gold sickle and hammer with a radius of one-sixth the width of the flag in the upper left corner, above the sickle and hammer, a red five-pointed star edged in gold; the diameter of the star equal to one-tenth the width of the flag.[119]

When the Soviet Constitution was amended in 1936 the reference to scarlet (*alyi*) was dropped, leaving the colour specification as red.[120] On 19 August 1955 an edict further clarified the size and position of the emblems relative to the overall appearance of the flag. Essentially, the new description was meant to standardise the way in which the symbols were depicted, as well as how they were situated on the field of the flag. The new specifications made the appearance of the star, hammer, and sickle more geometrically precise and was intended to ensure that all Soviet flags produced in the country shared a common design.[121]

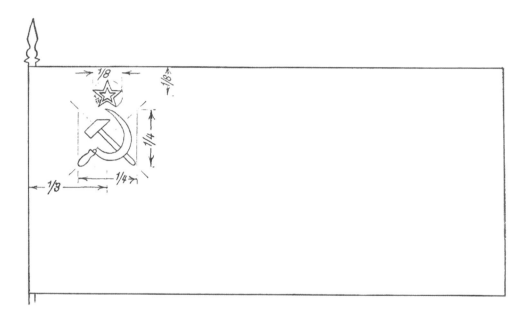

Figure 2.13. National Flag of the Soviet Union as specified in '*Ukaz Prezidiuma VS SSSR ot 19.08.1955 ob utverzhdenii Polozheniia o gosudartsvennom flage SSSR*' (19 August 1955).

The edict prescribed official uses of the flag, but also permitted it to be flown 'on buildings of enterprises, social organisations, and institutions, as well as on dwellings' on designated Soviet holidays, and also 'in connection with ceremonial and other festive measures carried out by state or social institutions and organizations'. Essentially, the Soviet flag was a state flag, but usage by the citizens of the USSR was permitted within specified contexts. In this way the use of the Soviet flag differed significantly than that of national flags in countries where wide-spread usage is common among the citizenry.[122]

Descriptions of national flags and the directives for their use are key elements of national symbolism. However, the use of the flag is just part of the civil religious function of the symbol. For a national flag to function as an effective tool for communication and a representation of a nation's sovereignty, there must be specific symbolism ascribed to the elements of the flag and that symbolism must be defined for the citizenry. The *Great Soviet Encyclopedia* explained the meaning behind the flag to its readers:

> The red color symbolizes the heroic struggle of the Soviet people, led by the CPSU, to construct socialism and communism. The hammer and sickle stand for the unshakable union of the working class and the kolkhoz peasantry. The red five-pointed star is a symbol of the ultimate triumph of the ideas of communism on the five continents of the earth.[123]

This entry from the encyclopaedia clearly defines the multivocality of the Soviet flag. The messages conveyed included the concepts of Soviet sovereignty, the unity of the workers and peasants, and the common goal of the Soviet people under the leadership of the Party – the building of communist society. Citizens were taught this symbolism early on and should have understood the meaning of the symbol, even if they did not consciously acknowledge it.

The flag design combined the two most important symbolic elements from the state emblem with the *krasnoe znamia* – the red banner of revolution. In an article from the *Great Soviet Encyclopedia*, the origins of the red banner as 'the symbol of the revolutionary liberation struggle' were traced to popular uprisings in eighth-century Iran, the sixteenth-century Great Peasant War in Germany, and the French Revolution of 1789-1799. Most notably, the lineage of the red banner was tied to political actions of the masses: 'With the revolt of June 5-6, 1832, in Paris, the red banner became a symbol of the blood spilled by the people and thus the banner of revolution, and after the Paris Commune of 1871 it became the banner of proletarian revolution and the world revolutionary workers' movement.' As such, many revolutionary movements in Tsarist Russia adopted this colour as a primary symbol used in their protests, as the encyclopaedia explained:

> In Russia the red banner was first raised in 1861 by rebellious peasants in Penza Province. During the first political demonstration in Russia, on Kazan Cathedral Square in St. Petersburg on Dec. 6, 1876, the worker Ia. Potapov raised a red banner as a symbol of the struggle against autocracy. The first May Day meetings and rallies of striking workers occurred under the red banner, and it flew at the barricades of the Revolution of 1905-07 and during the February Revolution of 1917. After the triumph of the October Revolution of 1917 it became the state flag of the Soviet state (Decree of the All-Russian Central Executive Committee of Apr. 14, 1918) and the combat banner of its armed forces.[124]

The 'red banner of revolution' had no set design specifications other than the general colour of the field. Typically, within the context of the Russian revolutions and Soviet usage, they took the form of long banners bearing revolutionary slogans or simple flags with or without writing. Red flags and banners were pervasive in the Soviet Union. In the form of the national flag they were displayed in public venues such as government buildings and schools. However, because the field of the national flag was 'the red banner of revolution' the wide variety of red flags and banners used throughout Soviet society would have served as substitutes for the official national flag. They were meant to instantly signal a patriotic message subliminally, even without the presence of the star, hammer, and sickle. Additionally, the flags of the union republics were derivatives of the USSR flag and should have also evoked a connection between the republic and the larger union of which it was a part (see Appendix).[125]

Several additional uses of the red banner bear discussion here, as they illustrate the wide variety of ways in which citizens encountered this symbol. In Chapter 3, it will be shown how children were taught to value this symbol through exposure to special flags designed for communist children's organisations and patriotically themed toy flags. In addition, the scarves worn by members of the Young Pioneer movement were described as a child's own fragment of the red banner of revolution to be cherished and cared for. In adulthood, Soviet citizens may have encountered their own special red banners through either military service or in the workplace.

It should be no surprise that military banners were first, based upon the red banner of revolution, and second, acquired a sacred nature of their own through the established military traditions in many European countries which linked such banners to state religion. In Russia, this connection resulted in a military tradition of carrying banners with the image of a famous icon of Christ, usually referred to as the *Spas nerukotvornyi* ('Our Saviour, Not Made of Hands'). This icon style emerged from the Orthodox tradition related to the first icon, the 'Image of Edessa'. According to Orthodox belief, an image of Christ miraculously appeared on a rectangle of cloth without the intercession of an artist's hand. A relationship between the military tradition of the tsarist period and Soviet unit banners bearing the face of Lenin and/or Stalin, is likely not coincidental. It should also be noted that within the military context there were ceremonies in which soldiers kneeled and kissed the flies of military banners, perhaps emulating ways in which icons have been venerated in the Russian Orthodox faith.[126]

Red banners bearing Soviet leaders were also used in various contexts in civilian life. Lane noted that, as in the military ritual of kissing the flag, this practice was sometimes seen in civilian enterprises:

> Among the many symbolic objects utilized in the new socialist ritual a few stand out as having a sacred character and may be described as holy ritual attributes. Examples are the Red Banner of an enterprise or organization, in front of which people kneel and which they kiss during a ritual performance, and the Eternal Flame of war memorials.[127]

The flag that Lane mentioned was likely a 'challenge red banner' – a special reward used to incentivise workers in factories and other fields to exceed their production quotas. The *Great Soviet Encyclopedia* explained that these banners were 'one of the forms of rewarding winners in socialist competition'.[128] The article further explained:

> Red banners are awarded and monetary prizes given to the winners in socialist competition according to two different principles: enterprise staffs (with the exception of seasonal sectors of industry) are judged according to quarterly results, and kolkhozes and sovkhozes and raions, oblasts, krais, and autonomous and Union republics are judged on an annual basis.[129]

While numerous examples of these challenge red banners exist in museums and in private collections, there has been little scholarly discussion of the flags and how they were used as production incentives. Symbols on challenge red banners included portraits of Lenin, portraits of Stalin, combined portraits of Lenin and Stalin together, the state arms of the USSR, collections of the arms of the USSR with those of one or more union republics, the quote from the *Communist Manifesto* from the state arms (sometimes in multiple languages), and inspirational quotes about the value of labour.[130]

It is important to recognise the significance of the colour red in Russian culture. The word for red – *krasnyi* – shares the same linguistic root with, and is often synonymous with, the word *krasivyi*, which means 'beautiful'. Therefore, red has traditionally represented the concept of beauty in Russian culture. While the name of Moscow's Red Square originally meant 'beautiful square', it took on a unique double meaning during the Soviet era when red became the colour associated with communism and the Soviet state. In addition, it should be noted that red has a strong psychological impact on the observer, making it an especially powerful colour in civil religious contexts. As clinical psychiatrist Wolfgang G. Jilek noted in his discussion of the psychophysiological effects of totalitarian symbols, red 'has several unique physiological and psychological characteristics'. He explained that because red is the colour of blood and fire, it is thus linked to basic survival instincts of the human species. As a result, 'red is the first colour to which infants react and which they recognise'. Jilek contended that, as a consequence of the relationship of red to the positive and negative emotions associated with blood and fire, the colour 'will elicit ambivalent emotions in humans but its immediate effect on the central nervous system is one of stimulation, excitation and arousal with transient increase in blood pressure and pulse rate'.[131]

Gloria Calhoun's study also suggested a linkage between the colour red and Russian Orthodox iconography. In the discussion she evokes the story of the prophet Elijah and notes that red glories:

> ... were especially prominent in Elijah's icons, in which the glories typically were shaped as a red circle, cloud, or banner. Regardless of the glory's precise form, however, its meaning was consistent: the red glory not only symbolized God's sanction of Elijah as a major prophet, it further signified Elijah's divine connections by evoking the whirlwind and the fiery chariot drawn by fiery horses in which the prophet, according to the Old Testament, was swept up to heaven.[132]

In the story of Elijah, and in iconic representations of the prophet, his cloak or mantle – often shown in red – symbolised his prophetic power as a gift from God. As Elijah ascended to heaven, his cloak fell to Earth and was thus passed on to his heir, Elisha. Therefore, Calhoun suggested that the red glory – both in Russian Orthodoxy and as reused by the Soviets – served as a symbol of legitimacy.[133]

Within Soviet society the red banner was meant to remind the viewer of the red banner of revolution and the historical struggle of the proletariat. The banner represented the unity of all the Soviet peoples within the boundaries of the USSR; the unity of the workers and the peasants who, under the revolutionary red banner, established the first socialist state in what had been the Russian Empire; and the brotherhood of the Soviet people with all the working people of the world under the red banner of socialism.

The third official state symbol of the Soviet Union was the national hymn (*gimn*). For several decades, *The Internationale* – an international socialist anthem – was used in the USSR in lieu of a national anthem. Originally written in French, it had been popular with Russian communists and, in translation, adopted as the official hymn of the Russian SFSR in 1918. The first USSR state anthem was introduced on 15 March 1944 as Soviet troops were advancing westward through eastern Europe, eager to avenge the losses that they had suffered during the fascist invasion and occupation of their country in the 'Great Patriotic War'. While officially titled the *State Anthem of the Soviet Union*, it was also known as *Slav'sia, Otechestvo nashe svobodnoe!*, meaning '*Be glorious, our free homeland!*'. This new distinctly Soviet hymn celebrated the *Soiuz nerushimyi* or 'unbreakable union'. The original lyrics (see Appendix) reflected the time in which they were written, when Iosef Stalin was leader and the country was at war.[134]

After Stalin's death in 1953, Party leadership initiated a policy of destalinisation. Little by little it whittled away at the policies and practices that Stalin had used to maintain and abuse power, including the most excessive abuse – the *GULAG* system. As part of this process Stalin's status as a symbolic figure was significantly reduced and his role in Soviet history was gradually deemphasised. Politically, two symbolic acts defined the new view of Stalin in the Soviet Union. First was Khrushchev's 'secret speech' which he delivered to the twentieth party congress in February 1956. In the speech, he denounced Stalin's abuse of power and the 'cult of personality' associated with his rule. The second symbolic act took place following the party congress of 1961. In the dead of night Stalin's body was removed from Lenin's mausoleum, where he had been laid to rest after his death, and he was buried just in front of the Kremlin wall.[135] As a result of destalinisation, the lyrics of the state anthem fell out of favour because one verse mentioned Stalin by name and another seemed too militaristic for the peaceful image of the USSR that Soviet leaders wanted to project to both domestic and international audiences. During this period, the anthem was performed as an instrumental piece only. It was not until 1971 that one of the original lyricists was commissioned to revise the words, with the new version officially adopted in October 1977 (see Appendix).[136]

In a review of both versions of the lyrics, it is significant that the first verse of the song was the only section that was retained without change in the updated version:

> Great Russia has united forever the unbreakable union of free republics.
>
> Long live the united, mighty Soviet Union created by the will of the peoples!

These words touched on concepts that were vital to Soviet symbolism. First, it described the Soviet Union as an 'unbreakable union of free republics'. Additionally, the first verse explained that the unbreakable union had been 'united forever by Great Russia'. This emphasised the relationship of many of the territories as part of the former Russian Empire and recalled that the revolutionary might of the Russian people led to the dissolution of that empire, allowing the newly freed peoples to join willingly to form the Soviet Union. The lyrics further stressed the idea of a voluntary union by noting that it was formed through the will of the peoples, with the use of the plural referring to the many nationalities in the USSR. Finally, the last line of the verse tied it all together so that the listener was meant to understand that it was the unity of the Soviet peoples, following the leadership of the Russian people, that made the Soviet Union a mighty state.

The 'unbreakable union of free republics' celebrated in the state hymn was one of the most important notions in Soviet symbolism. This concept promoted the idea that the Soviet Union was a multinational family of free peoples who were not only equals, but also united in their common goal to build communism. Soviet symbolism visually portrayed this concept in a variety of ways. Examples include the use of the 15 republic languages such as on the Soviet emblem, flag displays showing the national flag along with a full collection of republic flags, images showing groups of people wearing national costumes of each republic, as well as other forms. These visual portrayals of unity will be discussed further in Chapter 4.

This view of the Soviet Union as a permanent union of many nationalities was reinforced through the lyrics of the first verse every time it was sung. The equality of all people in the Soviet Union, regardless of their ethnicity or social function, was demonstrated by addressing each other using the terms 'citizen' (*grazhdanin*) or 'comrade' (*tovarishch*). This practice was found in every strata of society – workplaces, the military (where 'comrade' preceded a person's military rank), and even to how one referred to national leaders (Comrade Lenin, Comrade Stalin, for example).[137]

As with many states the capital of the USSR became an important symbol of the country, both domestically and internationally. The 1923 Soviet constitution declared Moscow to be the capital of the new country, reflecting the fact that the Bolsheviks had moved the seat of government for the RSFSR from the imperial capital of Petrograd back to Moscow on 12 March 1918. Moscow, and the Kremlin fortress that lies at its centre, became synonymous with Soviet power. In terms of visual imagery, Soviet sources portrayed Moscow as the heart of the country through images focused on Red Square and the Kremlin. Those of Red Square typically showed the portion of the square around Lenin's mausoleum with the wall of the Kremlin and Saviour Tower in the background. Other common symbolic portrayals of Moscow as the centre of the USSR included images of the Soviet flag on the top of the dome of the Kremlin Senate or of the shining red stars atop the Kremlin towers. Chapter 4 discusses Moscow and Red Square as national symbols in further detail.

One of the most important symbols in the Soviet Union outside of the official state symbol set was Lenin. Like the sacred red banner, representations of Lenin were ubiquitous. Following his death in 1924, Soviet leaders decided not only to create an elaborate tomb for Lenin on Red Square, but also to scientifically preserve his physical body and place it on display as an object of reverence and pilgrimage. Many have theorised that the decision to preserve and display Lenin's remains was linked directly to the popular belief in Russian Orthodoxy that a true saint was incorruptible, and therefore their physical remains would not decay.[138] While the preservation was achieved through scientific means, the psychological connection to the older religious tradition of the country was meant to imbue Lenin with saint-like status in Soviet society. In addition, his glass coffin served as a reliquary and his mausoleum became the primary shrine of Marxism-Leninism, as well as the most important location for pilgrimage in Soviet civil religion. By locating Lenin's tomb on Red Square, this historic location at the heart of Moscow was sanctified as a Soviet holy place and transformed into the symbolic heart of the entire USSR.[139]

Daily, citizens queued to pay homage to Lenin in long orderly lines that usually extended well beyond the boundaries of Red Square. Excerpts from Hedrick Smith's classic book, *The Russians*, illustrate what it was like to wait in the queue and experience the opportunity to be in the presence of the great leader of the Soviet Union. Smith describes how, as the line approached the mausoleum, militia (police) members collected women's handbags and organised the visitors into two straight lines – arranging couples with the man on the right and the woman to his left. As the queue reached the middle of the square, the line executed a sharp right turn toward the mausoleum. Guards instructed people to remove their hands from their pockets and the men to remove their hats, and everyone assumed a solemn demeanour appropriate to a visit to a holy shrine. When the queue at last entered the mausoleum, the pilgrims moved along a clearly defined path until they reached the crypt room. Smith recounted:

> The column made a swift circuit around the coffin. The crypt room is constructed so that visitors enter, immediately turn right and walk up half a flight of steps along the wall, turn left and walk along another wall on a balcony overlooking the glass tomb of Lenin, turn left again and descend another half a flight of stairs, and exit the room. This semicircular route

permits a view of Lenin from both sides and from the feet, but never at closer than ten to twelve feet and never with an instant to pause and simply look.[140]

Once the visitors had paid their respects to Lenin, they proceeded to the exit of the mausoleum and passed along the part of the Kremlin wall in which the most important heroes and political figures of the Soviet state had been interred. Soviet children experienced this spiritual journey either accompanied by their parents or in the company of their Pioneer comrades. The experience would have been the culmination of their education about Lenin, and it was intended to have a strong emotional impact on the participants.[141]

It also became common practice to display portraits and sculptures of Lenin within both private and public contexts throughout the country. From a civil religious perspective, it is especially interesting to note how Lenin corners (localised shrines to Lenin) replaced the traditional icon corners of Russian Orthodoxy. Again, the linguistic relationship between the Russian words for 'beautiful' and 'red' made this transition easier. In traditional Russian Orthodox homes, the standard practice was to have one corner in the home devoted to a household Christian shrine. This corner was the location where the family displayed their icons and it served as the locus of religious activities in the residence. In Russian, the icon corner was known as the 'beautiful corner' or alternately as the 'red corner'. After the October Revolution, the Communist Party began an anti-religious campaign aimed at changing the culture to replace Orthodoxy with atheism in line with Marxist philosophy. With the death of Lenin and his 'canonisation' as a 'saint' of the communist cause, it seemed only natural that images of Lenin would replace the religious icons in the home. Eventually, 'red corners' became known as 'Lenin corners'. In addition to 'icons' of Lenin, it was quite common to display other Soviet symbols in this location. Lenin corners were also found outside the context of the home. It was a common project for Young Pioneers to create their own Lenin corners or even miniature Lenin museums in their schools. Additionally, Lenin corners were found in workplaces and public buildings. In communal living environments, Lenin corners served not just as centres of civil religious observance, but also as the expanded social space shared by all the residents.[142]

In her analysis of Soviet political posters, Gloria Calhoun described how 'A ruling regime can assert its membership in the relational category legitimate by visually associating its leaders with images that culturally or historically convey legitimacy.'[143] Citing the example of how portraits of Marx were carried in early Bolshevik demonstrations, she explained that:

> We might refer to this practice as establishing 'relational legitimacy,' a practice that
> continued as the Soviet regime changed leadership. Relational legitimacy explains why
> Stalin's succession to Lenin was often legitimized by including Lenin in images of Stalin,
> thus representing Stalin as 'Lenin's intellectual and spiritual heir.'[144]

As with other protocols of Soviet symbolism, this usage is another example of cultural recycling. During the tsarist era it was common practice to portray images of the tsar and his heir to convey the natural order of succession for the nation's leadership. Lenin's portrait eventually became an important element in the symbols of Soviet children's organisations, the emblem of the Young Communist Union, and the official symbol of the Communist Party of the USSR. In this way, all these organisations were shown to be continuing Lenin's work. Chapters 3 and 4 discuss further the use of Lenin's image in various contexts in Soviet society.[145]

There were, of course, other individuals who were symbolically significant in the Soviet Union. Among the earliest were Karl Marx, and to a lesser extent, Friedrich Engels – the authors of *The Communist Manifesto*. Soviet imagery frequently showed Marx and Lenin together in a manner to portray Lenin as the heir and inheritor to Marx's legacy. Lenin's successor, Stalin, enjoyed equal symbolic status during his time as leader of the Soviet Union. While it was common to see portraits or sculptures of later Soviet leaders displayed in public places, none were ever elevated to the level of Lenin and Stalin. Finally, it is important to note that Khrushchev never intended for his condemnation of Stalin's 'Cult of Personality' to extend to Lenin. He continued to be one of the most important symbols in the Soviet Union until its dissolution in 1991. In many ways, images of Lenin not only commemorated his importance as a revolutionary and political leader, they also served as a visual metonym for the Communist Party.

One final personification of the Soviet state is worth noting in this discussion – national heroes of the Soviet Union. This broad category incorporated a variety of individuals, and not just recipients of the official 'Hero of the Soviet Union' citation. In the Soviet state, heroes served as exemplars of the communist principles to which all people should aspire. Ideal citizens included military heroes, cosmonauts, athletes, chess players, scientists, and others deemed worthy to serve as role models for the citizenry. In addition, national heroes could also take the generic form of an idealised Soviet soldier or sailor, a factory worker or communal farmer, a scientist or engineer, an athlete, or even a good student or member of the Soviet youth movement. These people were portrayed as exemplars of the best devotees of Marxism-Leninism and their contributions to the building of communism were widely promoted. Heroes of the Soviet Union, like Christian saints in Russian Orthodoxy, were held up as examples for all who were on the Leninist path. In this way, Lenin's memory was kept alive, and his legacy would live on in the new communist utopia that they were all working to build. In Chapter 3, examples of how Lenin and national heroes were used as role models in political education for children will demonstrate how the concept of *Sovietness* was symbolised throughout Soviet society.[146]

Conclusion

In his classic study *Political Power*, political scientist Charles Edward Merriam acknowledged the importance of the use of symbols and symbolism in the consolidation of power:

> Organization as well as interpretation is a key to the use of symbolism upon a mass scale. It is not enough to dream or devise a catching symbol, for the techniques of modern mass action, of advertising, of assembly must be invoked, so that the symbol is impressed upon millions. In organized form this is sometimes called propaganda, popular education in special appeals. But the propagandist does not sow the seed to the four winds of heaven. He systematically surveys the field and spreads the seed mechanically in spots where it may most quickly or most deeply take root.[147]

Merriam's quote aptly describes the Soviet view of national symbols. The Bolsheviks and the Soviet government thoroughly understood the importance of symbols and quickly developed a distinct symbol set and a well-defined symbolic vocabulary to accomplish their goals. Symbols and symbolism were important tools for both official communications from the central government and in conveying a linkage to national priorities throughout the various institutions and enterprises in the society.

This chapter has presented a discussion of the role that national symbols play in the communication of shared values and in the formation of national identity. Further, it has introduced the Soviet *simvolika*, emphasising the meaning assigned to specific elements and explaining how the combination of those elements in official state symbols conveyed the importance of union and unity in the country. Symbols were a vital element in the construction of a sense of Soviet identity and in the civil religion of the USSR. The article on 'patriotism' in the *Great Soviet Encyclopedia* made it clear that the concepts of 'union' and 'unity' in Soviet patriotism meant more than just showing devotion to, and taking pride in, the country. It also embodied the spirit of socialist internationalism in the common goal of building communism not just in the USSR, but on a global scale:

> Under the conditions of the consolidation and development of a new historical community of people – the Soviet people – all-Union political and sociopsychological values are being established. There appears in the Soviet man a national pride that embraces the Soviet Union as a whole; such pride is an important element of socialist patriotism. With the formation of the world socialist system, 'the patriotism of the citizens of socialist society is embodied in devotion and fidelity to one's homeland and to the entire community of socialist countries' (Programma KPSS, 1974, p. 120). The ideas and feelings of socialist patriotism are an important factor in the political and labor activity of the masses during the construction of communism. The CPSU considers the education of the Soviet people in the spirit of an organic union of socialist patriotism and internationalism to be one of its most important tasks.[148]

In Chapter 3, the discussion will turn to how educators used the symbols in the political socialisation of children, both within the educational system and through official children's organisations. German pedagogist Friedrich Kuebart noted that, during the period of developed socialism, there was renewed emphasis:

> …to create an emotional identification with the political system by means of rituals related to state symbols, for example, the national flag, emblem and national anthem. Since the adoption of the new constitution in 1977 it has become evident that school rituals are paying increased attention to state symbols.[149]

As will be demonstrated, political education was clearly designed to instil a specific set of shared values, and a shared sense of Soviet identity, in the youngest citizens of the country.

Most adults in the USSR would have had the same basic patriotic upbringing. The hope was that the lessons of childhood would produce a sense of *Soviet* national identity and socialist responsibility that would be inherent in the work and life of the individuals in adulthood. Chapter 4 will discuss the concept of banal nationalism and how national symbols were present in the everyday life of Soviet citizens. Combined with the discussion in this chapter, examples of the role of Soviet *simvolika* in the lives of children and adults in the USSR will demonstrate how seemingly mundane items, such as national symbols, are vital to the governmental functions of modern states and the creation of relationships between citizens and their countries.

Figures 2.14-2.17. Four postal cards for May Day demonstrating the way that Soviet symbols were used on holiday greeting cards. *Top Row (Left to Right):* '1 May' and 'With the holiday 1 May! *Bottom Row (Left to Right):* 'Peace. Labour. May' and 'With the holiday 1 May! *See discussion in Chapter 4.*

Chapter 3
Little Leninists: Symbols and the Political Socialisation of Soviet Children

The Pioneer Movement has enormous significance. It captivates children at that age when a person is still forming, develops children's social instincts, helps in the creation of their social skills, the creation of social consciousness.[150]

– Nadezhda Krupskaia

As with any religion, the precepts of civil religion as well as its associated symbols and rituals are taught to each new generation. While children are sometimes exposed to these elements in the home, in most cultures basic political socialisation is achieved through the country's system of formal education. Schoolchildren worldwide learn to read the symbols of their countries as they are instructed in the basic political values of their societies. In many countries, flags are displayed at educational venues – on flagpoles outside school buildings, in entryways, in gymnasiums, and in individual classrooms. Schools may also display photos of the head of state or national heroes within the buildings. In addition to national symbols, students are typically introduced to the basic rites and rituals of their national culture of patriotism. These can include a formal recitation of values, singing the national anthem or other patriotic songs, or performing a ritual such as the American Pledge of Allegiance. Throughout a child's education, the basic elements of civil religion are continuously reinforced and given deeper meaning through formal history and civics lessons as the child matures.[151]

National symbols are so closely linked to the political socialisation process that social scientists can use them to gauge the development of national identity in children throughout the years of formal education. Through multiple studies scholars from a variety of fields were able to determine how children's knowledge and understanding of national symbols increases because of the political socialisation process. These studies, although not conducted in the Soviet Union, can be used to understand the role of symbols in the political socialisation of children in the USSR. In a study of American children conducted in 1940, sociologist Eugene Horowitz found that even as early as the first grade, children had already begun to acquire some attachment to their national flag, and that by the tenth grade the attachment was nearly universal. While the youngest children explained their choice of the US flag in simple terms ('because I like it'), the older children were able to verbalise their preference by explaining that they selected it because it was the flag of their country. Follow-up studies conducted on American children by sociologist Eugene Weinstein (1957) and psychologist Edwin Lawson (1962) confirmed Horowitz's findings that, as children progress through their education, their attachment to their nation's flag shows a steady progression in terms of the popularity of the flag and the children's sophistication in the explanation of their preferences. These early studies continue to be relevant because they focused on attitudes toward national symbols as indicators of political socialisation.[152]

Based upon his results, Weinstein was able to chart out distinct stages in the child's development of the concept of flag and their sense of national identity (summarised in Table 3.1).

Stage (ages)	Child's Concept of Flag and National Identity
Level 1 (5-6 years)	The child has no knowledge of other countries or flags; associates flags with various celebrations.
Level 2 (5-6 years)	The child has begun to develop the concept of countries; begins to understand that flags are used to identify with a country; only knows their country's flag, but understands that other countries have different flags; exhibits the initial stages of understanding symbols, but has not fully processed the flag as a symbol.
Level 3 (7 years)	The child has a better understanding of countries as a geographic area; understands that flags can show ownership, but interprets the relationship as the country 'possessing' the people; recognises that people 'possessed' by a country will prefer that country's flag; indicates that their country's flag is 'the best'.
Level 4 (7 years)	The child begins to display more knowledge about their nation's flag and flags in general; begins to acquire a basic understanding of the concept of government; learns that people and flags are attributes, rather than possessions, of a country.
Level 5 (8 years)	The child understands the notion of 'a multiplicity of flags'; begins to understand that countries are subdivided; dramatically changes their estimation of how many countries there are; recognises that their country's flag is best because their country is best.
Level 6 (8 years)	The child begins to grasp the full extent of symbolism associated with their nation's flag; recognises that singing the national anthem is a way to honour the flag and that raising the flag to honour a past leader indicates that leader was one of the 'greatest leaders'.
Level 7 (9 years)	The child has a 'better notion of country' as not only a geographic unit, but also 'a group which has certain common purposes and allegiances'; understands flags as a conventional symbol that can represent not only countries, but also smaller entities and groups of people; understands national identity not in terms of 'being possessed by a country', but as 'identification with a group and the goals of that group'.
Level 8 (10 years)	The child fully comprehends that the national flag 'stands for loyalty to a set of goals and the group holding those goals'; understands that people in other countries who agree with their own country's goals would prefer their own national flag.
Levels 9 & 10 (11-12 yrs.)	The child fully understands the relationships between flag, people, and government; progresses from one level to the next through an 'increased knowledge of rituals associated with the flag'.

Table 3.1. Summary of Weinstein's stages in the child's development of the concept of flag and their sense of national identity.

Examining Weinstein's scale, it is obvious just how quickly the educational process helps children progress from the stage where they just 'like their national flag', to developing a symbolic understanding of, and a personal relationship with, that flag as a symbol of their national identity.

He concluded that 'the order in which the elements are acquired and the types of relationships perceived among them is fairly stable from child to child'. In addition, he drew a parallel between the child's development of self and their development of a sense of national identity. This sense of national identity, according to Weinstein, is 'predicated upon an awareness of other countries and the identification of people within those countries'.[153]

In their study of American children, political scientists David Easton and Robert D. Hess explained the need for political socialisation from the perspective of both the regime and of the individual child. From the regime's perspective, political socialisation is one of the tools that is used to promote stability of the political system itself. Easton and Hess noted that the procedures that are typically used by different regimes to attain this goal include 'coercion, perceived satisfaction of the needs and demands of the members, generation of positive motivation and identification through manipulation of symbols, verbal and otherwise, regulation of communications, and the like'. They also acknowledged the importance of the educational system in the political training of the youngest citizens, so that a sense of national identity will be instilled in such a way that it is greater than any tribal loyalties that might be at play. From the government's perspective, it is important that each new generation form an attachment to, and positive sentiments toward, the regime. As with previously discussed studies, this work stresses the importance of the early years of formal education, as Easton and Hess contend that by the time a child reaches the age of 14, his or her political attitudes are already formed. In the early years, it is concrete symbols such as the flag or a leadership figure that are the most important at this stage of development. It is only as the child matures that they can relate to abstract and more impersonal political symbols. The authors also pointed out that, in the case of American children, many 'associate the sanctity and awe of religion with the political community' and that those in the 9-10 age group 'sometimes have considerable difficulty in disentangling God and country'. It is this aspect of the political socialisation process that is key to the growth of civil religious feelings in the developing child. Finally, the authors emphasised that the process of political socialisation is beneficial not just for the state, but also for the individual child. They suggested that, faced with the authority of adults, children develop a sense of helplessness and vulnerability:

> By idealizing authority and by actually seeing it as benign, solicitous, and wise, the child is able to allay the fears and anxieties awakened by his own dependent state. A potentially threatening figure is conveniently transformed into a protector.

The result of political socialisation and the state's ability to provide this sense of protective authority to the child is the formation of a social bond that reinforces the child's national identity and produces the civil religious feelings associated with political symbols and rituals.[154]

Researchers have also used symbols to assess the development of a sense of national identity in schoolchildren in other countries. Cross-cultural studies between American and Canadian children have shown similar patterns of flag preference in both countries. Symbol studies conducted in Scotland have examined how Scottish children negotiate their dual identity of being both Scottish and British. Other studies in the United Kingdom have demonstrated how children relate to national flags, as well as to other political symbols such as the national anthem and the monarch.[155] A study of Hungarian children conducted by social psychologist György Csepeli confirmed that this relationship between symbols and the development of national identity is not just an American or British phenomenon. Csepeli concluded that 'national attitude is developed in the early years of school life, reflecting both the influence of curriculum and of the teaching and school rituals'.[156]

In addition, each of these studies further validated the age progression in the development of national identity suggested by Weinstein and others.

Why are these psychological and sociological studies of children relevant to the examination of national symbols? Quite simply, it is because of the civil religious aspects of national identity and the role that symbols, and national rituals, play in the process of political socialisation. Considering that children in the United States, the United Kingdom, and the Soviet Union lived in different types of societies and experienced political socialisation through different educational contexts, the basic psychological and sociological processes involved in the development of their sense of national identity were basically the same. While the methodology of political socialisation employed in a constitutional democracy, a constitutional monarchy, or a single-party communist state may at first seem quite different, in reality, the psychosocial educational process through which the culture of patriotism is taught and the sense of national identity is formed in different political systems is actually quite similar. Finally, as sociologist Adam Gamoran suggested in his study of civil religion in American schools, the role of civil religious education and the development of a strong sense of national identity in children is particularly important in societies where there is a wide range of ethnic, racial, and/or religious diversity. This is because a common sense of identity helps to integrate diverse populations into the broader society. In a country such as the Soviet Union, that included more than 100 distinct ethnicities, this aspect of civil religion is particularly relevant to the development of the detailed system of political symbols and rituals in the USSR.[157]

Soviet Schools and Formal Education

With this understanding of the role of symbols in civil religion and how children develop a knowledge of national symbols in the early years of formal education, it is now possible to examine these concepts within the context of the Soviet Union. The first step is a discussion of the basic institutions through which the political training of Soviet children was conducted. In the USSR there was a well-developed, systematic, and universal mechanism through which children were taught the elements of Soviet civil religion and were given formal instruction in patriotism. Soviet civil religion was deliberately and strategically integrated into the national education system with the goal of developing a strong sense of national identity and a cohesive culture of Soviet patriotism among the population of the entire country. While this discussion will briefly review the history of the Soviet educational system and children's organisations, most primary source material will be drawn from the era of mature socialism.

One of the primary architects of the early Soviet education system was Nadezhda Konstantinovna Krupskaia, an influential Bolshevik and wife of Vladimir Il'ich Lenin. Following the October Revolution, Krupskaia served as deputy to Lunacharskii in the People's Commissariat for Education. She played an influential role in the development of Soviet education, libraries, and youth programmes. In her writings on communist pedagogy, Krupskaia attempted to clarify the differences between bourgeois educational methods and those that should be employed in a communist society:

> The Soviet system of education aims at developing every child's ability, activity,
> consciousness, personality and individuality. That is why our educational methods differ
> from those in bourgeois public schools, and they are radically different from the methods
> employed in the education of bourgeois children. The bourgeoisie tries to bring up its
> children as individualists who set their ego above all else, who oppose the masses.

44

Communist education employs other methods. We are for the all-round development of our children – we want to make them strong physically and morally, teach them to be collectivists and not individuals, bring them up not to oppose the collective but on the contrary to constitute its force and raise it to a new level. We believe that a child's personality can be best and most fully developed only in a collective. For the collective does not destroy a child's personality, and it improves the quality and content of education.[158]

The emphasis on collectivism and instilling a sense of communist morality was just as important to the goals of Soviet education as the teaching of basic skills such as reading, writing, mathematics, and other traditional academic subjects. Educational authorities ensured that every aspect of the curriculum was designed with the teachings of Karl Marx, Friedrich Engels, and Vladimir Lenin in mind. This was key to the process through which children were prepared for their future roles in helping to build the communist society.[159]

Children of preschool age in the Soviet Union had a diverse range of experiences. During the workday, some children remained home in the care of grandparents, while others were taken to day care centres or kindergartens. Those who remained at home may have had little formal introduction to Soviet civil religion, but those enrolled in state childcare and kindergartens certainly did. In the day care system, the primary pedagogical goal was to help children adjust to life as a member of a collective. This was accomplished through group activities and positive reinforcement where children were praised for playing together and sharing with their comrades.[160]

Soviet kindergartens were designed for ages three to seven. A Soviet book published in English for an international audience in 1957 clearly defined the goal of Soviet kindergarten education:

> The aim of the educational work and care of the children in the kindergartens is to instil in them a collective spirit, to teach them to play together, to do things together and help one another to perform simple tasks. Thus the children's 'collective' becomes a social environment in which their abilities and inclinations are developed.[161]

In addition to learning about how to be a good group member, the children in kindergarten would have had a good introduction to a few of the basic symbols of the Soviet state. For example, in addition to the colourful decorations usually found in kindergartens in any country, photographs of Soviet kindergartens frequently show that these institutions had portraits of Lenin on the walls. In 1971, Kitty D. Weaver, an observer of the Soviet educational system, described seeing a family portrait from Lenin's childhood displayed on a table with flowers in one preschool, as well as a patriotic celebration of the October Revolution that she witnessed in one kindergarten:

> We took seats in the front row of chairs, and the musical director sat down at the piano and started to play 'Moya Rodina [My Motherland]' as the children marched in, carrying red flags.[162]

Through the performance, the children created their own version of the Great October celebrations held in cities across the Soviet Union. One group of children portrayed the bus carrying the demonstrators to the celebration, while others played passengers:

> The passengers sang:
>
> *One, two; left, right. We march with a song.*
> *No other holiday October has been as wonderful as this.*

The seated group of children sang back:

Holiday, holiday, holiday October!
The flags, the flags, the red flags are exciting
Faces are joyous, everyone is merry.
The red flags are exciting.[163]

Activities such as this gave the kindergarten students an early start in their formal lives as Soviet citizens. In addition to learning the basic skills taught in kindergartens around the world, they were introduced to the Leninist path, along which they would become politically trained in collectivism and Soviet patriotism.[164]

Formal education for all children in the Soviet Union began at the age of seven.[165] On 1 September – the Holiday of the First School Bell – seven-year-old children were introduced to life in the collective of Soviet schoolchildren. On their first day of school, children dressed in their new school uniforms carried flowers intended for presentation to their teachers. In the welcoming ceremony, the teachers greeted the new students at the entrance to the school. Then the tenth graders came forward, and each took a new student by the hand to lead them in a procession to their classroom, as illustrated in a book for the leaders of Little Octobrist groups. In the classroom, the second graders presented each student with their own copy of the textbook and welcomed them into the collective of the student body. From this point forward, the children were not just individuals but also members of a group. Throughout every stage of their education, children were encouraged to put the group ahead of themselves and to help their comrades. A glimpse of the first day of school can be found in two documentaries that focused on the last years of the Soviet Union. American filmmaker Robin Hessman's documentary, *My Perestroika*, featured interviews with a group of friends who grew up together in the last two decades of Soviet power. They reflected upon their school years and experiences in the children's organisations. The interviews were supplemented by documentary footage from the Soviet era. The second film, *Age 7 in the USSR*, by Sergei Miroshnichenko, was a documentary about Soviet childhood that was broadcast as part of the British *Up* television series.[166]

Figure 3.1. Young Pioneers escort Little Octobrists to their classroom in this illustration from a 1959 book for leaders of the Little Octobrists.

Initially, the age at which children entered the formal educational system was eight years. It was later lowered to seven and was being lowered to 6 across the country when the Soviet Union broke up. In addition, in the early years of the Soviet Union education was mandatory for seven years, while in the years following the Second World War the period was expanded. By the 1950s, education was mandatory for all children for ten years, with some students completing their secondary education in college-preparatory courses and others in polytechnic schools.[167]

The Soviet campaign to expand educational opportunities for all children had multiple goals. First was the reversal of educational policies in the tsarist era that basically trapped children in the life-path of their parents. Prior to the October Revolution children of the nobility, the wealthy, and the merchant class had access to formal education, while the children of peasants and workers received little or no formal education and often entered the work force at an early age. Soviet sources estimated that before the October 1917 revolution the illiteracy rate among men was 70%, while for women it was nearly 90%.[168] In their lessons, Soviet children learned about the inequality of the old educational system and received frequent reminders that it was because of communism that all children had an equal opportunity to get an education in the USSR. The national curriculum included the same basic goals of any educational system – to teach the student to read and write, to teach them mathematics and science, and to give them a good background in the humanities and social sciences. Children in each of the Soviet republics received instruction in the language and literature of their own republic, but all children in the Soviet Union regardless of their nationality studied and were expected to achieve fluency in the Russian language, as it was the common language for all citizens of the USSR, as well as the language of bureaucracy and administration.[169]

It is the second goal of the Soviet educational system, political socialisation, that is of interest to this study. Technically, the curriculum in each of the 15 Soviet republics was directed by that republic's Ministry of Education. However, the Communist Party and the national education authorities were involved in shaping the curriculum in every republic. The ideology of Marxism and Leninism was central to teaching all subjects and not just limited to instruction in history and civics. At every stage of their education students not only were trained to be 'good communists', but also received instruction in other subjects that was presented within the framework of the Marxist-Leninist worldview. Political education was intended to teach the children to be patriotic citizens and, more importantly, to instil in them a sense of *Soviet* national identity that would be dominant over their ethnic identity. While the formal educational system was designed to teach Soviet political philosophy and communist morality, it is impossible to completely understand how Soviet children were politically socialised without a discussion of the role of the children's organisations. These organisations were directly linked to the formal educational system and embedded into the schools. Teachers and leaders of the children's organisations shared the responsibility for teaching children to be good Leninists and patriotic citizens of the Soviet Union.[170]

Children's Organisations in the USSR

In the Soviet Union, there was only one organisation for children – the Vladimir Lenin All-Union Pioneer Organisation (*Vsesoiuznaia Pionerskaia organizatsiia imeni Vladimira Lenina*) – better known as the Young Pioneers. This organisation was administered under the authority of the All-Union Leninist Young Communist League, better known as *Komsomol* – an abbreviation of 'Young Communist League' (*Kommunisticheskii soiuz molodezhi*). *Komsomol* was an organisation open to individuals aged 15-28 who had proven themselves worthy through their participation in the Young Pioneers. Pioneers ranged in age from 10-15 years, but to become members of the organisation children first had to demonstrate their worthiness in the Little Octobrists (*Oktiabriata*). Therefore, the ideal progression in the political life of a Soviet citizen would start as a Little Octobrist (age 7), continue in the Young Pioneers (age 10), advance in youth as a member of *Komsomol* (age 15), and culminate with membership in the Communist Party as an adult.[171]

This study focuses on the initial years of formal education from ages 7-15. These years correspond not only to the age-span of the Little Octobrists and Young Pioneers, but also have been shown through the previously-discussed studies to be the period when children acquire their sense of national identity and ability to recognise and understand the symbols of their country. Nadezhda Krupskaia, one of the architects of the Young Pioneer Organisation, understood the importance of political education in preparing the next generation:

> The Pioneer Movement has enormous significance. It captivates children at that age when a person is still forming, develops children's social instincts, helps in the creation of their social skills, the creation of social consciousness. It places before children a great goal – that goal, which is put forward by the current era, for which the working class of the whole world is fighting. This goal is the liberation of workers, the organization of a new system, wherever there are divisions by class, there would be no oppression, exploitation, and all people would live a full happy life. This goal is such that it can illuminate the life of a growing generation with a bright light, fill it with deep support, with extraordinary rich experiences. Under certain conditions the Pioneer Movement could actually raise that young generation which could deal with those tasks which will arise before it.[172]

Krupskaia and others worked to build a coeducational organisation that would give children similar opportunities as those available through Scouting organisations in other countries, but would also train children to be good citizens of the Soviet Union. Through the Young Pioneer organisation children had access to a wide variety of extracurricular activities such as games, field trips, camping, handicrafts, theatre and the arts, and more. Activities were also designed to encourage teamwork and good social habits, with an emphasis on collective accomplishments and socially beneficial work. According to Krupskaia,

> The Young Pioneer organization instils in its members collective instincts and accustoms them to share joy and grief, teaches them to make the interests of the collective their own, to regard themselves as members of the collective. It develops collective habits, i.e., the ability to work and act collectively and in an organized manner by subordinating their will to the will of the collective, displaying their initiative through the collective and teaching them to respect the opinion of the collective. Lastly, it enhances children's communist consciousness by helping them to realize that they are members of the working class which is fighting for mankind's happiness, members of the huge army of the international proletariat.[173]

Political training was both the responsibility of the school system and the children's organisations, so that it was impossible to really separate the two. Krupskaia contended that this connection between the school and the organisations was the main strength of the Young Pioneers and kept the group relevant to Soviet society. Probably the easiest way to clearly define what was expected of children in this area is to look at the laws and principles for each level of the children's organisations, which were frequently reiterated in literature and formal textbooks designed for each age group.[174]

The Little Octobrists and Young Pioneers

As the youngest age group of the Young Pioneer organisation, the Little Octobrists were an introductory group used to prepare children for membership in the Pioneers. The programme was first introduced in 1924 and was named in honour of the heroes of the October Revolution using the diminutive form of the word 'Octobrist' (hence, *Oktiabriata* or 'Little Octobrist'). Nearly every child in the Soviet Union participated in the group when they were in grades 1-3. Octobrist groups were organised within each school or children's home. The Little Octobrists were usually led by schoolteachers with the assistance of *Komsomol* members and older Young Pioneers.[175]

The rules of the organisation, as articulated in manuals for Young Pioneers and their leaders, clearly defined the ideal child of this age group:

Rules of the Little Octobrists

Little Octobrists are future Pioneers.

Little Octobrists are diligent children, study well, love school, [and] respect their elders.

Only those who love work are called Little Octobrists.

Little Octobrists are honest and truthful children.

Little Octobrists are amicable children, they read and draw, play and sing, [and] live cheerfully.[176]

School books and recreational reading for Octobrist-aged children reinforced these ideals with illustrations of happy children, proudly wearing their Little Octobrist badges while working with a group of their peers or helping at home. More discussion about Octobrist symbols and the imagery used to portray the ideal Little Octobrist will follow in the section on how symbols were used in the political socialisation process.

When a child advanced to membership in the Young Pioneers (*Molodye Pionery*), they were expected to live up to a higher ideal and to accept much more responsibility for themselves and their comrades. Promotion to the Young Pioneers was not automatic, but nearly every Little Octobrist aspired to achieve that goal and very few children were excluded from participation in the organisation. The promotion ceremony was a solemn affair, and usually was held in the Pioneer Room of their school or at a place of symbolic significance in their city, such as Red Square for children in Moscow. As part of the ceremony, an older Young Pioneer tied the coveted red neckerchief of the Pioneers around the neck of the new member, and they were given the badge of the organisation to wear on their chests.[177] The newly initiated Pioneers swore the solemn promise of the Young Pioneer and agreed to live by the laws of the organisation, such as these examples from the 1961/1962 school year:

Solemn Promise of the Young Pioneer of the Soviet Union (1961)

I, a Young Pioneer of the Soviet Union, before my comrades solemnly promise:

to passionately love my Soviet homeland,

to live, study, and fight as great Lenin bequeathed and as the Communist Party teaches.

Laws of the Young Pioneers of the Soviet Union (1961)

A pioneer loves the homeland, the Communist Party of the Soviet Union. He prepares himself to become a member of the VLKSM [All-Union Leninist Young Communist League].

A pioneer reveres the memory of those who have given their life in the fight for the freedom and flourishing of the Soviet Homeland.

A pioneer is on friendly terms with children of all countries of the world.

A pioneer diligently studies, is disciplined, and polite.

A pioneer loves to work and protects the national good.

A pioneer is a good comrade, cares for the younger, [and] helps the elders.

A pioneer grows up courageous and is not afraid of difficulties.

A pioneer tells the truth, he values the honour of his detachment.

A pioneer toughens himself, does physical exercises every day.

A pioneer loves nature; he is a defender of green plants, beneficial birds, and animals.

A pioneer is an example to all children.[178]

Throughout the history of the organisation, the oath and laws were updated on several occasions, bringing them closer in line with the priorities of the nation at the time. For example, there were fewer laws in the 1920s and they were simpler. The Pioneers were expected to be 'faithful to the cause of the workman class and in the precepts of Ilich'; to be 'the younger brother and helper of the Young Communist and the Communist'; to organise other children and join with them in their lives, as well as being an example for all children; to be 'a comrade to other Pioneers, and to the workman and peasant children of the whole world'; and to strive for knowledge, because 'Knowledge and understanding are the great forces in the struggle for the cause of the workman'.[179] There were also five customs that described the personal habits of the ideal Young Pioneer. By the 1980s, the list of laws from the previous two decades had been combined and simplified so that there were eight. While the laws and customs of the Young Pioneers varied throughout the history of the organisation, the basic principles guiding the lives of the organisation's members were all designed to help the children develop a sense of Soviet identity and to prepare themselves for their future role as a builder of communism. To achieve this, the programme incorporated the symbols, rituals, and pilgrimages that were inherent in the civil religion of the Soviet Union.[180]

Soviet Symbols and the Socialisation of Children

While Soviet children initially were exposed to national symbols either in their home environments or in public places, formal introduction to and instruction about the symbols and their meanings began when they entered school. As German pedagogist Friedrich Kuebart noted, 'on a cognitive level, state symbols provide a starting point for explaining basic elements of state organisation and the ideological and constitutional foundations of the political system in a form suited to various age groups'. As the child matured and advanced through the educational system the connection between the symbols and the concepts they represented became more sophisticated.[181]

Beginning Readers

An examination of books designed for children, who were at the early stages of learning to read, highlights the importance of national symbols in every aspect of the educational process. The basic alphabet book *Azbuka* (1990) demonstrates this point very clearly. When the book was opened, on the first pages after the title page the child saw an image of a wise, but friendly-looking, Lenin. On the opposite page were three lines from Maiakovskii's famous poem: 'Lenin lived, Lenin lives, Lenin will live'.[182] On the following pages the child saw a 2-page image of Red Square – the heart of the Soviet state.

Figure 3.2. Image of Red Square showing pilgrims waiting in the queue to pay their respects to Lenin.

In this image were illustrated many of the key elements of Soviet civil religion. First and foremost, just to the left of centre, was the Lenin Mausoleum. A long line of Soviet citizens – men, women, and children together – wound its way from the mausoleum entrance back towards the Historical Museum, which was to the right out of the frame. Behind the mausoleum was the massive red wall of the Kremlin – the centre of the Soviet government. At far left in the image was Saviour Tower capped by an immense red star. During the Soviet era, this was the entrance through which high party officials entered the Kremlin complex. Behind the mausoleum and to the right was Senate Tower (*Senatskaia bashnia*) and behind that the dome of the Kremlin Senate (*Senatskii dvorets*), on the top of which waved the red banner of the Soviet Union. In this one image, the child was presented with many of the symbols that would be key to their understanding of what it meant to be a Soviet citizen. The flag was described much later in the book when the student was learning the letter 'я' (ia) – the final letter in the Russian alphabet, as well as in the word for banner – *znamia*:

Krasnoe znamia – znamia Oktiabria. (The red banner is the banner of October.)

Na krasnom znameni – serp i molot. (On the red banner is the sickle and hammer.)

51

This text gave a basic introduction to the national flag. As with the image of Red Square, this simple text presented a visual introduction to four of the major symbols of the Soviet Union: the October Revolution, the red banner of revolution, the sickle, and the hammer.[183]

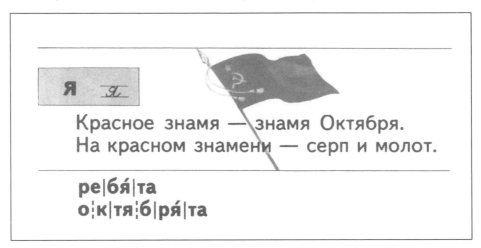

Figure 3.3. Explanation of the Soviet flag from a children's alphabet book. Beneath the text are the words for 'children' and 'Little Octobrists'. *See colour on plate C-4.*

With the alphabet now mastered, the student was then ready to read basic texts on a variety of topics. Among these were texts that gave them more information designed to help develop their Soviet identity. For example, a 2-page section on Lenin showed an illustration of him as a child and identified his place of birth – 'Vladimir Il'ich Lenin was born in the city of Simbirsk. This city now is called Ul'ianovsk. It is located on the bank of the great Russian river, Volga.' Next was a short text by Nadezhda Krupskaia, titled 'How Volodia Ul'ianov Read'. In this text the child learned how much Lenin loved to read, how much he valued learning, and how quickly he read because he had a remarkable ability to concentrate while reading. And which author did Lenin love most? The answer was Pushkin, one of the most-revered Russian poets. In a short story later in the book, the children read about a young boy who met Lenin. It is also important to note how children's books referred to the founder of the Soviet state. Of course, he was called 'Lenin' or 'Comrade Lenin', but many books used more familiar forms of his name. When talking about Lenin's childhood, a diminutive form of his given name, Volodia, was often used. The intent was to make him more relatable for the children. In other instances, he was called by his patronymic – Il'ich. This usage related to a practice among the peasants where calling an elder by just his patronymic was considered both familiar and respectful. Linguist Genevra Gerhart explained that 'this use of the patronymic alone often appears in the Soviet press to invoke these feelings of folksiness, familiarity, and respect: Lenin is referred to as *(nash) Il'ich*', meaning 'our Il'ich'.[184]

Finally, there were several places in the book where the child was introduced to some of the abstract symbols, themes, and rituals of Soviet civil religion. In a poem called 'May song', the student read about one of the most important holidays on the Soviet calendar – May Day. On this holiday Soviet citizens participated in mass demonstrations to show their solidarity with the workers of the world. It was also a favourite holiday because it marked the end of the long winter. The illustration next to the text showed two children – a boy carrying a flag on a pole and a little girl who carried a toy flag in one hand and a couple of balloons in the other. Over their heads three white birds were flying – perhaps doves of peace. At the end of the book was a two-page spread that could also relate to May Day. In the picture, a multi-ethnic group of children held flowers, balloons, a large portrait of Lenin, and two signs in Russian – one that said 'Peace' and another that read 'To the world, peace'. The text repeated the three lines about Lenin by Maiakovskii, while on the right was a poem by L. D'iakonov regarding Soviet children singing about peace. On the last two pages of the book was a group of 15 children – each wearing the traditional costume of a different Soviet republic. The Russian child, who appeared to be the leader of the group, was waving a large Soviet national flag on a pole. His comrades held hands with each other, and waved small flags and flowers. The text below the picture included the first verse and the refrain of the national anthem, again stressing the idea of the 'unbreakable union of free republics'.[185]

Figures 3.4-3.5. *Left:* Children march with flags on May Day. *Right:* A group of fifteen children celebrate the 'unbreakable union of free republics'. *See colour on plate C-4.*

Many of the themes from *Azbuka* could be found in another early reading book by the same authors intended for children in the first grade, entitled *We Read Ourselves* (*Chitaem sami*, 1982). On the cover of the book were two children, wearing school uniforms and Little Octobrist membership pins, who are working together to read a book. The text was designed to teach children about the qualities of the Little Octobrists, who 'live cheerfully in friendship', 'read stories and guess riddles', 'draw with pencils and paints', and 'know many amusing games'. There was also a story about 'Moscow – the mother of all cities'.

> …Moscow, the capital of the homeland, lives in the heart of everyone… Shining over the land are the stars of the Kremlin. The whole world listens to the striking of the hours of Saviour Tower. People from everywhere come to Red Square to visit the mausoleum of the great Lenin.[186]

Other readings in the book included 'The Lenin Way', and several other entries about the Communist Party and the Soviet homeland.[187]

The examples from these books match the findings of British educator Felicity O'Dell, presented in her study of the thematic content of three Soviet textbooks from the early 1970s – readers used for grades 1-3. She found Soviet patriotism to be the central theme of many of the lessons. Students were taught about the political structure of government including local Soviet councils and the CPSU. They were presented with the merits of socialism and the evils of capitalism – a simple dichotomy intended to portray the Soviet Union as the champion of all working people. Of course, Lenin was presented as the primary role model for all children for his love of learning, revolutionary passion, and brilliant leadership in the creation of the world's first socialist state. O'Dell also identified other themes mentioned in the above examples, such as peace, the military, collectivism and the family, labour and the merits of all types of professions, as well as discussions of the seasons and the broad geography of the Soviet Union. In addition, she recognised several trends in how content was presented in the textbooks. For example, heroes – both named and generalised – were used to illustrate the ideals of Soviet morality and the virtues inherent to the best Soviet citizens. O'Dell noted how the lessons were linked to daily life in order to help children better relate to the material and see themselves as part of a greater collective than just their families and schools. Throughout the books there were simple contrasts between 'good', represented by the Soviet state, and 'bad', represented by capitalism and the tsarist regime. Most importantly, for the topic of this study, she stressed how important symbols were in the Soviet educational context: 'From his first years at school – as these readers plainly demonstrate – the Soviet child is instructed in the significance and mystique of his system's symbols.'[188]

These examples illustrate several key trends in Soviet education. First, all subjects were taught in such a way that the students could learn the basic symbolic themes of Soviet civics. Lenin, in both his childhood and as an adult, was portrayed as a role model for all citizens. Symbols of the homeland featured prominently in the texts, in such a way that the student would begin to recognise them, associate them with the state, and gain an initial understanding of their meaning. For example, the red banner became a reminder of the October Revolution and the national flag. The red star was connected to the Red Army, the flag, and the Kremlin. Additionally, the hammer and sickle were visual reminders of the union of workers and peasants, as well as the value of labour in the Soviet Union. As the Soviet child progressed through the educational system and participated in the children's organisations, these lessons were constantly reinforced, and the young citizen was meant to develop personal connections with these symbols. To understand how this worked, it is useful to examine books written for Little Octobrists and Young Pioneers to see how national symbols were explained to the different age groups and how their organisational symbols were directly linked to the national symbol set.

Symbols and the Little Octobrists

Russian Studies scholar Jim Riordan described how children were prepared for membership in the Little Octobrists during their first months of school. They were taught about Lenin, the Revolution, and the Soviet Union. Through games and group play, students formed their own collective with their classmates. While every child was welcomed into the organisation, the implication of their pre-initiation lessons gave the children the impression that membership in the Octobrists was a privilege that they had to earn. The induction ceremony was usually held on 7 November, the date on which the anniversary of the October Revolution fell on the Gregorian calendar. Once inducted into the Little Octobrists, children set out on the path that would lead them to membership in the Young Pioneers. As the youngest members of the communist family, the Little Octobrists were often called 'Lenin's grandchildren'.[189]

Figures 3.6-3.8. Three variations of the Little Octobrist badge combining the red star and an image of Lenin as a young child. The plastic badge at *left* is from the late 1950s. Dates for the other two specimens are unknown. *See colour on plate C-5.*

During the induction ceremony, Young Pioneers pinned a membership badge on each of the new Little Octobrists. The badge was their own personal copy of the emblem of the group – a red star in the centre of which was a portrait of Lenin as a young child. Star symbolism extended to how the children were organised – a group of Octobrists was subdivided into patrols of 5-6 children that were called 'little stars' (*zvezdochki*). Each little star was guided by a Young Pioneer from the same school. Little Octobrists in the school were also given their own small red banner with the Octobrist emblem to use in their activities. In a book written for Little Octobrists, the explanation of the group's emblem and flag was symbolically linked to the history of the Soviet Union:[190]

> Little Octobrists wear a little red star on their chests. Look at it. Isn't it really like the stars, which shine over the Moscow Kremlin? And the entire world knows the Kremlin stars. Those are the stars of our mighty motherland.
>
> The Soviet red star began to shine over the world in the year 1917, when the Great October Revolution took place in our country. On those glorious days Vladimir Il'ich Lenin and the Communist Party led the workers and the peasants, soldiers and sailors in the storming of the Winter Palace. There in that palace, is where the government of the capitalists and the landowners met.
>
> The people seized power in their own hands. They drove away the bourgeois, the landowners, the merchants – all those, who did not work themselves, but lived at the expense of the labour of others.
>
> In honour of the famous victory of the October Revolution, you are called Little Octobrists. After all, you were born in a happy country, under the Soviet red star.
>
> Therefore, you also wear upon your chest a little red star on which is represented the person who is most dear for all of us – Vladimir Il'ich Lenin.
>
> In each Little Octobrist group is their own little red flag. That little flag is a fragment of the renowned banner of the motherland. Under the red banner your grandfathers went to fight against poverty and lawlessness, and they won a better fate.
>
> Right after the October Revolution the white generals attacked the young Soviet country from all directions. They wanted to suppress the world's first free state of workers and peasants.

In the grim civil war our people defended the Soviet people's power – they crushed all the White Guard gangs.

In 1941 the worst enemies of humanity, the fascists, deviously attacked our peaceful land. They destroyed and burned villages and cities, trampled down rich crops and fields. And then your fathers and brothers again stood up under the military red banners. In bloody battles they defended the freedom and happiness of the homeland. The heroic Soviet Army liberated from the fascists not only our land, but also many other countries.

And this is why all honest people of the world look upon the red banner with respect. They see in its flame-red colour the dawn of a new life of all humanity – the dawn of communism.

Here your Little Octobrist flag is a piece of that wonderful banner.[191]

Once the child joined the Little Octobrists they were meant to see themselves as a participant in the Soviet fight for the victory of communism. Stereotypical Little Octobrists wore the red star proudly on their chests and marched under their very own piece of the revolutionary red banner both at Pioneer assemblies and when their groups went on field trips outside of their schools. In their second-grade readers, they not only read stories about everyday life; they also learned more about Lenin, the October Revolution, Soviet holidays, and the behaviour that was expected from Little Octobrists.[192]

Figure 3.9. Flag of the Little Octobrists from 1986. *See colour on plate C-5.*

During their time as Little Octobrists, children regularly interacted with the Young Pioneers and attended assemblies in which they witnessed Pioneers in full uniform performing their ceremonies. This connection between the younger and older children was meant to build enthusiasm among the Octobrists to prepare themselves for membership in the Pioneers. They were told that achieving this goal would require them to study hard and to live up to the ideals of the Little Octobrists. During their third Octobrist year, the children were expected to learn the rules of the Pioneers, to demonstrate an understanding of the symbols of the Soviet Union, and to exhibit a sincere desire to do their part in the building of a communism. Children would declare their intent to join the Young Pioneers and wait until their 'little star' was selected for advancement near the end of the year.[193]

Symbols and Young Pioneers

What were the new members of the Young Pioneers taught about the official symbols of their country? The answer was clearly illustrated in books written for the children, such as a Pioneer handbook entitled *Comrade* from 1961. In the passage, the children were introduced to the importance of the flag and arms as 'distinctive symbols (emblems) of the state'. In describing the elements of the Soviet flag, the children were introduced to the primary messages communicated by the symbol:

> The red colour of the banner – the colour of blood, spilt by the best people in the fight for freedom and deliverance from all kinds of oppression – has become the international symbol of revolutionary struggle for liberation. After gaining power and the establishment of the Soviet system by our people in October 1917, the red banner became the symbol of the struggle for the complete victory of communism.

> The sickle and hammer symbolise the labour that creates everything for the life and work of the people and, therefore [work] is highly respected in our country. People who selflessly give their labour for the people's benefit are the people who are most esteemed among us, the pride of the country, and her honour and glory.

> The red five-pointed star is the symbol of the unity of workers of the entire world. The Soviet Union is the hope and a stronghold of all honest people on Earth who think about peace, work, and happiness for our people and for the peoples of all countries.[194]

Many of the symbolic elements of Soviet civil religion are present in this text. First, the child was taught how the official state symbols signified the values of the USSR. From this point on, when Young Pioneers saw these symbols in use, they were expected to remember that the symbols represented the state and their country. The history of the class struggle and the victory of the Soviet communists were reflected in the description of the flag. Red was clearly defined as the colour of revolution and the child was reminded that the struggle for the ultimate victory of communism was ongoing. This links directly to the Pioneer summons, which called upon the Young Pioneers to be ready to play a role in the fight. The importance of labour, whether it was industrial or agricultural, was stressed and they were taught that those who worked hard for the benefit of all the people would be praised and honoured for their contributions to the country. This point is also important because, unlike in the capitalist countries where the class struggle often defined a person's value to society, in the Soviet Union all work was to be considered prestigious and all workers were to be valued for their contributions. In addition, the Young Pioneer was reminded that their country was a multinational union where all peoples were equal. They were also informed that the people of the USSR were united by their common goal to build communism and defend all the workers of the world who were still struggling against their oppressors. The Soviet Union, they were told, served as an example and stronghold for 'all honest people on Earth who think about peace, work, and happiness'.

With their promotion to the Young Pioneers, the children traded in their little red star for the badge of the Pioneer Organisation. As with the oath and laws, there were different variants of the badge design during the history of the Soviet Union. The very first emblem of the Young Pioneers, used prior to April 1923, was a simple depiction of the Pioneer campfire with five logs representing the continents and three tongues of flame symbolizing the connection between the three generations working to build socialism – Communists, Young Communists, and Pioneers. While there were a variety of emblem designs, all subsequent designs incorporated elements from the national symbol set of the Soviet Union. An excellent example is the badge used during the 1920s, which was in the shape of the red banner of revolution. In the centre of the banner was the three-tongued Pioneer campfire, overlapping a hammer and sickle. The arrangement of these last two symbols was quite different from that usually used in Soviet symbols – the sickle, with a much larger blade than normal, was turned upside down from its usual alignment. On the blade was inscribed the motto *'Bud' gotov'*, meaning 'Be Prepared'. The hammer, with a much longer handle than in other uses, was angled behind the campfire with the handle at upper hoist and the head of the hammer at mid fly. In an article in the magazine *Iunyi tekhnik*, V. Nikolaev summarised the history of the Young Pioneer emblem. According to his account, a contest was held in July 1925 to design a new emblem for the organisation and a sketch of a new emblem was released at the end of the year, but it is unclear if this emblem was widely used. The design showed the red banner, topped with a red-star finial. In the foreground was a saluting Young Pioneer standing in front of the Lenin Mausoleum.[195]

In 1927 a new emblem was issued in the form of a tie clip, comparable to the neckerchief slide or 'woggle' worn by many Scouts and Guides. In this version of the emblem, the orientation of the hammer and sickle were flipped on the horizontal axis so that the head of the hammer was to the left and the handle of the sickle was on the right. The most noticeable change beginning in 1929 was that the text on the clip read *'Vsegda gotov!'*, meaning 'Always Prepared!' – the form that remained in use until the breakup of the Soviet Union. Nikolaev explained that the motto change on the badge was a result of the first All-Union Rally of Young Pioneers during which every Pioneer detachment reported on their readiness to fight for the cause of the workers and the Communist Party. Because all Pioneers were always ready, Nikolaev suggested, this was the impetus for the alteration of the badge.[196]

The similarity of the Young Pioneer motto to that of the Boy Scouts and Girl Guides/Girl Scouts is not a coincidence. Boy Scouting had already been established in Russia prior to the October Revolution. However, after the Bolsheviks gained power, they determined that bourgeois principles were so ingrained in Scouting[197] that the existing organisation could not be sufficiently adapted to serve the communist cause. Several experienced Scout leaders were recruited to assist in the creation of a new, distinctly Soviet, organisation for children. According to E. Tiazhel'nikov, 'Krupskaia advised the adoption and assimilation of the styles for external forms, the concreteness and comprehensibility of tasks, slogans, and rules of conduct from the previous experience of the children's movement, and the inculcation of children with various practical skills and the utilization of their tendencies toward romantic adventures, marches, and games.' However, in his history of the Pioneer Movement, S. Furin credits Lenin with the 'Be Prepared' motto, citing an account related by Krupskaia in one of her letters to the Pioneers:

> 'Be Ready!' Lenin said to the members of the Party, and Lenin's party ... was not afraid of even the most routine, depressing work. And when the time was ripe for revolution, Lenin's party 'was ready', and led forward the workers and peasants. Young Pioneers had not yet come into existence at the time Lenin called those who were fighting for the workers' cause to 'be ready', but the Young Pioneers made a firm decision to be faithful to Lenin's bidding ... they want to learn to build a new life, they want to continue Lenin's work...[198]

While clearly the Boy Scout connection was the most likely origin of the motto, it makes sense that the credit was shifted to Lenin via Krupskaia. In her letter, Krupskaia cites Lenin's treatise, *What is to be Done*, which was written in 1901-1902. Lenin wrote 'We must always conduct our everyday work and always be prepared for every situation, because very frequently it is almost impossible to foresee when a period of outbreak will give way to a period of calm.' By alluding to this work as the source of the motto, Krupskaia was not only able to credit Lenin, thus giving the motto a proper communist linage, but also succeeded in backdating the origin of the motto to a time preceding its adoption by the Scouts in 1907. This rewriting of the origin story helped distance the Young Pioneer motto from the bourgeois baggage associated with the World Scouting Movement. It is also quite likely that the desire to disassociate the Pioneers from Scouting was the impetus for changing the motto on the badge from 'Be Prepared' to 'Always Prepared'. Interestingly, the full motto for the organisation included both versions. During meetings and assemblies, the Pioneer leader issued the summons 'To fight for the cause of the Communist Party, be prepared!' and the assembled Young Pioneers gave the response 'Always prepared!'[199]

According to Nikolaev, the next emblem change was the result of the Great Patriotic War. This badge design was a red star with the Pioneer campfire in the centre. The words of the motto were centred top and bottom over the flames. Nikolaev explains that the red star was a symbol of the military valour and bravery of the Soviet people. During the war, the country's metal and manufacturing capability was devoted to the production of weaponry and ammunition for the war effort. For this reason, on 15 September 1942 new Pioneer regulations were issued that called upon each Pioneer to make their own badge, either using paint and scrap tin or by embroidering the emblem on scraps of red cloth.[200]

Figures 3.10-3.14. Emblems of the Young Pioneers. *Top to Bottom, Left to Right:* Badge (1923-1927) with motto 'Be Prepared'; tie clip (1929-ca. 1942) reading 'Always Prepared'; badge design used during the Second World War; badge used 1946-1962; emblem used 1962-1991. *See colour on plate C-6.*

After the war, a new Pioneer emblem was introduced, which Nikolaev described as reflecting 'the return of the Soviet people to peaceful constructive labour'. For nearly two decades, the symbol of the Young Pioneers met the description in the handbook from 1961:

> It is a five-pointed star with the sickle and hammer shown on it. That is the emblem of our
> beloved homeland – the Union of Soviet Socialist Republics. Above the star rise up 3
> tongues of flame, a reminder of the connections of the three generations: Communists,

59

Young Communists, and Pioneers. In the lower part of the star is a ribbon with the inscription 'Always Prepared!' The badge is worn on the left side of the chest.[201]

In 1962 the All-Union Young Pioneer Organisation was awarded the Order of Lenin. The emblem was redesigned to reflect this recognition. In the place of the hammer and sickle, the badge featured a portrait of Lenin, the namesake of both the award and the Young Pioneer Organization. The motto was reduced in size and moved down to accommodate the portrait. This was the final version of the design in use until the breakup of the Soviet Union.[202]

Banners and flags of the Young Pioneers all reflected the red banner of revolution emblazoned with the badge of the organisation. Young Pioneer groups (or troops[203]) representing an entire school were issued a banner that included not only the Pioneer badge, but also the full motto including both the summons and the response. Detachments, which comprised all the Pioneers from one grade in the same school, were issued flags with simple designs showing just the Pioneer emblem on a red field. Pioneer banners were also typically fringed, while the flags usually were not. Troop banners and detachment flags were kept in the school's Pioneer room, along with the bugles and drums used during Pioneer ceremonies and assemblies. In addition, Furin describes a 'main' Pioneer banner that was kept at the headquarters of the organisation in Moscow. What distinguished the main banner from those used by troops was the addition of two streamers (ribbons) for the Order of Lenin, which had been awarded to the organisation in 1962 and 1972. This very special banner was used at All-Union Pioneer rallies and was carried at the head of the flag group when the Young Pioneers paraded on Red Square.[204]

Figures 3.15-3.17. *Top Left:* Banner of the school-level Pioneer troop showing the emblem in use from 1962-1991. *Top Right:* The flag of a Young Pioneer detachment from the same period. *Bottom:* Reverse side of a Pioneer banner showing the honorary name of the detachment. The text reads 'Pioneer detachment, school 500, in the name of Iurii Gagarin, Lenin Region, City of Moscow'. *See colour on plate C-7.*

60

The reverse of the flag often bore the honorary name for detachments or troops that had earned the privilege. According to Furin, the regional or town Pioneer council could confer the honour on a troop, and the troop council could confer it on a detachment, as a reward for 'good achievements in study and work, and for loyalty to the Pioneer flag'. Appropriate namesakes included war heroes, cosmonauts, writers, or other luminaries of Soviet society. Furin observed that popular namesakes included Cosmonaut Iurii Gagarin, children's writer Arkadii Gaidar, and heroes from World War II such as Oleg Koshevoi, Liuba Shevtsova, and Ivan Turkenich. The Pioneers in the honoured detachment or troop were encouraged to learn as much as they could about their namesake and to endeavour to be like him or her.[205]

Perhaps the most coveted token of membership in the Young Pioneers, though, was the red neckerchief (galstuk, 'tie'). In images of the initiation ceremony, Little Octobrists were shown standing at attention with their brand-new neckerchiefs draped over one arm. As each child was inducted into the organisation, they would say the solemn promise of the Pioneers and an older member of the organisation tied the neckerchief around their neck. The meaning of the neckerchief was explained in the following way in the manual:

> Every Young Pioneer, as a sign of membership in the Pioneer Organisation, wears the red neckerchief and the Pioneer badge 'Always Prepared' on their breast pocket.
>
> Why is the pioneer neckerchief that you wear on your chest red? It is red because it is a fragment of the Red Banner, saturated with the blood of hundreds and thousands of brave fighters for the cause of communism.
>
> The three ends of the Pioneer neckerchief – that is a symbol of the indestructible friendship of three generations: Communists, Young Communists, Pioneers.
>
> Value your scarlet Pioneer neckerchief. Wear it every day and always act such that no one can reproach you as unworthy to wear it.[206]

In this ceremony, the newly initiated Young Pioneer was symbolically wrapped in their own piece of the revolutionary red banner. They were entrusted with this relic and reminded that the knot with which it was tied bound them to the three generations that were working together to build a communist society in the Soviet Union. More importantly, they were told that, as a wearer of the red neckerchief, they must conduct themselves according to the highest communist ethics. The implication was that bad behaviour would not only reflect poorly upon themselves but would also disgrace their Pioneer group and dishonour the memory of all those who had given their lives fighting under the red banner. For a ten-year-old child, this level of responsibility was deemed quite prestigious and many Soviet Pioneers took it quite seriously.[207]

Figure 3.18. A row of Little Octobrists (***right***) wait with their scarves over their right arms as they participate in the induction ceremony for the Young Pioneers. The children are from School No. 54 (Moskvoretskii District, Moscow) and the ritual was held at the pavilion-museum of Vladimir Lenin's Funeral Train, 1 January 1984.

For the Young Pioneer, the sacredness of the red banner and their neckerchief – a piece of that banner personally entrusted to them by the state – was often accepted without question. In fact, as a story purported to be from the Great Patriotic War illustrated, they were expected to protect this relic above all else:

> The following story took place in a Ukrainian village in the fall of 1941. A German soldier broke into the house of Galia Dotsenko, a Pioneer. He began rummaging through the things on the shelves, in drawers, closets and trunks.
>
> Galia was holding her school bookbag.
>
> The German approached her… and began taking everything out…. Suddenly, it was as if the German was scorched by a flame. A new Pioneer tie fell out of the bag.
>
> '*Klein Kommunist!*' yelled the infuriated German, grabbing the tie. He threw it on the floor and trampled it with his feet.
>
> Galia sprang on the fascist.
>
> 'Why are you trampling my Pioneer tie?' she screamed, and she pushed the German as hard as she could…. She snatched her tie from under the German's feet, ran out of the house, and headed for the forest. She heard shouts and assault rifle fire behind her, but she managed to hide from the pursuers in the woods.
>
> Galia spent the next two years with a guerrilla unit. In October 1943, the Red Army liberated her village from the German invaders. Now Galia goes to school again, and a Pioneer tie glows red on her neck – the same tie that she tore away from a German bandit's hands in the fall of 1941.[208]

Evaluation of this story leads to some interesting historical questions. Was Galia Dotsenko a real child and did this incident really occur? That is difficult to determine, and not particularly important from the point of view of Soviet authorities. Does it even matter if the story is historically accurate, or if it was simply meant as a fable used to teach societal values? Even if young Galia was just an idealised representation of a Young Pioneer used to illustrate the importance of protecting the red banner, the message conveyed to the child receiving the account was still clear – it was the duty of every Soviet citizen, no matter how young, to defend the homeland in whatever way they could. Without thinking about her own safety, or the safety of her family, Galia acted instinctively as any good citizen of the Soviet Union should, to defend the sacred relic of the revolution. While in other countries children her age were able to attend school, Galia's fate was inextricably linked to that of the continuous struggle of communism as she fought alongside other partisans to help drive the foreign invaders from the Soviet homeland. The final line of the story is key... with peace restored, thanks to the intervention of the Red Army, Galia was once again able to live the life of a schoolgirl and Young Pioneer of the Soviet Union. To the Soviet schoolchild, the authority of the state was portrayed as the ultimate protector that ensured that all citizens were free to live their lives in peace.

The story of Galia Dotsenko was just one example of the mythic stories told about Pioneer heroes who, each in their own way, fought to protect the Soviet way of life. The 1954 edition of the Young Pioneer *Book of the Leader* included numerous accounts of young heroes who all shared the lineage of the Young Pioneers. Each vignette was labelled 'He [or she] was a pioneer' and illustrated with a drawing of the person, typically wearing their Pioneer neckerchief or military dress. One of the earliest Pioneer heroes was Pavlik Morozov, a young boy from a rural village who informed Soviet authorities that his father was a *kulak* – a peasant farmer who refused to share their crops with the collective. As most versions of the story go, after his father's arrest Pavlik was murdered by his family – martyred for living by communist morals and attempting to look out for the good of the community. While it is generally accepted that Pavlik was a real child who may have actually informed upon his own father, it is doubtful if he was ever actually a member of the Young Pioneers because at the time of his death in 1932 the organisation was not yet established in the more rural parts of the country. Nevertheless, Pavlik was always portrayed wearing the red neckerchief of a Young Pioneer and the story was considered part of Pioneer history by leaders and children alike. Along with Pavlik Morozov, there were other Pioneer martyrs, most from the time of the Great Patriotic War, who were well known amongst Young Pioneers. In fact, four Young Pioneers were awarded the title 'Hero of the Soviet Union' for their actions in the Great Patriotic War and honoured with a monument in Moscow.[209]

It is highly significant that the symbols of the Little Octobrists and the Young Pioneers incorporated elements from the national symbol set of the Union of Soviet Socialist Republics. That linkage was used as a way not only to teach children about the symbols of their country, but also to give them their own symbolic connection to the Communist Party and the Soviet state. As part of their formal education and through their participation in the children's organisations, each young Soviet citizen was expected to acquire a practical knowledge of the symbols that, almost quite literally, would surround them throughout their lives. They were provided with numerous role models – child heroes and adults – who illustrated the attributes of the ideal Soviet citizen. In addition, they participated in civil religious rituals designed to convey symbolic meaning and reinforce the values of Soviet patriotism that they had been taught through their formal education and the traditions of the Young Pioneers.

Soviet Children and Civil Religious Rituals

At this point in the discussion, it is important to again review West's neutral definition of civil religion: 'A civil religion is a set of beliefs and attitudes that explain the meaning and purpose of any given political society in terms of its relationship to a transcendent, spiritual reality, that are held by the people generally of that society, and that are expressed in public rituals, myths, and symbols'. Rituals are quite simply the 'prescribed form or order of religious or ceremonial rites'. In his book *The Symbolic Uses of Politics*, political scientist Murray Edelman offered more insights into the value of ritual in the realm of politics.

> Ritual is the motor activity that involves its participants symbolically in a common
> enterprise, calling their attention to their relatedness and joint interests in a compelling way.
> It thereby both promotes conformity and evokes satisfaction and joy in conformity.[210]

With these definitions in mind, it is imperative to look beyond the symbols and their meanings to the types of rituals through which the sacredness of these symbols was reinforced. In civil religion, rituals are meant to form an emotional connection between the participants and the symbols of their nation. Each time the citizen participates in a ritual, the lessons of political socialisation are reinforced through an emotional experience. It is the combination of symbols and rituals that help children develop their sense of national identity and a personal connection to the values of their society.

The previously described rituals – those associated with the first day of school, joining the Little Octobrists, and induction into the Young Pioneers – were just a few of the rites associated with Soviet childhood. Children participated in Soviet civil religious rituals in many different contexts. As with the patriotic culture of other countries, children in the USSR experienced these rituals with their families, with their classmates, and through participation in the youth organisations.

Children and Soviet Rituals

In her study of Soviet textbooks, O'Dell commented on how children were taught about the ceremonies inherent to Soviet civil religion and how those rituals related to the symbols of the country. She observed: 'Ceremony is but an extended form of a symbol with the same inherent social advantages (providing foci for the individual's identification with the group) and, for the individual, if not always for the authorities, the same snags (discouraging realistic thought).' Her discussion of Soviet ceremonies illustrated that the use of symbols was part of the general methodology of character training meant to prepare children for their roles in those rites. For example, traditional holidays were described to the children as colourful and festive, showing the joy inherent to life in a communist society.[211]

The Soviet calendar was filled with many different official holidays, each offering the citizenry an opportunity to acknowledge a different element of Soviet society. In many ways, Soviet holidays were designed to replace the elaborate calendar of Orthodox religious holidays that existed in tsarist Russia. In some cases, traditions associated with a religious holiday were directly transferred to a secular holiday with Soviet elements added. For example, several of the traditions from Christmas (celebrated on 7 January on the Orthodox calendar) were transferred to New Year's Day. These practices included gift giving, visits by *Ded Moroz* (Grandfather Frost) and *Snegurochka* (Snow Maiden), and the *elka* – the Russian version of the Christmas tree. In the Soviet era, the *elka* was topped with a red star and decorated with miniature red banners and

64

decorations having symbolic connections to the Soviet state. As the school year progressed, children were taught about various Soviet holidays because textbooks were arranged in such a way that the texts would be read at the appropriate time of year.[212]

One of the first national rituals that even the youngest child might have witnessed was a mass demonstration associated with May Day, or International Worker's Day, celebrated on 1 May. The youngest children would have attended these parades with their parents or grandparents, while older children often participated with their Pioneer detachments. A children's book about Soviet holidays offered three short readings related to this highly important Soviet holiday:

1 May – May Day

1 May is the blossoming of Spring and the biggest holiday of the workers; joyous, terrible 1st of May.

It is joyous for the people of labour. Terrible for capitalists. On that day the workers go out for demonstrations in all countries. They carry banners on which are written:

'We won't allow the capitalists to start a war!'

'Long live the friendship of the peoples!'

'He who works is the owner of the land!'

Red Banners

People even in ancient times thought up banners. They were different colours. They were hoisted in battle on tall staves, so that soldiers could see where were their own and where were the foreigners.

Now we also distinguish friends from the enemies by the colours of their banners.

Workers of all countries have red banners. Workers of all countries are friends.

And You Go Out

If on May Day you were to look at the Earth from space, it would appear as a red sphere. The workers raise so many of our banners.

And you should go outside with your little flag. Let the Earth be even more red.[213]

These readings were similar to those found in textbooks, and clearly illustrated the major themes of the May Day holiday – it was a celebration for all the workers of the world (not just the people of the Soviet Union) and it was a holiday focused on peace. It was also explained to the child that on this day all citizens should participate either as official marchers in the mass demonstrations that were held in every Soviet city or as part of the large crowds that gathered to watch the parades. This motif of public participation was key to the imagery associated with May Day demonstrations. Postcards and greeting cards celebrating the 1st of May often showed children emulating the behaviour of the demonstrators by marching with their own little red flags or participating with the Young Pioneers.

Figures 3.19-3.20. Two postcards for May Day. Little Octobrists march with toy flags, emulating the behaviour of adults participating in the annual mass demonstrations. *See colour on plate C-8.*

Figures 3.21-3.22. Two postcards for May Day. *Left:* Young Pioneers march with their comrades. *Right:* Columns of Soviet citizens march through Red Square. *See colour for figure 3.21 on plate C-8.*

Two other holidays on which there would have been large parades were Victory Day (9 May), which commemorated the end of the Great Patriotic War, and the anniversary of the Great October Revolution (7 November). Children were taught about, and perhaps celebrated, other patriotic holidays either in the school or with the Octobrists and Pioneers. These might have included the Day of the Soviet Army and Military Fleet (23 February), the Day of Cosmonautics (12 April), the Day of Remembrance of Vladimir Il'ich Lenin (22 April), the Day of the USSR Constitution (7 October), and the Day of the Friendship of the Peoples (30 December). In addition, there were holidays that celebrated different professions and even a day marking the anniversary of the founding of the Young Pioneer Organisation.[214]

Little Holiday Flags

One particularly interesting aspect of Soviet flag culture was the creation of special flags for children that were linked thematically to different holidays. These flags were known in Russian as *prazdnichnye flazhki*, which means 'little holiday flags'. Russian vexillologists consulted by the author explained that these little flags were just toys. They were inexpensive (costing around 20 kopeks) and could be purchased in toy stores throughout the country. The flags were given out to participants in holiday or Pioneer events and allowed children to emulate adult behaviour at mass demonstrations and parades. One Russian vexillologist remembered that the flags also had a practical use. When Pioneer detachments went out on excursions, the leaders often carried these small flags at the front of the columns as a way of signalling the children. In addition, they were used at Pioneer camps. For example, when an American schoolgirl named Samantha Smith visited the Artek Pioneer camp in 1983, she was greeted by children using signs, balloons, and little holiday flags.[215]

Figures 3.23-3.24. Little holiday flags designed for Young Pioneers and illustrating the theme of a happy childhood. *Left:* 'Let there always be sunshine', the title of a favourite song among Young Pioneers. *Right:* Little holiday flag depicting the flames of the Pioneer campfire, representing the three generations working to build communism.

Young Pioneers were taught to be friends to all the children of the world. The concept of international friendship was typically illustrated using the three-races theme or the word 'friendship'. In addition, the theme of peace was illustrated through use of text that read 'peace' or 'to the world, peace'. Peace-themed flags often portrayed doves or flowers, especially poppies which are associated with revolution in Russian symbolism. The primary Soviet holiday connected to the theme of peace was May Day.

Figures 3.25-3.26. Two holiday flags related to the theme of friendship. The flag at *left* illustrates the friendship of the world's peoples (the three-races theme) with the word 'friendship' in Russian, while the flag at *right* says 'friendship' in Latvian.

Figures 3.27-3.28. *Left:* Little holiday flag reading 'To the world, peace'. In Russian, the word *mir* means both 'peace' and 'world'. *Right:* Little holiday flag which reads 'peace' in Latvian.

Figures 3.29-3.30. Holiday flags designed for May Day. *Left:* 'Peace, May'. *Right:* 'With the holiday'. Doves and flowers were meant to illustrate the 1st of May as a celebration of peace, the unity of the workers of the world, and the beginning of Spring.

Some little holiday flags incorporated elements of the national symbol set, such as the Soviet arms, the red star, and the hammer and sickle. These flags most likely served as substitute national flags for children, since a small replica of the national flag would have been inappropriate for use as a toy. Imagery of the Kremlin and Red Square served to promote a sense of Soviet identity. Landmarks shown on the flags included Saviour Tower and the dome of the Kremlin Senate Building with its Soviet flag. While the Lenin mausoleum was not specifically shown, its presence was implied through the portrayal of the other two landmarks. Red was the dominant colour used on the flags, with three colour combinations being typical – yellow or white imagery on a red field, and red printing on a white background.[216]

Figures 3.31-3.34. Examples of little holiday flags with national symbols. *See colour for figure 3.31 on plate C-8.*

One Russian vexillologist commented that, 'It was pretty typical to see a Soviet child holding a flaglet of this kind in hand.'[217] It is interesting that Russian flag scholars emphasised that these flags were just toys, and not considered as 'real flags'. An examination of the symbols on many of the flags clearly illustrates that even these inexpensive toys were meant to fulfil a role in the political socialisation of children. As the illustrations from textbooks and May Day cards have demonstrated, it was clear that this type of patriotic display by children was not only encouraged but was also considered to be a pleasing and appropriate way to illustrate Soviet patriotism.[218]

Figures 3.35-3.38. Four little holiday flags that would have reminded children of the advances made through the building of communism. *Top:* Flags for the Anniversary of the Great October Revolution showing the Cruiser Aurora and a *budenovka* cap – a broadcloth helmet worn by Red Army soldiers and by Young Pioneers. *Bottom:* Flags for Cosmonautics Day celebrating the Soviet space programme.

Pioneer Rituals

The Young Pioneer organisation of the USSR had its own set of rituals which incorporated elements from Soviet civil religion, drew upon Soviet military traditions, and promoted patriotic behaviour. The manuals for Pioneer leaders explained that the organisation's rituals were an important tool for nurturing highly patriotic feelings and collectivism, and a venue for Pioneers to show pride in their detachments and in the Young Pioneer organisation. It was the leader's responsibility to learn the rituals and to instruct their Pioneers in the proper conduct of the ceremonies. In this way, they were to guide their charges through the emotional aspects of the rituals, and to have a positive moral influence upon the children. Each rite was to be explained and performed in such a way that the Pioneers were able to understand its meaning. Through instruction and participation in Pioneer rituals, it was hoped that the members would fully appreciate the sacred traditions of the organisation, rather than just mechanically fulfilling their roles.[219]

In addition to the ritual for reception (or induction) into the Pioneers, there was also a ritual for the Creation of a New Detachment each year for the new Pioneers in the fourth year, and one for saying Farewell to the Pioneers in the eighth year, (who had reached the maximum age for the organisation and presumably were going to join the *Komsomol*). The leader's manual recommended that these two rituals could be held together as a way of allowing the older children to 'pass the torch' to the newest Pioneers. As a way of doing this, the departing Pioneers could ceremonially pass on their detachment flag to the newly formed detachment. In addition, the older Pioneers would promise, 'to not forget the Pioneers, to be friends with them, and to help them'. This combined ceremony was intended to reinforce the friendship between these two youngest generations – the Young Pioneers and the *Komsomol* – as they worked together to help build communism in their homeland.[220]

Many Pioneer rituals included flag displays accompanied by bugles and drums, as well as military-style line-ups. Furin describes the Pioneer line-up as 'festive', noting that 'the voice of the bugle is ardent, the rub-a-dub of the drum is vibrant, and the children's hands on their own accord fly up to salute the troop flag'. This ceremony was a regular feature of troop assemblies and an important part of the tradition at Young Pioneer camps. During the line-up, patrol leaders reported on their activities to the detachment leaders, detachment leaders gave a report for their detachment to the troop leaders, and troop leaders gave their reports to the Pioneer council.[221]

Within the Pioneer detachment it was considered quite prestigious to be the colour-bearer and the child thus entrusted swore an oath to protect the flag:

> I [given name, family name], standard-bearer of the detachment named for [namesake's name], in the presence of our comrades swear to carefully protect the banner of the Pioneer division, precisely carry out all rules about the handling of the banner, and justify the trust put in me.[222]

After taking the oath, the standard-bearer placed the base of the staff on their right leg. The leader of the detachment gave the command, 'Under the banner, attention! Alignment on the banner!'. On this command the bearer reset the banner from the 'attention' position to the position for movement and, having quietly given the command to the assistant standard-bearers to 'forward march', carried the banner from the left flank to the right. At this point, all the Pioneers and leaders in the formation and the assistant standard-bearers gave the Pioneer salute. The salute was executed by raising the right hand about the head, with the five fingers pressed tightly together and the palm upright. Young Pioneers saluted when responding to the Pioneer summons and during the presentation of the red banner. They also saluted during the hoisting of the national flag or flags of the Union Republics, and during the singing of the national anthem or republic hymns. Additionally, salutes were performed at the Lenin Mausoleum or other monuments honouring Soviet heroes. As a sign of respect, Young Pioneers greeted their leaders and members of the military with a salute. The standard-bearers, buglers, and drummers all learned the appropriate positions for different commands, and how to execute the movements required for each aspect of the Pioneer ceremonies.[223]

Figures 3.39-3.41. Positions of the standard-bearers. ***Left to Right:*** '*Smirno!*' ('Quietly!' or 'Attention!'), '*Ravniais!*' ('Equal!' or 'Present colours!'), and '*Vol'no!*' ('Freely!' or 'At Ease!').

There were several other traditions associated with the banners and flags of the Young Pioneers. For example, there was a prescribed procedure for 'Carrying out the Banner'. In this ceremony, either the standard-bearer or the 'best Pioneer' (as selected by the leaders) brought out the red banner of the Pioneer group or detachment. The colour guard was comprised of the standard-bearer, two assistant standard-bearers, buglers, and drummers. As the banner was brought out, the assistant standard-bearers saluted the banner. When the ritual was performed as part of an assembly including multiple detachments, the troop banner led the procession with the detachment standard bearers falling in behind the buglers and drummers.[224]

During assemblies and troop celebrations, an honour guard of one standard-bearer and two assistants stood watch over each of the banners and flags. The guard was changed every 5-10 minutes, through a specified ritual, with the guards selected from among the best Pioneers in each detachment. During the changing of the guard, on the command 'Change stand!' the new guards approached those holding the banners from behind and placed a hand on the staff of the flag. On the next command – 'Change!' – the new standard-bearer took possession of the banner. The relieved watch waited for the command 'On the left (or right) quick march!', after which they joined the ranks of the other Pioneers. Instructions for the ceremony stressed that all commands were to be given 'accurately, but very quietly'.[225]

Most likely, many Soviet children took these responsibilities very seriously. By fulfilling their duty in the execution of the ritual, they were meant to demonstrate their ability to contribute to the Pioneer collective, as well as their dedication to the Communist Party and the Soviet state. In a manual for Young Pioneer leaders, S. A. Shmakov noted the value of such responsibility for the development of the Young Pioneer, both as an individual and as a member of the collective:

> The strength of children's imagination is so great that it can overcome any difficulty. The child becomes stronger in his own eyes when he can fulfill his duty, no matter what. In a Pioneer summer camp, the girl on flag duty did not leave her position, even when her mother arrived unexpectedly. She asked to relate to her mother, 'I am on guard duty, the change will come in two hours, please don't feel hurt and wait, or come tomorrow.'
>
> Makarenko[226] was right when he said, 'Respect for the banner symbolizes not only love toward our country, but also efficiency in performing a task in the collective.'[227]

In this account, we see confirmation that many of the aims of political socialisation had been attained with this Young Pioneer. First, she took her responsibility as guardian of the sacred red banner very seriously. She understood that her commitment to this duty, and her obligation to uphold her obligations to the Pioneer collective, were of primary importance. They are so significant, that when her mother arrived at the camp unexpectedly, she stayed at her post. Like the Pioneer hero Pavlik Morozov, she placed the good of the collective and the country above her desire to see her own mother. These were the qualities of a good Young Pioneer and a true patriot, according to Soviet standards.

There were also regulations for how members of the organisation payed homage to the Soviet national flag and the flags of the republics. As the Pioneer Leader's manual explained, 'Pioneer homage given to the state flag of the USSR is an integral part of instilling in Pioneers Soviet patriotism, civic consciousness, class consciousness, [and] loyalty to the revolutionary, military, and labour traditions of the Soviet people.' The manual also stressed that the national flag was 'the symbol of state sovereignty of the USSR and the indestructible union of workers and peasants in the struggle for construction of communist society'. According to the regulations, the national flag was to be hoisted at Pioneer rallies and events, daily on the masts at Pioneer camps, during stays by Soviet Pioneers at international Pioneer camps, and on buildings and tents that served as accommodations for Soviet Pioneers at international Pioneer camps. Regulations also specified that the national anthem was to be performed during the hoisting of the Soviet flag. In addition, Pioneers followed regulations specifying that the flags of the Union Republics were to be raised after the national flag, and that the hymns of the republics were to be performed while those flags were raised.[228]

Pioneer Pilgrimages

In addition to various rituals associated with Pioneer meetings and assemblies, members of the organisation would have participated in pilgrimages appropriate for their age group. Communist pilgrimages typically involved a journey to a place with a sacred connection to Lenin, the Revolution, or the Soviet state. For Young Pioneers, these spiritual journeys involved a detachment going together to a hallowed place in their community, such as a war memorial, Lenin monument, or monument to a Hero Pioneer. While there, they would perform a Pioneer ritual involving the laying of flowers or a wreath, 'reporting to Lenin' on their efforts to build communism, or other such practices.[229]

One interesting object used in these ritual journeys was the Pioneer Wreath of Honour. Furin described the wreath as 'a symbol of Pioneer loyalty to the heroic military and ritual deeds of previous generations'. The wreath was made either of natural flowers or of the branches from an oak, pine, or laurel tree. Depending on the nature of the pilgrimage destination, the wreath was wrapped in a special ribbon – a red ribbon when it was intended for a memorial to Lenin or to heroes of the Revolution, or a 'Guards' ribbon when the wreath was to be laid at a Soviet war memorial. The laying of the Wreath of Honour was a solemn occasion and involved paramilitary style practices appropriate to a war memorial.[230]

In the leader's manual from 1968, there was a recommendation for a local pilgrimage that could be completed in any region of the country. The book suggested that the Pioneers undertake an 'Expedition on the Precepts of Lenin'. As part of the expedition, the Pioneers would travel to sites in their city or region that either had a direct connection to Lenin or could be used to illustrate the teachings of Lenin. For example, when visiting a location where Lenin had lived, worked, or studied, it was believed that the children could feel a physical connection to the founder of their country. Of course, not every community in the Soviet Union had such a place, but nearly every region had a location named after Lenin. These places, it was suggested, could be used as substitutes. The authors also recommended visiting locations that demonstrated how 'Lenin's precepts are realised in life'. Examples included places associated with electricity (the fulfilment of Lenin's desire for electrification of the country), a factory (Lenin called for the development of heavy industry), a farm (Lenin envisioned the mechanization of agriculture throughout the country), or a location associated with the arts (Lenin supported a cultural revolution and development of the arts). This physical journey was meant to help children understand what it meant to be 'on the Leninist path' – a phrase that reinforced the importance of dedicating oneself to the study of Leninism and fulfilment of Lenin's precepts.[231]

The most important pilgrimage site in the Soviet Union, for children and adults alike, was the Lenin Mausoleum on Red Square. This most sacred of places in Soviet civil religion was also the location of other Pioneer rituals. It was a favourite site for children to visit with the purpose of laying flowers or wreaths in honour of Lenin. The sacred nature of the mausoleum extended well into the square, adding an extra element of solemnity to the Pioneer induction ceremony or the rite in which Young Pioneers joined the *Komsomol*. And, of course, Red Square was also the site of parades and mass demonstrations associated with May Day and the anniversary of the October Revolution. All of these connections were meant to suggest that the Lenin Mausoleum, Red Square, the Kremlin, and Moscow itself, should be understood as the focal point of the Soviet citizen's worldview, and the ultimate destination in their practice of the rites and observances of Soviet civil religion.

Figure 3.42. Young Pioneers prepare to pay tribute to Lenin with flowers during a visit to his mausoleum on the 98th anniversary of his birth (22 April 1968).

Taken as a whole, the rituals and pilgrimages practiced by Soviet children as members of the Young Pioneer organisation illustrated how the symbols of Soviet civil religion were sanctified, and how the principles of Marxism-Leninism were reinforced through ritual practice. For many children, aged seven through fifteen, these practices would likely have been performed with the highest reverence. To this age group, the supremacy of the Soviet state was meant to be unquestionable, the wisdom of Lenin highly valued, and the responsibilities of the average Soviet citizen taken to heart. Such feelings were meant to contribute to the political socialisation of the youngest citizens, preparing them for the next step in their political evolution – elevation to the status of *Komsomol* member. In the Party's view, these were vital steps in helping children to develop a sense of Soviet identity and a communist worldview.

Conclusion

In his book, Hedrick Smith suggested that Soviet patriotism had become 'the most unifying force in Soviet society, the most vital element in the amalgam of loyalties that cements Soviet society'. Soviet patriotic practices were designed to develop a sense of Soviet identity among the citizens. It was this sense of *Sovietness* that was meant to unite Russians, Kazaks, Moldavians, and persons of other ethnicities into a cohesive population. The Soviet people, working together, did accomplish a great many things in the seven decades of the country's existence. They electrified the country, they expanded the nation's transportation network, they repelled the fascist invasion, they developed a highly successful programme of space exploration, and they elevated their country to superpower status. While many in the West liked to believe that all of these accomplishments were possible only because of the autocratic nature of the Soviet government and the strong control exercised by communist authorities over the population, this belief cannot completely explain the successes of the Soviet state. Clearly, there were other types of cohesive forces evident in the USSR. Many citizens, no matter how cynical they might have been about the messages of state-sponsored propaganda, likely took pride in the successes of their Soviet homeland.[232]

As this chapter has shown, both the formal educational system and the children's organisations were used to encourage children to develop a sense of Soviet identity in childhood. The state invested a great deal of effort into the political socialisation of its youngest citizens. As has been demonstrated, the educational system was designed and operated in such a way that it was meant to instil in the citizenry a strong sense of Soviet identity, rooted in the teachings of Marx and Lenin. From the very first day of school, children were taught to think of themselves as members of a collective; to put the needs of the group above their own; to honour their country and those who had died in its defence; to value labour and the contributions of the working people; and to dedicate themselves to the building of communism. The Young Pioneer Organisation supplemented the formal school lessons while also giving millions of children their own role in achieving national goals. Little Octobrists and Young Pioneers throughout the Soviet Union were encouraged to perform socially meaningful work and to help accomplish the goals of communism as prescribed by Lenin. Through these organisations, the children were meant to experience the 'happy Soviet childhood' envisioned by Lenin and Krupskaia in the early years of the Soviet state.[233]

Chapter 4
Banal Nationalism in the USSR: State Symbols
in the Daily Lives of Soviet Citizens

> The metonymic image of banal nationalism is not a flag which is being consciously waved with fervent passion; it is the flag hanging unnoticed on the public building.[234]

– Michael Billig

It is impossible to understand the importance of national symbols in any country without first examining the nature of national identity and the culture of patriotism in that society. The concept of 'civil religion' is useful for understanding symbol usage and how those symbols spiritually connect individuals to their country. One thing that is sometimes missed in a discussion of a country's civil religion, though, is how it relates to the concept of nationalism. Exactly what does nationalism mean?[235] How is it different from patriotism? In many contexts the term 'nationalism' has been used to describe the desire of a distinct people to achieve self-determination and to have their own independent state.[236] It is often used to explain why smaller ethnic groups in established countries do not completely identify with the mainstream culture of the nation in which they are citizens.[237] Nationalism is also applied when examining why people sharing a common language and cultural identity feel a closer connection to people of the same ethnic group in other countries than they do to the majority group of their own country.[238] In the modern era, nationalism has been applied to extreme cases where the concept of national exceptionalism has been used to justify conflicts with other countries, discrimination against or the mistreatment of ethnic and religious minorities, and even genocide.[239] For this reason, 'nationalism' has often been applied to other peoples and other countries without a recognition of the nationalist tendencies within one's own country. Many, when describing their own loyalty to their home countries, refer to their 'patriotism' or 'love of country' without recognition that the feelings they have could be characterised as 'nationalism'. Finally, nationalism has been conveniently applied to specific ethnic or cultural groups without recognition that it is also a source of unity in multinational and multi-ethnic states.[240]

The literature on nationalism has often focused on groups that aspire to have their own independent state. While the patriotism of the majority can provide legitimacy to a state, minority nationalism is frequently viewed by scholars and politicians alike as a threat to the status quo. Recognising the inconsistency between using 'patriotism' to explain one's own connection to country, while applying 'nationalism' to others agitating for their own states, social psychologist Michael Billig challenged the idea that nationalism is typically a characteristic of groups seeking statehood or a transient condition. He posited that there was a form of nationalism at work in stable, established states. Billig recommended 'stretching the term "nationalism", so that it covers the ideological means by which nation-states are reproduced.' In his 1995 book *Banal Nationalism*, Billig suggested a new term to describe how people in established states develop and retain their sense of nationality:

> The term **banal nationalism** is introduced to cover the ideological habits which enable the established nations of the West to be reproduced. It is argued that these habits are not removed from everyday life, as some observers have supposed. Daily, the nation is

indicated, or 'flagged', in the lives of its citizenry. Nationalism, far from being an intermittent mood in established nations, is the endemic condition.[241]

For Billig, it seems, the real question was why people in established countries can recognise the nationalism of people in other countries without acknowledging the nationalist tendencies that are at play in their own lives. How is it that citizens overlook elements in their societies that tie them psychologically and socially to their own country? Billig suggested that, 'As far as nationality is concerned, one needs to look for the reasons why people in the contemporary world do not forget their nationality.' His thesis was that, 'in the established nations, there is a continual "flagging", or reminding, of nationhood.'[242] In his book Billig demonstrated how a study of political language in the press could be used to investigate the linguistic 'flagging' of national identity. His 'Day Survey'[243] of the British press illustrated how the language of 'us' and 'them' is used in modern countries to enable the populace to recognise their own national identity while distinguishing themselves from people in other countries. This flagging is so much a part of everyday life that people often do not register it on a conscious level.[244]

According to Billig, the daily communication inherent to banal nationalism is not just verbal. It also extends to the visual display of nationhood that is part of daily life in most countries. Expanding on the quotation at the beginning of the chapter, Billig wrote:

> In so many little ways, the citizenry are daily reminded of their national place in a world of nations. However, this reminding is so familiar, so continual, that it is not consciously registered as reminding. The metonymic image of banal nationalism is not a flag which is being consciously waved with fervent passion; it is the flag hanging unnoticed on the public building.[245]

It should be no surprise that flags are a primary visual symbol discussed in Billig's book. Typically, nations represent themselves symbolically with at least three top-level symbols: a coat of arms or state emblem, a national anthem, and a national flag. In many countries the state emblem is used primarily in formal contexts – on currency, postage stamps, government documents, and on other official materials. This symbol is rarely used by the people themselves, although symbolic elements contained therein might be. National anthems, similarly, are usually associated with special events in the lives of citizens. In the routines of life, they likely do not hear the state hymn daily. Of all national symbols, flags are perhaps the most recognisable means through which nationhood is visually represented. Many national flags are known not just by the citizens, but also are familiar to international audiences as well. In many countries the national flag is not only used at official government locations, but also is encountered in various contexts among the populace. Flags are often flown outside schools, are displayed in classrooms, are flown by private citizens and at commercial locations, are shown on vehicle license plates or adhered to vehicles in the form of a decal, and they are used in many other ways. Often, citizens see the flag without consciously registering its presence. Subliminally, though, the 'unsaluted' flags are working to reinforce an individual's psychological attachment to their country and their sense of national identity. As Billig explained:

> National identity in established nations is remembered because it is embedded in routines of life, which constantly remind, or 'flag', nationhood. However, these reminders, or 'flaggings', are so numerous and they are such a familiar part of the social environment, that they operate mindlessly, rather than mindfully (Langer, 1989). The national flag, hanging outside a public building or decorating a filling-station forecourt, illustrates this forgotten

reminding. Thousands upon thousands of such flags each day hang limply in public spaces. These reminders of nationhood hardly register in the flow of daily attention, as citizens rush past on their daily business.[246]

Billig's work focused on examples from the United States and the United Kingdom. For him, the best examples of banal nationalism seemed to come from the established nations of the West. However, his book has become a classic work in the field of nationalism, patriotism, and identity studies. It has inspired numerous scholars to examine different states around the world, demonstrating that banal nationalism is not an American or British phenomenon, or even a trait limited to just western nations. As Billig noted, banal nationalism has become a cultural feature in established nation states and helps citizens to locate themselves within a broader global context:

> There is a further reason for looking carefully. We are not just noticing our own identity, or even the identity of others. All those identities do not float in some sort of free psychological space. Identities are forms of social life. National identities are rooted within a powerful social structure, which reproduces hegemonic relations of inequity. Moreover, the nation-state is rooted in a world of such states.[247]

While the Soviet Union had ceased to exist by the time that Billig published his book, his ideas about symbols and identities are valuable for an examination of the culture of patriotism in the USSR.

Before proceeding, it is useful to review how the concepts of nationalism and patriotism were explained within the context of Marxism-Leninism. Soviet patriotism was defined not just as the love of the USSR, but also as a form of socialist internationalism. This internationalism was both internal and external, meaning that it was intended to create a bond between Soviet citizens from fifteen republics and over 100 ethnic groups, and also was meant to connect them to the citizens of all other socialist countries. The inward and outward nature of Soviet patriotism is closely tied to Vladimir Lenin's writings on 'the nationalities question' and how Marxism-Leninism viewed the concept. Lenin clearly established the Soviet view of nationalism as 'a bourgeois and petit bourgeois ideology and policy, as well as the outlook that raises the national question'.[248] He explained the historical role that nationalism had played in the economic evolution from feudalism to capitalism:

> Throughout the world, the period of the final victory of capitalism over feudalism has been linked up with national movements. For the complete victory of commodity production, the bourgeoisie must capture the home market, and there must be politically united territories whose population speak a single language, with all obstacles to the development of that language and to its consolidation in literature eliminated. Therein is the economic foundation of nationalist movements.[249]

Lenin warned that, when thinking about nationalism, it was imperative that Marxists remember the 'powerful *economic* factors that give rise to the urge to create national states'. Because of these factors, the bourgeoisie would be certain to champion nationalist demands. He further advised that, 'For the proletariat, however, the important thing is to strengthen its class against the bourgeoisie and to educate the masses in the spirit of consistent democracy and socialism.' Furthermore, Lenin assessed how the working class viewed 'the nationalities question':[250]

While recognizing equality and equal rights to a national state, it values above all and places foremost the alliance of the proletarians of all nations, and assesses any national demand, any national separation, from the angle of the workers' class struggle.[251]

He also argued that workers would understand the benefits of a large economically integrated market and state, and thus would only resort to secessionism in the absence of the equality of nations.

In his interpretation of Marxist theory, the realities of the class struggle would be enough to make the people (in the sense of the working masses) understand that they had more in common with the workers of other nations (in the sense of different cultural groups) than they did with the bourgeoisie of their own national or ethnic group.[252] He wrote:

> The interests of the working class and of its struggle against capitalism demand complete solidarity and the closest unity of the workers of all nations; they demand resistance to the nationalist policy of the bourgeoisie of every nationality.[253]

Contrasting Billig's ideas about banal nationalism with how Marxist theorists understood the concepts of patriotism and nationalism, it becomes clear that authorities in the USSR would have denied that the core of Soviet identity was linked to any type of nationalism. In the Soviet Union, the concept of nationalism was attributed to individual ethnic groups and would not have been an appropriate descriptor for the process that created a sense of Soviet identity among the citizens of the USSR.[254]

An examination of the material culture of the country appears to tell a different story and suggests that a form of *Soviet* banal nationalism was clearly at play. This aspect of the Soviet culture of patriotism has yet to be examined in detail in the historical literature. Using a variety of everyday objects as primary source material, this chapter will demonstrate how Billig's concept of banal nationalism can be used to examine the role of symbols in Soviet culture. How were flags used to reinforce a sense of Soviet identity among the populace? What other symbols were used to reinforce political socialisation and to foster a feeling of *Sovietness* in people from many ethnic groups? And how was banal nationalism in the Soviet Union meant to help citizens recognise their place in the world of nation states? With these questions in mind, this chapter will demonstrate the many ways in which Soviet citizens might have encountered national symbols in their daily lives and will reveal the nature of banal nationalism in the Union of Soviet Socialist Republics.

Flags and Banners

When looking at the role of flags and banners in the banal nationalism of the USSR, it is important to remember that the field of the Soviet flag was the red banner of revolution. This meant that any red banner or flag could serve as a visual substitute for the national flag. In addition, as evidenced by how children in the Young Pioneer organisation were taught about their red neckerchiefs, even a piece of red cloth could be a symbolic fragment of the red banner, and thus a visual reminder of the Soviet flag. This type of symbolic substitution of red banners for the national flag resulted in a convenient double benefit in the civil religion of the Soviet Union. The national flag with the hammer, sickle, and red star could be reserved for formal display contexts while red banners of many different varieties were used in other contexts within Soviet society. Throughout the USSR, especially on national holidays, this type of red banner use was common.

Figures 4.1-4.2. Photo of the author and her companion on Nevskii Prospekt in Leningrad (December 1982). Notice the red banners and street decorations in the enlarged section at right. These were holiday decorations in place for the celebration of the New Year.

One of the most common motifs used to portray the unity of the Soviet republics was through the display or portrayal of state symbols – those of the Soviet Union and those of the union republics – in groupings intended to show the republics as equals, yet as part of a bigger Soviet whole. Flagpole sets flying the Soviet national and republic flags were situated in public places such as large squares. The author witnessed such a union flag display on Palace Square in Leningrad, just in front of the Winter Palace in December 1982 (see Fig. 4.3). The flags matched a description of unity displays provided by David G. Wagner, a United States Foreign Service officer who was stationed at the embassy in Moscow:

> In several squares around the city there are sets of permanent flagpoles from which the union and republic flags are flown on holidays. The union flag is always given prominence and the order of precedence among the republics always follows the standard Soviet listing of the republics – the R.S.F.S.R., the Ukraine, Byelorussia, Uzbekistan, Kazakhstan, Georgia, Azerbaidzhan, Lithuania, Moldavia, Latvia, Turkemenia, Tajikistan, Armenia, Kirghizia, and Estonia.[255]

The order of precedence identified by Wagner almost matches the 1977 'Constitutional order' as discussed in Chapter 2, except that he seems to have made a slight error, having switched the position of the Turkmen SSR and Kirghiz SSR in his list. Regardless, to the observer the message conveyed by unity displays should have been obvious: despite all their differences the Soviet republics were portrayed as united and as integral parts of the Soviet Union. The similarity of the republic symbols was intended to symbolise that while the people of those republics had retained their cultural diversity, the unity of purpose in their common goal of building a developed socialist society meant that the unity of the proletariat was far more important than the nationalist interests of any of the peoples of the USSR.

Figure 4.3. Union flag display on Palace Square in front of the Winter Palace, December 1982.

Perhaps the most visible unity displays of state symbols were those placed on Moscow's Red Square for the celebration of important Soviet national holidays. Patriotic images frequently used a portrayal of the Kremlin and/or Red Square to convey unity, Soviet identity, and national pride. Located in the centre of the city, Red Square and the Kremlin have been the symbolic heart of Russia (and the Soviet Union) for centuries, even when the capital was in St. Petersburg. In this one location the long history of Russia was clearly on display. Symbolically the square was important because it was a place for the common people with the backdrop of the Kremlin – the centre of government for the country.[256]

A description of the geography of this location will set the stage for the grand celebrations that occurred there during the Soviet era. The borders of Red Square were defined by the Cathedral of Vasilii the Blessed (St. Basil's Cathedral, #3 in Figure 4.4), the Kremlin wall, the State Historical Museum (#7), and the *GUM* State Department Store (#13).[257] Red Square was the symbolic centre of the Soviet Union, but it was also a location that was rich in visual symbolism. For example, Saviour Tower, the tower with the gate closest to St. Basil's, had long been notable for its large clock faces. The addition of the large red star made it a prominent venue for the display of this important Soviet symbol (#5). Near the tower, positioned in front of the Kremlin wall, the Lenin Mausoleum (#1) was intended to be the focal point for visitors to the square. Marble viewing stands on each side of the tomb were used for patriotic parades and mass demonstrations held on Soviet holidays and other occasions (#2). On the opposite side of the Kremlin Wall was the domed Kremlin Senate building (behind Senate Tower, #8). This building served different roles throughout history. In the Soviet era, it was notable as the location of Lenin's apartment and study, Stalin's study, and the executive branch of the Soviet government. On top of the Senate's dome was an iconic flagpole where a large Soviet flag fluttered in the breeze. This flagpole was an essential part of many images illustrating the heart of the nation. Behind Lenin's Mausoleum was the Kremlin Wall Necropolis – the burial site of Soviet dignitaries and heroes in individual tombs and wall creches between Saviour Tower (#5) on one end and *Nikolskaia* Tower (#9) on the other. Finally, it is important to note that the Soviet Tomb of the Unknown Soldier was located along the Kremlin wall perpendicular to and just outside of the square (#12).[258]

80

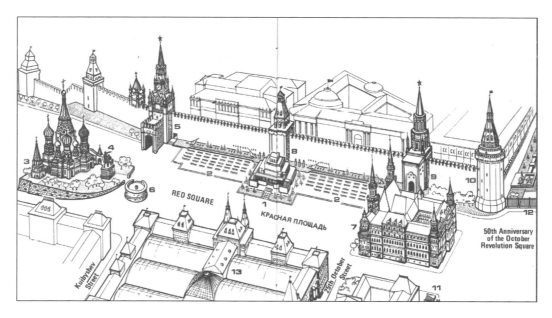

Figure 4.4. Diagram of Red Square from a Soviet guidebook of Moscow.

For Soviet citizens and foreign observers, Red Square was clearly the focal point of the Soviet culture of patriotism and civil religion. During public holidays, on which parades and demonstrations were held, Red Square was decorated with large placards and banners bearing Soviet symbols and Communist Party slogans. Red banners, flags, and posters were carried by participants in the civilian mass demonstrations resulting in visual waves of symbols flowing through the square on these occasions. In addition, the large red stars atop the Kremlin towers, the red Soviet flag fluttering over the Kremlin Senate, and the stately mausoleum of Lenin all lent an air of sacredness to Red Square.[259]

Figures 4.5-4.6. *Left:* Image of a Kremlin star. *Right:* View of Red Square during the 1981 celebration of the anniversary of the Great October Revolution. Note the large Soviet flag on the Kremlin Senate, the Soviet state emblem on Senate tower, the republic coats of arms on the wall to either side, and the republic flags in the foreground.

Vexillologist Whitney Smith observed that the 'great mass of fluttering colors in all shapes and sizes and designs is far more meaningful than decorative, for every flag is a communication from one human being or group of people which may be received and responded to by others.'[260] Billig reminded us, though, that not every flag seen in daily life will be perceived as sending a specific

81

message. The communication is not always consciously received and processed by the observer. He wrote:

> One can distinguish between the ways in which national flags are treated. Some are consciously waved and saluted symbols, often accompanied by a pageant of outward emotion. Others – probably the most numerous in the contemporary environment – remain unsaluted and unwaved. They are merely there as symbols, whether on a forecourt or flashed on to a television screen; as such they are given hardly a second glance from day to day.[261]

Therefore, it can be tempting to discount red banners as just street decorations, or unity displays as just colourful collections of flags. For the average citizen, these objects quickly became part of the background environment and thus were easy to overlook. However, when flags and banners are examined as part of the broader material culture of the modern nation state it becomes clear that banal nationalism, or everyday nationalism, is a regular part of life in many countries. By studying the broader culture of symbol usage in a state such as the Soviet Union we can learn more about the role of flags and symbols in modern societies.

Monuments, Markers, and Public Art

Red flags and banners were obvious expressions of Soviet patriotism from the perspective of visitors to the Soviet Union, even if citizens seemingly passed by without noticing them. Similarly, people encountered a wide range of monuments, markers, and public art that all contributed to the distribution of Soviet symbols throughout the USSR. In his study of Leninist 'monumental' propaganda, semiotician Sergei Kruk observed that:

> The proliferation of large statues and the creation of immense, expensive monumental frescoes, bas-reliefs and haut-reliefs helped the Communist Party to monopolize social space. The size and quantity of monuments were very important as they were the expressive form of the regime's stability.[262]

Historian Michael Ignatieff, in his study of a Soviet war memorial in Kiev, acknowledged the role of monuments in the formation of Soviet collective memory and identity. They were more than memorials and artwork. Ignatieff suggested that 'The statues are little sermons in stone. As with all sermons, the question is who is listening.'[263] While a thorough discussion of Soviet monuments and public art is outside the scope of this study, a few examples that focus on the primary symbols of the USSR will serve to illustrate how this form of banal nationalism was present in cities, towns, and villages throughout the country.

The presence of Lenin was a given in public spaces of the Soviet Union. In addition to the symbolic architecture of the Lenin mausoleum on Red Square, historical markers were placed in locations associated with Lenin's life, and statues or imagery of Lenin were common. Sociologist Victoria Bonnell noted that the standard elements of *Leniniana*[264] had already started to develop even before Lenin's death in 1924. Typical aesthetic qualities noted by Bonnell included 'the superhuman qualities of the *vozhd'* [leader], his simplicity and humaneness, the *narodnost'* [national character] of the *vozhd'* and his power (*moch'*).'[265] Imagery of Lenin was meant to portray him as an intellectual, but also as a friend of the workers; as a revolutionary, but also as a statesman; and as the founder of the USSR, as well as the 'beloved father' of the Soviet people. Once introduced, standard poses of the leader were repeatedly used in a variety of media. One such pose – where Lenin stands gesturing forward – is an excellent example of how Soviet artists played upon the multivocality of Lenin's arm position to help create the 'Cult of Lenin'. An example still stands at Finland Station in Saint Petersburg, the rail station through which Lenin returned from exile prior to the October Revolution. Lenin is dressed in a vested suit and coat without a cap. His right arm extends forward with the hand sideways and the thumb up. There are multiple interpretations associated with this gesture. First, he is not only pointing the way forward for his followers, but also indicating movement toward the bright future of communism. Additionally, poses of Lenin with his outstretched arm may have intentionally played upon traditional portrayals of Christ in Russian Orthodox art and icons, thus appropriating religious symbolism for the purpose of elevating Lenin to god-like status in Soviet culture. In this way, a single image or monument of Lenin showed him in multiple roles – as the revolutionary who led the Bolsheviks to power, as a statesman who set the people on the path to a bright future through communism, and as a supernatural figure who, after death, continued to bless and guide the work of building socialism. The concept of Lenin as a continuing participant in Soviet life was further suggested by the invocation of his presence through imagery and text in public spaces throughout the country.[266]

Figures 4.7-4.9. Three portrayals of Lenin from Leningrad/St. Petersburg. *Left:* Lenin statue at the Finland Station (2017). *Centre.* Portrait of Lenin surrounded by pictures of Soviet children on the Palace of the Pioneers in Leningrad (December 1982). *Right:* Building plaque reading 'V. I. Lenin was a regular reader of the Public Library in the years 1893-1895.'

A popular artistic theme in the Soviet movement of socialist realist art was the glorification of work – in factories and in the fields. It was important to demonstrate that all types of labour were valued and that workers in all sectors were vital to the success of building advanced socialism. Perhaps the best personification of this theme was a sculpture by Soviet artist Vera Mukhina entitled 'Worker and *Kolkhoz* Woman' (*Rabochiy i kolkhoznitsa*).[267] Created for installation on the Soviet pavilion at the 1937 World's Fair exhibition in Paris, the sculpture portrayed two young Soviet citizens – a factory worker and a collective farm worker. Each held a tool raised above their heads and, as the figures appeared to move forward, their tools combined to form the hammer and sickle emblem – the symbol of labour and of the first socialist state. Mukhina described the inspiration for her sculpture in her memoir:

> B. Iofan, the architect of the pavilion, acquainted me with the theme: a young worker and collective farm woman triumphantly raising aloft the emblems of their labours—a hammer and sickle—which were to cross high in the air and form the main part of the State Emblem of the Soviet Union.

...
     I did not have to invent the prototypes of the figures, they surrounded me at every step in my daily life—people who were full of the joy of living and sure of themselves and of their victory.[268]

Following the exhibition in Paris, the sculpture was moved to Moscow where it stood in front of the Exhibition of Achievements of the National Economy. Mukhina's sculpture was reproduced on postage stamps, on greeting cards, and was a key element in the production logo of the Mosfil'm movie studio. It would have been familiar to most citizens of the USSR, regardless of whether they had ever seen the sculpture in person.[269]

Figures 4.10-4.11. *Left:* Vera Mukhina, sculptor, 'The Worker and the *Kolkhoz* Woman' *Right:* Front view of the sculpture as used in the logo of the Soviet film company Mosfil'm.

Public artwork such as sculptures and monuments are typical conveyors of the sentiments of banal nationalism in many societies. Visitors to the capital cities of any country will be able to find national symbols displayed in many different venues. Examples include the Cenotaph and memorials in Whitehall (London, UK); an immense flag flown on state holidays at the Arc de Triomphe (Paris, France); the National Mall in Washington, DC (USA); and the statue of Nelson Mandela on the Union Buildings grounds in Pretoria (South Africa). In the Soviet Union, however, the use of symbols in public works was a strategic form of agitation and propaganda designed to instil in citizens and visitors alike an impression of the many advancements achieved under the Soviet system. An excellent example of such usage was in the subway stations of the Moscow Metropolitan railway system. As Russian art historian Olga Kostina noted, 'From its inception it was clear that the metro was destined to become the embodiment of the image of socialism. This was presented as a thing of celebration, a flourishing movement upward and onward'.[270] Not only was the entire Metro system a monument to Soviet achievements in construction and technology, but the stations themselves were designed to celebrate the cultural achievements of the Russian and Soviet people. Soviet architects and artists were commissioned to create formal structures, artwork, and design elements which depicted the story of the USSR and the development of an advanced socialist society. Most notable for visitors were the sculptures, mosaics, and paintings that decorated the walls and alcoves of many stations. More subtle, and perhaps a better illustration of Soviet banal nationalism, were the design elements people passed as they rushed through the stations to get to their final destinations. A few examples show how familiar symbols of Soviet identity were used as part of the ornamentation in Metro stations.

Figures 4.12-4.15. Examples of the use of Soviet symbols in the ornamentation of Moscow Metro stations. *Top Left:* Chandelier at the Kurskaia station (2018). *Top Right:* Red star under the dome of a vestibule in the Arbatskaia station (n.d.). *Bottom Left:* Detail from the Komsomolskaia station (2012). *Bottom Right:* Decorative element from the Prospekt Mira station (2018). *See colour on plate C-9.*

Currency

In his discussion of banal nationalism, Billig frequently cites the 'unsaluted flags' which reinforce a person's national identity. However, in this usage he is not just talking about actual flags. The iconography of national identity is found on a variety of objects which the citizen encounters on an almost daily basis. Many of these icon-bearing items are deliberately designed and deployed by central authorities of the modern nation state. As Billig noted, 'Flags are not the only symbols of modern statehood. Coins and bank notes typically bear national emblems, which remain unnoticed in daily financial transactions'.[271] In his analysis of the relationship between money and national identity, political scientist Eric Helleiner cited several important factors that have made currency an important vehicle for the communication of identity. For example, he noted that 'images on money were guaranteed a much larger audience than images carried by other media' and that 'images on money were particularly effective in conveying messages to the poor and illiterate'. Helleiner suggested that in the modern era 'images on money may also have been particularly effective tools of propaganda because they were encountered so regularly in the context of daily routines'. For this reason, he concluded that 'national currencies may have acted as much more effective purveyors of nationalist messages than flags or anthems'.[272] Following up on Helleiner's work, communication historian Josh Lauer also linked the symbols on banknotes and coins with the civil religious processes that tie citizens to their home country. He explained that 'ultimately, the quasi-religious faith imbued in national currencies is not merely symbolic or emotional; it is also functional and material. The imagery of national currencies actually validates them as real and credible'. For Lauer, money is a mode of communication from the political elites to every citizen of the state. The importance of a national currency extends beyond its role in the national economy, for it also serves as a vehicle to demonstrate sovereignty. National symbols, whether on currency or in other contexts, are the language through which governments communicate the cultural values of their societies to their people. According to Lauer, 'Nationalist iconography provides an important channel through which the authenticity and legitimacy of national currency is communicated, and through which social trust is reaffirmed in its taken for grantedness'.[273]

As Helleiner observed, on any given day more citizens may encounter their national symbols on banknotes and coins than through any other communication channels, whether they consciously notice them or not. In the Soviet Union, the importance of *Soviet* identity symbolism on money was highly significant. While the Constitution of the USSR defined a union republic as 'a sovereign Soviet socialist state that has joined the other Soviet republics in the Union of Soviet Socialist Republics', many of the traditional responsibilities related to sovereignty were exclusively reserved for the central government – protection of international borders, control of the military, and management of the integrated economy of the USSR. In terms of banal nationalism, one of the most significant prerogatives of sovereignty related to the economy was the issuance of currency.

The act of issuing money as a mark of sovereignty predates the modern national state. It was perhaps one of the earliest manifestations of national identity. In the ancient world the face or cypher of a sovereign was often used to 'brand' coins of the realm, but the two-sided nature of these objects provided a venue for the use of additional symbols as marks of national sovereignty. For centuries the coins of the Russian Empire bore the name of the tsar, the royal cypher, or a portrait of the sovereign. In the seventeenth century other national symbols such as the double-headed eagle and St. George were added to Russian coins. By the early twentieth century, the imperial double-headed eagle was a standard feature on most Russian coinage. On the early coins of the Russian Soviet Federative Socialist Republic the state emblem of the new Soviet republic replaced the imperial arms. In addition, they added the abbreviation of the republic's name – R.S.F.S.R. – and the quote from the *Communist Manifesto*, 'Proletarians of all countries, unite!' On the reverse was the five-pointed star.[274]

Figures 4.16-4.17. One-ruble coin issued by the Russian Soviet Federative Socialist Republic in 1922.

In terms of how national symbols were used in the designs, the coinage of the Soviet Union was remarkably consistent. Perhaps influenced by tsarist designs or the early coins of the Russian SFSR, the prominent symbol on Soviet coins was the state emblem of the USSR. The coat of arms had multiple symbolic functions in this usage. First and foremost, as the primary symbol used in governmental contexts and on official documents, it was the symbolic representation of Soviet authority. The state emblem on coinage illustrated the sovereign authority of the Soviet government to issue currency and, in terms of a centrally managed economy, also demonstrated the importance of the state in controlling economic activity in the country. Secondly, the Soviet arms conveniently conveyed the primary symbolic messages of Soviet Marxism-Leninism

Figures 4.18-4.19. One-ruble coin (obverse and reverse) issued by the USSR. This basic design was used until the breakup of the Soviet Union. On ruble coins the full name of the country was used, while lower value coins typically read *SSSR* (USSR).

Like many countries, the Soviet Union also issued commemorative coins on special occasions. Distinctive coinage intended for circulation provide excellent exemplars of how governments use money to communicate key points about a nation's history. Examples of Soviet commemorative coins included those issued on the anniversaries of the birth of Lenin, the Bolshevik Revolution, the creation of the Soviet Union, and the Soviet victory in the Great Patriotic War. They were also used to celebrate accomplishments in science and technology, the triumphs of Soviet athletes, and notable figures in the arts from the different republics. On most such designs, one side of the coin communicated Soviet identity through the state emblem and the abbreviation 'USSR', while the other side was used for commemorative purposes. In many cases, important national symbols were used in the designs. Any Soviet citizen versed in the national symbol set, the history of the country, and the cultural values of Marxism-Leninism should have been able to easily recognise and interpret the imagery used on the coins.[275]

Figures 4.20-4.23. *Left:* Obverse and reverse of a commemorative 15-kopek coin from 1967 celebrating 'Fifty years of Soviet power'. *Right:* Obverse and reverse of a commemorative 50-kopek coin from the same set. Coin images are not shown to scale.

Soviet banknotes exhibited a similar usage of national symbols as coins, relying on the state emblem as the primary symbol of national identification. Following the death of Lenin in 1924, his portrait became a prominent addition to the Soviet symbol set. Reflective of this practice, images of Lenin were added to banknote designs beginning in 1937. In the later years of the Soviet Union, images of state venues within the Kremlin grounds were also shown on currency.[276]

Figure 4.24. Obverse of Soviet banknote from 1937, the first series to include a portrait of Lenin. This note was valued at one *chervonets* (ten rubles).

An examination of Soviet paper money reveals the strategic use of language on currency. While not all writing on banknotes was multilingual, the practice of writing the denomination and monetary unit in each of the republic languages was established early on and continued throughout the history of the country. Considering that the Russian language was established as the common language among all citizens of the USSR and bearing in mind that even citizens who did not have fluency in Russian would likely have been able to read the numerals on the notes, it seems clear that the most likely rationale behind this design element on Soviet money was to demonstrate the unity of the Soviet peoples. However, re-examination of the display of the languages reveals an additional message encoded in the design of the banknotes. In his study of banknote design in multilingual states, sociolinguist Mark Sebba found a distinct difference between multilingual note designs which emphasised the equal status of languages versus those in which one language is favoured over the others. Sebba observed that in multilingual states where languages were given equal status, banknote designs tend to follow several standards. These practices include the symmetrical arrangement of the languages on the notes, presentation of the languages using equal-sized fonts, conveying the information content equally in all the languages used, and alternating the precedence of the languages in the layout of the notes. When Soviet banknotes are viewed with Sebba's principles in mind it becomes clear that, while Soviet authorities included the languages of all the republics on the notes, they were also demonstrating the dominant status of the Russian language. On the currency of the USSR, only the denominations of the bills were multilingual. All other text appeared only in Russian. Additionally, the font size for the republic languages was such that the total space used on most banknotes to list the denomination in Russian was typically equal in size to the region used for all the other languages combined. Clearly, the intended message was to recognise the different republics as an important part of the Soviet whole, while illustrating the leadership role of the RSFSR as well as the importance of Russian as the common language used by all Soviet peoples.[277]

Figure 4.25. Reverse side of a Soviet five-ruble banknote from 1961 showing the use of fifteen languages (Series used 1961-91).

Propaganda Posters

Soviet posters have been a popular topic of study as propaganda, art objects, and cultural artefacts. Scholars such as Victoria Bonnell and Anita Pisch, an art historian, focused on the evolution of the Soviet poster and its use in the leader cults of Lenin and Stalin. Bonnell's study is valuable as it examines the establishment of the basic iconography used in poster design throughout the history of the USSR. The study of Soviet political posters and their iconography is useful in the broader study of Soviet symbols, as they share many characteristics with other physical artefacts of banal nationalism and civil religion in the Soviet Union.[278]

In addition to Bonnell's study, the works of art historian Ulf Abel and historian Gloria Calhoun demonstrated how Soviet artists drew upon the symbolic traditions of Russian Orthodox icons to contribute to the civil religious nature of Marxism-Leninism in the USSR. As previously mentioned, this practice was especially important in the early Soviet period before mass literacy campaigns and universal education policies significantly increased the literacy rate among the population. For example, the traditional role of red as a symbol for life, blood (especially the blood of Christ), and of martyrdom was also linked to the relationship between the colour and the concept of beauty in Russian culture. Conveniently, red was also the colour of revolution and socialism, making it the logical national colour for the Soviet state. As a result, it was easy to appropriate the psychological connection between red and sacredness for the propaganda of the Soviet era.[279]

Recalling Calhoun's discussion of relational legitimacy, propaganda posters clearly conveyed this idea by grouping certain individuals. Posters combining Lenin with Marx, and those portraying Stalin with Lenin, clearly sent a message about how authority and power were transferred in the society. Soviet posters played upon the transfiguring power of light, another symbol of legitimacy, in the way that Lenin or Soviet heroes were illuminated. Two other important uses of light in Soviet symbolism were depictions of the red star and the rising sun. Similarly, the use of the red banner of revolution as a backdrop or simply red as the prominent colour on a poster would have signified legitimacy through its connection to revolution, the Communist Party, and the Soviet state.[280]

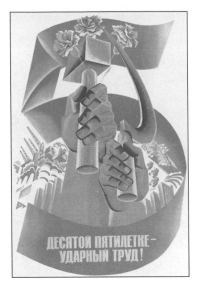

Figures 4.26-4.28. Three Soviet propaganda posters showing different ways in which symbols were used on this mode of communication. *See colour on plate C-9.*

The poster of Lenin dates from 1967 and shows him with the Soviet flag in the background. At upper right is the stanza by Maiakovskii ('Lenin lived, Lenin lives, Lenin will live!'). Notice the white line illuminating the form of Lenin on the left and how the red ribbon on Lenin's lapel is flapping in the wind like the flag, creating a visual connection between the two. On the centre poster, published in 1976, the text reads 'To the tenth five-year plan – high-powered labour!' Five-year plans were used by the Soviet government to focus national efforts on various goals of economic development. A red ribbon, reminiscent of that worn by Lenin or seen on the state emblem, forms the number five and encircles the hands from Mukhina's famous sculpture. The tools held in their hands form the combined hammer and sickle, while in the background we see evidence of industrialisation on the left and agricultural production on the right. At right the third poster, from 1972, illustrates the unity of the Soviet peoples. Fifteen women, each wearing traditional costume and holding produce from their republic, form a human 'ribbon' wrapped around a wreath of grain such as that on the Soviet arms. Behind them we see the rising sun and the five-pointed star at the top. The text on the poster reads 'The union of the republics is indestructible!' reminding the viewer of the lyrics from the Soviet national anthem.[281]

Postage Stamps

Another prerogative of sovereign states is the issuance of postage stamps. As with currency, it is quite common for countries to incorporate national symbols into stamp designs. However, states typically release many different stamps annually while currency designs can be used over a span of many years. For this reason, postage stamps present much more opportunity for a nation to define, or redefine, itself through imagery. Another important difference between currency and postage stamps is that currency is intended for use within the state's borders, while postage stamps can reach both domestic and international audiences. Additionally, the sale of postage stamps for use on letters and parcels, as well as for the collectors' market, generates revenue for the state.[282]

In his study of the symbolism on postage stamps as a source for research, historian Donald M. Reid observed that 'Stamps resemble government buildings, monuments, coins, paper money, flags, national anthems, nationalized newspapers, and ambassadors as conveyors of official viewpoints'.[283] As such, Reid contended that postage stamps can serve as historical evidence as artefacts and 'as *bearers of symbols, as part of a system of communications*'.[284] He recommended that historians focus on postage stamps as a form of communication, considering the messages conveyed by the stamps and observing how symbols and imagery are used to transmit those messages. Additionally, Reid suggested that 'For modern times, the symbolism of stamps is more useful to the historian than that of coins because stamps are more varied and less conservative'.[285] His article offered useful guidance for how postage stamps can be used to study banal nationalism in the modern state. A set of stamps issued for the 60th anniversary of the Soviet Union in 1982 clearly demonstrated Reid's observation that postage stamps are 'conveyors of official viewpoints'. The messages on the stamps illustrated six themes common in Soviet propaganda.[286]

Figures 4.29-4.34. Set of stamps celebrating 60 years since the founding of the USSR and portraying major themes of Soviet propaganda. **Left Column:** The Constitution of the USSR (**top**) and the friendship and unbreakable unity of the Soviet peoples (**bottom**); **Centre Column:** The creative work of the people (**top**) and benefits gained through industrialization and progress in agriculture (**bottom**); **Right Column:** The ability of the Soviet Union to defend itself (**top**) and the USSR as a peaceful nation (**bottom**).

Three studies of Soviet postage stamps confirmed Reid's thesis, demonstrating the ways that these small artefacts reveal how the state used stamps to communicate societal values. Historian Jonathan Grant examined how the Soviet government worked to redefine the hobby of stamp collecting, used stamp sales as a source of revenue, and most importantly, how they viewed postage stamps as tools for communicating state propaganda:

> Because the Soviet government so intimately tied the themes on its postage stamps to political goals, Soviet stamps can be regarded as visual statements of the values that the regime espoused and desired to foster among the population. In this light, these visual representations revealed the regime's conception of how Soviet society should be structured. Put another way, Soviet stamps made graphic declarations about the desirable composition of the new socialist society and what social groups would form the components of that society.[287]

Following up on the idea of stamps as propaganda, historian Alison Rowley studied the themes of Soviet stamps to show the variety of messages communicated. She noted that designs were vetted not just by officials of the Ministry of Communications, but also by experts in the subject matter portrayed on the stamps. Rowley's work demonstrated how the Soviet Union used stamps to convey messages about the values of Soviet society. For example, she sees the images of citizens as visual portrayals of the 'New Soviet Person' – workers, peasants, soldiers, heroes, aviators, explorers – showing how each citizen contributed to the construction of socialism through their labour.[288]

Stamps were also used to illustrate the history and political values of the USSR through the portrayal of prominent individuals from the development of Marxism-Leninism, images of Russian revolutions and the masses seizing power, and the heroic victories of the Bolsheviks and Soviets. In addition, stamps depicted the Soviet Union as a technologically and culturally developed country by celebrating science and technology, art and literature, athletics and physical culture, the emancipation of women in the USSR, and the ethnic diversity of the Soviet peoples. And finally, there were stamp issues clearly designed to appeal to collectors. An article by geographer Stanley D. Brunn, focused on a comparison of the themes of Soviet and post-Soviet Russian stamps, reaffirming how images portrayed on postage stamps can be used to study political transition and societal change.[289]

Figures 4.35-4.37. Three examples of stamps featuring images of Lenin. *See colour on plate C-10.*

Recalling Gloria Calhoun's observations about posters, images of leaders on stamps served as symbols of legitimacy. Stamps which showed Marx with leaders of the USSR illustrated continuity in the development of communist theory. Likewise, Lenin's image lent legitimacy on stamps such as on the example at upper right, which commemorated the 1981 Congress of the Communist Party of the Soviet Union. His profile on the red banner of revolution alluded to the membership badge of the CPSU, and symbolically portrayed the legitimacy and authority of the party.

An examination of stamp catalogues spanning the full history of the Soviet Union revealed the wide array of symbols used by the regime. Most notable were the official state symbols of the USSR and their constituent parts – the red banner of revolution, the Soviet national flag, the official state emblem, the red star, the hammer and sickle, and the abbreviation 'USSR' in Russian. There were individual issues and sets of stamps designed to show the unity of all the Soviet republics through official symbols (flags and coats of arms) and by the inclusion of national ornaments (design patterns associated with specific ethnic groups). In addition, single issues used the symbols of specific republics to celebrate the anniversaries of their entry into the union. Revolutionary themes, victories of the Red Army in the civil war, and the heroic success of the Soviet armed forces in the Great Patriotic War all showed the importance of the citizens in seizing power and the might of the military for defending the homeland. Marxist-Leninist ideology was illustrated with images of communist theorists and Soviet leaders, as well as through the portrayal of people in all strata of Soviet society engaged in their work and thus, contributing to the building of a socialist society. The latter category is especially significant, as there were stamp designs which could have given any citizen a direct connection to the goals of the state. Stamps with members of children's and youth organisations were meant to show the contributions of even the youngest Soviet citizens, as well as the 'happy Soviet childhood' made possible through the implementation of Soviet policies. Agricultural, industrial, and intellectual workers could have seen themselves in stamps showing the advancements of the USSR in productive capability and technology. In addition, athletes and cultural workers could have recognised their contributions through stamps related to physical culture, the arts, and literature.[290]

Figures 4.38-4.40. Three holiday stamps showing the use of Soviet symbols. *Left:* Stamp for the New Year. *Centre:* Souvenir sheet for May Day. *Right:* Stamp for Great October. *See colour for figures 4.38-4.39 on plate C-10.*

Stamps issued for various holidays would have appealed to collectors as well as to citizens sending greetings to their friends and families. Many stamps in this category feature national symbols in the design. The stamp at left read 'With the New Year!' and portrayed the Soviet state emblem centred above, with the clock from the Kremlin's Saviour Tower striking midnight at lower right. A stamp for May Day showed a hint of the red banner, but when viewed within the context of a souvenir sheet designed for collectors it becomes part of a mass demonstration of marchers. On the stamp reading 'Glory to Great October' the red banner of revolution was shown flying above the products of labour, with the hammer and sickle emblem in the foreground. The date '1917' and the rocket at left illustrated the many achievements accomplished since the revolution. Postage stamps featuring national symbols were not reserved just for national holidays. They were issued throughout the year.

Figures 4.41-4.42. *Left:* Stamp showing the Soviet flag, with the Kremlin flagpole below. *Right:* Lenin stamp on a souvenir sheet showing a unity flag display. *See colour on plate C-10.*

In his article, Grant discussed the complicated relationship between Soviet authorities and philatelists in the USSR. On the one hand, stamp collecting was considered to have bourgeois roots – especially when it came to the sale of postage stamps and exchanges between collectors. Even in the later Soviet period this was a concern, with articles appearing in the press about collectors who had been convicted of currency speculation or business dealings related to coin or stamp collecting.[291] In order to assert control over philately in the country, Soviet authorities enacted strict regulations limiting the trading of postage stamps to exchanges only for the purpose of completing an individual's collection. Additionally, control was asserted through the creation of an officially sanctioned society for stamp collectors. From a different perspective, Soviet authorities recognised the financial benefits of marketing their own stamp issues to collectors both at home and abroad. Domestically they promoted the sale of postage stamps to generate revenue for socially meaningful causes such as famine relief. Internationally, the Soviet government reserved for itself the right to sell Soviet stamps to foreign dealers. Regardless of the regulations, authorities understood the value of stamp collecting as a source of revenue and a mode to communicate Soviet values.[292]

Figures 4.43-4.44. Examples of postal covers intended for stamp collectors. Envelopes were designed with cachets – illustrated regions on the envelope intended to provide more information about the stamp or the event commemorated. *Left:* 'Transcaucasia '84' Philately Exhibition with the flags of the Georgian SSR, the Azerbaijan SSR, and the Armenian SSR. *Right:* 40 Years of the Estonian SSR. *See colour for figure 4.44 on plate C-10.*

94

Znachki: Badges and Pins

Another hobby in the Soviet Union was the collecting of *znachki*, small metal badges which were found in all levels of society. To the casual observer, these small pins could easily be dismissed as having little value to the historian. However, the variety of badges produced in the USSR can shed light on the importance of symbols in the material culture of the country. In his catalogue of Soviet badges from 1917-1991, exonumist I. I. Likhitskiy suggested that *znachki* had value as more than just collectables:

> The history of the Soviet period, like no other, is vividly reflected not only in documents and scientific research but to a great extent in small pieces of metal which combine laconism, vividness, neatness and original expression of a certain idea. The badges have much to tell a thoughtful researcher. Half a century old rewards are undeservedly abolished and forgotten.
>
> When collected together, read and described without prejudice and political declaration, they build a whole picture of the past when our ancestors lived.[293]

Likhitskiy acknowledges that, to some, these small badges might be discounted as mere trinkets. However, the passage of time lends relevance to these items as artefacts of the Soviet era. 'After 50-60 years or even a century the thing finds its value as a reminder of the past. This is a history, this is a life story. It is full of beauty, romance, dreams and heroism and other everlasting spiritual values.'[294]

The variety of pins produced in the USSR served many different purposes in Soviet society. Some were distributed selectively while others were available for purchase at tourist attractions and in shops throughout the country. Badges designed for the collector's market were widely available and quite inexpensive, making them easily obtainable by people at all levels of the society. Likhitskiy identified six different categories of *znachki* produced in the Soviet Union:

> Reward badges are given for a definite progress in labour, sports, public and political activity, military service etc.
>
> Official badges are given to representatives of different services and positions such as postmen, taxi drivers, shop assistants, deputies etc.
>
> Academic badges are given for graduation from specialized higher and secondary educational institutions.
>
> Membership badges are given for membership in the different societies, clubs and unions.
>
> Anniversary badges are dedicated to anniversaries of events, holidays and are given to the participants of these events.
>
> Souvenir badges, as a rule, are dedicated to countries, cities, exhibitions, festivals etc.[295]

Thematically it should not be surprising to find Soviet symbols on badges in any of these categories, especially those issued for use in official contexts. To the outside observer of Soviet society, the repeated use of national symbols on anniversary and souvenir badges was immediately noticeable.

Figures 4.45-4.46. *Left:* Commemorative badge for International Workers' Day ('Peace / Labour / May'). *Right:* Anniversary badge for 60 years of the Soviet Union (1982).

It was not uncommon for foreigners visiting the USSR to accumulate a small collection of *znachki* reflecting places that they had visited, badges traded to them by children in exchange for chewing gum, and pins indicative of the point in time when they visited the USSR. Many western tourists to the Soviet Union (including the author) returned home with numerous examples of badges bearing the red banner of revolution, flags and emblems of the USSR and Soviet republics, images of Lenin, and badges emphasizing the role of Moscow as the heart of the USSR. An examination of the pins that the author brought back from her trip illustrated not only her interest in flags and the Soviet space programme, but also documented the four cities and three republics included in her group's tour of the country. They also commemorated important events from the period such as the 1980 Olympics and the 60th anniversary of the Soviet Union.[296]

Znachki were also a way to promote the friendship of the Soviet peoples and the unity of the republics. Collectors might have enjoyed acquiring badges that commemorated anniversaries of the founding of the USSR and working to collect full sets of pins representing the fifteen republics. In looking at examples from five different unity sets of *znachki*, it becomes clear that there were a variety of ways to use the republic symbols in this context. Often both the flag and emblem of the republic would be shown, although there were sets that used just one symbol. In many cases a badge included not just the symbols, but also a label identifying the republic. Notable in the set of examples that follow on the next page is the flag badge for the Armenian SSR (bottom left) which included the abbreviation of the republic using the Armenian alphabet. Each pin in the set identified the flag in the appropriate language.

Figures 4.47-4.48. *Znachki* (metal badges) for Soviet anniversaries incorporating unity flag displays (1972 and 1982). On both examples, highly simplified flags of the republics are arranged in 1977 Constitutional order from the top down. *Left:* Flags are tiled left to right, in four rows against the background of the Soviet national flag. *Right*: Flags are in order from left to right, starting at the top and arranged around the Soviet national emblem. The red banner of revolution bearing the letters *SSSR* tops off the display. *See colour on plate C-11.*

Figures 4.49-4.53. *Znachki* from five different unity sets. ***Top to Bottom, Left to Right:*** Ukrainian SSR, Armenian SSR, Georgian SSR, Latvian SSR, and Turkmen SSR (various dates). *See colour on plate C-11.*

Postcards and Holiday Cards

The Russian word for postcard is *otkrytka*, a shortened form of *otkrytoe pis'mo*, meaning 'open letter'. In the Soviet era, the production and use of postcards continued a tradition established in Imperial Russia, including the use of postcard images as state propaganda. Soviet postcards have been studied as a means of reproducing and distributing socialist realist paintings. In his analysis, art historian Matteo Bertelé focused on the use of postcards as a transmedial object, showing how their production and distribution transformed objects of mass culture into tools of ideological practice. As he noted, 'the relevance of a postcard was determined by its number of prints, and this information was unfailingly reported'. Soviet postcards were produced in large numbers, they were widely used, and they were popular collectables among the populace. Their original purpose, noted by Bertelé, was 'to create a unitary, organic and canonical Soviet imagery'.[297]

Other scholars have concurred with this assessment when analysing these seemingly mundane objects. In his introduction to a collection of postcards reproducing works of socialist realist art, published in 2008, deltiologist A. L. Rubinchik remarked on the familiarity of the images for Soviet citizens:

> For every Russian member of the generation that is older than 35-40 years, who vividly remembers his or her Young Komsomol (Pioneer) childhood and Komsomol youth, monuments to the revolution heroes and state leaders on the city squares, Soviet newspapers and magazines, at least one-third of the postcards in this collection will be familiar. We saw them on the pages of ABC-books and reading books in school, we wrote compositions about them and met them on the pages of magazines, on posters, in school newspapers, and May 1st and November 7th congratulatory cards. This is one of the peculiarities of the postcards: on one hand, they illustrate how our life was directed and regulated down to mere trifles; on the other hand, they show how the postcards united entire generations, creating symbols and subjects, integrating the artistic field, and composed of images that were clear for all.[298]

Clearly, postcards in the Soviet Union were more than just a mechanism for communication between individuals. They also played an additional role by reinforcing societal values through imagery that reflected Soviet aesthetics and affirmed the patriotic feelings that were meant to connect citizens to their homeland.

While scholars have shown interest in Soviet postcards that reproduced artwork, little attention has been spent on the more simplistic postcards used to send celebratory greetings on various holidays. One such assessment was cultural scholar E. G. Imanakova's study of postcards for Victory Day (9 May), celebrating the defeat of National Socialist Germany. Imanakova made several important observations assessing symbols on Soviet greeting cards and the role these objects played in the banal nationalism of the USSR. First, there was a linguistic process of substantivisation (or nominalisation), through which the expression '9 *maia*' (9th of May) was transformed into a synonym for 'Victory Day'. Imanakova noted that, for residents of the USSR, seeing this date would have immediately communicated this meaning.[299] Similar usage of dates as substitutes for holiday names were common on cards for 8 March (8 *marta*), 1 May (1 *maia*), and 7 November (7 *noiabria*). Additionally, Imanakova identified a distinct set of visual symbols commonly used on cards for Victory Day. These symbols included holiday salutes (using fireworks and/or artillery), a holiday (military) parade, the Soviet Banner of Victory (*Znamia Pobedy*), the Soviet Order of Victory medal, and the Guard's Ribbon (also known as the Ribbon of St. George – an orange and black ribbon used on military decorations in both the Russian Empire and the Soviet Union). Additionally, she cited the use of red as the primary colour on most cards for this holiday. In the context of a holiday related to a military victory, red represents the concepts of blood, sacrifice, and victory. It also served as a substitute for the national flag of the Soviet Union. Other symbolic uses of flags on the cards for Victory Day included unity displays of republic flags or the flags for the branches of the Soviet military. In addition to postcards designed for this specific holiday, there were also more generic military-themed cards that would have been suitable for any holiday dedicated to the appreciation of the Soviet armed forces.[300]

Figures 4.54-4.56. Three holiday postcards with military themes. *Left:* 'Glory to the Soviet Armed Forces!'. *Centre:* 'Glory to the armed forces of the USSR!' *Right:* 'Glory to the armed forces of the USSR!'. *See colour on plate C-12.*

Applying Imanakova's methodology, it was possible to identify a symbol set for specific Soviet holidays – a menu of visual icons that was meant to communicate the meaning of the holiday and to reinforce feelings of Soviet patriotism and identity. Looking at postcards designed for May Day it became clear that the set of symbols associated with this holiday was well-defined. For example, red as a symbol of international socialism and the national colour of the USSR was widely used. As tokens of labour the hammer and sickle were prominent for this holiday, although other symbols such as the national flag and red banners in general were also used. Many cards showed citizens marching in mass demonstrations or watching the parades with their families. Another major symbolic theme for May Day cards was internationalism, emphasising the importance of this holiday not just for residents of the Soviet Union but also for the working people of all countries. This concept was typically shown through use of the '3-races' theme in which the figures illustrate the friendship of the peoples inherent to international socialism. The theme of internationalism was also shown using the national flags of different nations.[301]

Figures 4.57-4.58. Two cards for May Day. *Left:* 'With the holiday 1 May!'; text in the background says 'peace', 'labour', 'May', and 'socialism' in various languages. *Right:* '1 May'. *See colour on plate C-12.*

Figures 4.59-4.60. Two May Day postcards using the 3-races theme to illustrate internationism. *Left:* Three children hold their own little parade with the European girl wearing a Young Pioneer tie and carrying the red banner of socialism. The text below reads 'Long live 1 May!' in Latvian. *Right:* The banners read 'Peace, May, and Labour'. Text below reads '1 May – Day of the International Solidarity of the Workers!' *See colour on plate C-12.*

As with May Day, the anniversary of the Great October Socialist Revolution was celebrated with a military parade and civilian mass demonstration. The primary symbols for this holiday were Lenin, the Soviet flag, the red star, and the hammer and sickle. Moscow, as the Soviet capital, was the focal point of the country's celebrations. For this reason, imagery of the Kremlin or Kremlin red stars were also common on this holiday.

Figures 4.61-4.62. Two cards for Great October. *Left:* 'Glory to Great October'. The hammer and sickle, held aloft by the worker and collective farm woman from Mukhina's sculpture, are seen against a backdrop representing industry and agriculture. *Right:* The hammer and sickle are formed from text reading '1917 October'. The greeting below reads 'With the holiday!' *See colour on plate C-13.*

In terms of civil religion, national holidays played an important role in that they served as a common set of festivals to be shared by all citizens of the Soviet Union regardless of their ethnicity or religious background. As previously mentioned, textbooks designed for younger Soviet children often used the calendar as a schema, interspersing texts on national holidays with other readings appropriate for the season. As a result, Soviet children would have been taught the meanings behind these holidays and about the rituals that marked the Soviet calendar. On greeting cards, Soviet unity was illustrated using symbols of the USSR and those of the Soviet republics in unity displays. When examined in detail, most of the cards show the symbols in Constitutional order, although in some cases it is not at first readily apparent.

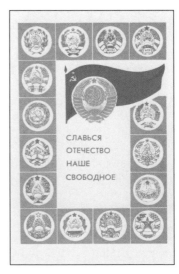

Figures 4.63-4.65. Postcards with unity displays of Soviet and republic symbols. *Left:* Card for May Day, reading 'Peace, Labour, May'. *Centre:* Card for International Women's Day with text '8 March' and 'Glory to Soviet women'. *Right:* 'Be glorious, our free fatherland', a phrase from the national anthem. *See colour on plate C-13.*

100

New Year's Cards and Ornaments

Not all holidays in the Soviet Union were overtly political in nature. Article 41 of the constitution guaranteed that 'Citizens of the USSR have the right to rest and leisure'.[302] Perhaps no holiday on the Soviet calendar illustrated this guarantee as much as *Novyi god*, the New Year. In the years following the October Revolution the Communist Party had worked to promote atheism and to discourage religious practices. However, in the mid-1930s the party tried a new strategy to discourage citizens from celebrating Christmas. Taking advantage of the fact that the revised calendar moved Orthodox Christmas to January, the Soviets were able to appropriate folk traditions for Christmas into a secular celebration of the New Year. Unlike Soviet holidays which focused on large public events, New Year's celebrations were typically observed with family and friends. The holiday was personified by *Ded Moroz*, who usually arrived in a traditional *troika* (three-horsed sleigh) accompanied by *Snegurochka*. Among the most beloved of New Year's traditions was the *elka* decorated with lights and ornaments.[303]

Reintroduction of the *elka* was prompted by a letter written by Pavel Postyshev, Second Secretary of the Ukrainian Communist Party, which was published in the newspaper *Pravda* on 28 January 1935. Postyshev noted that before the revolution the children of the workers could only enjoy a brightly lit *elka* by looking through the windows of the wealthy. He criticised those who had condemned the *elka* as an excess of the bourgeoisie, noting that in the Soviet Union this joyful celebration could be made available to all Soviet children. Postyshev called upon members of *Komsomol* and leaders of the Young Pioneers to 'organise a cheerful meeting of the new year for children, [and to] arrange a good Soviet fir tree in all cities and collective farms'.[304] In her discussion of Soviet New Year's celebrations, historian Karen Petrone traced the process through which Postyshev's suggestion prompted the reinvention of the New Year in the USSR.[305] Historian Alla Salnikova observed that 'The rebirth of the *elka* as an element of a new – Soviet – holiday culture required the "Sovietization" of its content, which could readily be represented and manifested by changing the *elka's* holiday "garb"'. Soviet symbols were quickly incorporated into holiday decorations and imagery related to the celebration of the New Year.[306]

Figures 4.66-4.68. New Year's postcards with Soviet symbols, reading 'With the New Year!'. On the card at right Mukhina's 'Worker and Kolkhoz Woman' are superimposed over the clock face of Saviour Tower. *See colour for figures 4.67-4.68 on plate C-14.*

The Russian term for tree ornaments – *elochnye igrushki* – means 'fir tree toys' and emphasises that the target audience for *elka* decorations were children. Tree decorations were meant to represent the joyful childhood enjoyed by Soviet children. In the early years of the Soviet *elka*, the 1938 Five Year Plan called for production of ornaments representing various elements of Soviet life including the Red Army, physical culture and sport, children, and city/village life. It should not be surprising that banal nationalism was also expressed in the design of many *elka* toys, as explained by Salnikova:

> A special place was accorded in the fir tree ornamental symbolic 'text' to the red star, hammer and sickle, now the universals [sic] symbols of Soviet (Bolshevik) culture. The five-cornered star sat easily on the pinnacle of the fir tree, was depicted on Christmas baubles, glass 'towers' and other Soviet ornamental toys.[307]

By emphasising the production of ornaments designed to instil feelings of patriotism in children, it became possible not only to justify the manufacturing of such items, but also to create a new distinctly Soviet *elka* as a socially acceptable replacement for the bourgeois Christmas tree. Salnikova noted that by the mid-1950s *elka* ornaments were commonplace throughout the USSR. The designs of fir tree toys did not remain static but changed with the times during the latter decades of the Soviet era. For example, during the 1960s space exploration was a popular theme for ornaments, while by the 1970s those featuring elements of the Soviet symbol set were phased out. However, because ornaments were collected and passed down through families, fir tree decorations with Soviet symbols would have remained in personal use until the breakup of the USSR.[308]

Figures 4.69-4.71. Soviet fir tree decorations including a red-star tree topper and ornaments. *See colour on plate C-15.*

Soviet symbols were present in other aspects of the New Year's celebration. An examination of postcards related to this holiday reveals several important examples. First, the *elka* and fir tree toys were often shown on New Year's cards. The use of the red star as the traditional tree topper is reminiscent of the star-topped towers of the Kremlin, making the physical centre of Soviet society and civil religion a focal point of imagery on the cards. Conveniently the famous clock faces of Saviour Tower reinforce this linkage as, regardless of the time zone, the New Year for the entire country symbolically began in Moscow. Thus, the connection between the *elka* and the passage of time are evoked in winter imagery of Moscow, further reinforcing the role of the city as the spiritual and political centre of the Soviet Union. As illustrated by symbol usage on *elka* ornaments and greeting cards, even a seemingly non-political holiday such as the New Year was a forum for Soviet banal nationalism.

Figures 4.72-4.73. Soviet New Year's cards with imagery of the Kremlin. *See colour on plates C-14 and C-15.*

Conclusion

While Michael Billig recognised banal nationalism in the cultures of the United States and the United Kingdom, others inspired by his work have shown that it is not an exclusively western phenomenon. Instead, this need to reinforce a unified sense of identity among the populace seems to be an essential element of the modern nation state. In states where there are clear ethnic majorities, banal nationalism is often linked to the historical culture of the primary national group and incorporates symbols from their culture. However, in multi-ethnic states the tendency has been to develop a new system of national symbolism that ties multiple peoples together and reinforces a shared sense of identity among members of all groups.

The many examples evident in the material culture of the USSR suggest that Communist Party leaders recognised the need to promote Soviet patriotism among the many different ethnic groups in order to create a unified culture among all citizens of the country. Political socialisation began in childhood through the formal education system and Soviet children's organisations. It was reinforced in adulthood through various rituals and social conventions, and a well-developed calendar of public holidays. Finally, the material culture of the Soviet Union was rich with examples of banal nationalism, thus ensuring that symbols of the state were common in both public and private spaces throughout the country. Because people encountered these symbols as part of their everyday life, they seemed to go unnoticed and faded into the background of life in the USSR. However, subconsciously the symbols of the Soviet Union were intended to reinforce a shared sense of *Soviet* identity among the people of the country. Clearly, Billig's concept of banal nationalism can be applied not just in western democracies but also in one-party multi-ethnic states such as the Union of Soviet Socialist Republics.

Discussing his book *Banal Nationalism* two decades after its publication, Billig reflected that:

> One of the main themes of *Banal Nationalism* was that signs of nationalism can be too
> familiar to be noticed. Whereas ordinary citizens may fail to observe the national symbols
> on the stamps that they are affixing to their letters or on their banknotes that they are

103

spending in shops, it is less forgivable that social theorists should routinely be so unobservant. Social scientists have concealed the nationalism of Western nations by labelling it as 'patriotism', which they contrast favorably, but unjustifiably, with the 'nationalism' of others. As Calhoun comments, *Banal Nationalism* argued that ordinary people and social theorists have shared common blind-spots and that the book drew attention to signs of nationalism that often pass unrecognized.[309]

This chapter has demonstrated numerous examples from the material culture of the Soviet Union that document the presence of banal nationalism in the USSR. As the various studies examining Billig's concept in myriad cultures have shown, banal nationalism seems to be applicable to many different types of cultures and societies around the world. Viewing the patriotic culture of a country as banal nationalism can provide valuable insight into the relationships between nationalism, patriotism, and national identity – all key concepts in understanding modern nation states. Billig suggested that, 'As far as nationality is concerned, one needs to look for the reasons why people in the contemporary world do not forget their nationality'.[310] He postulated that the constant 'flagging' of identity through symbols (both audible and visual) was essential to the formation and reaffirmation of national identity. Billig emphasised that 'by noticing the flaggings of nationhood, we are noticing something about ourselves. We are noticing the depths and mechanisms of our identity, embedded in routines of social life'.[311] Billig's focus on the role of symbols serves as a valuable connector between the theoretical basis of national identity and the material culture of modern countries. Because visual representation of national identity relies heavily on flags, coats of arms, and symbolic elements from them, it is clear that Billig's ideas can also provide scholars with a model to study the importance of political symbols more broadly in society.

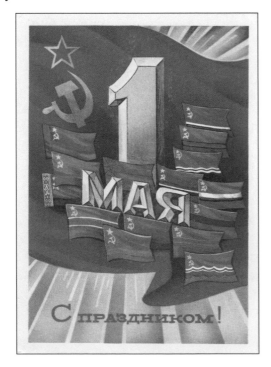 

Figures 4.74-4.75. Two Soviet holiday postcards using displays of republic flags to illustrate Soviet unity. *Left:* Card for May Day reading '1 May' and 'With the holiday!' *Right:* Card for the anniversary of the October Revolution reading 'With the holiday Great October!' *See colour on plate C-14.*

Chapter 5
Symbolic Afterlife: Legacies of Soviet Civil Religion

A spectre is haunting Europe – the spectre of communism.[312]

– Karl Marx and Friedrich Engels

In the first sentence of the *Communist Manifesto*, Karl Marx and Friedrich Engels described communism as a spectre haunting Europe. Three decades after they gained independence, many of the former Soviet republics still wrestle with the ghosts of their communist pasts. While a detailed examination of why and how the Soviet Union broke up is outside the scope of this study, an examination of the symbolic landscape of the former USSR is relevant. This study is focused on how symbols were used in Soviet civil religion and how they were linked to *Soviet* identity. In November 1989, when the Kremlin did not intervene with the removal of the Berlin Wall, it became a poignant symbol of the end of Soviet influence in central and eastern Europe. Back in the USSR, though, the fall of communism took much longer. When Lithuania unilaterally declared independence on 11 March 1990 it was unclear how the government in Moscow would respond. Over the next nine months Soviet authorities tried various strategies, including the imposition of an economic blockade on the breakaway republic, in the hope of bringing it back into submission. In January 1991 they initiated an attempt at military intervention, during which thirteen Lithuanians were killed. However, this action failed to crush the independence movement. By that time, pro-independence efforts were progressing in the other two Baltic republics and in Moldova[313], Georgia, and Armenia. Throughout the year the union essentially fell apart, culminating in the resignation of Mikhail Gorbachev on 25 December 1991. The following day, at 7:32 pm, the Soviet flag was lowered from the dome of the Kremlin Senate and, at 11:40 pm, the Russian tricolour was raised in its place. This last symbolic act signalled the end of the Soviet epoch both at home and abroad. What was once a vast multinational union had become fifteen independent countries, each working to define itself on its own terms.

Each of the ex-Soviet republics has faced challenges related to nation building. For example, every country has had to transform governmental structures, manage their own economy, establish foreign policy and diplomatic relationships, secure their borders, and attend to other basic concerns faced by any emerging state. In terms of this study, though, one of the most interesting challenges has been the creation of a sense of national identity amongst ethnically diverse populations, many of whom still had a strong sense of Soviet identity. A demographic snapshot from the 1989 Soviet census shows the ethnic composition and majority status in the Soviet republics just two years before the USSR disbanded. It is worth noting that there were only six republics where the titular majority represented over 75% of the population – the Russian SFSR, the Uzbek SSR, the Byelorussian SSR, the Azerbaijan SSR, the Lithuanian SSR, and the Armenian SSR. In addition, there were five republics where ethnic Russians comprised more than 20% of the population – the Ukrainian SSR, the Kazakh SSR, the Kirghiz SSR, the Latvian SSR, and the Estonian SSR.[314]

Republic	1989 Population	Largest Four Ethnic Groups (% of republic population to the nearest tenth)
Russian SFSR	147,021,869	Russian (81.5%); Tatar (3.8%); Ukrainian (3.0%); Chuvash (1.2%)
Ukrainian SSR	51,452,034	Ukrainian (72.7%); Russian (22.1%); Jewish (0.9%); Byelorussian (0.9%)
Uzbek SSR	19,810,077	Uzbek (71.4%); Russian (8.3%); Tajik (4.7%); Kazakh (4.1%)
Kazakh SSR	16,464,464	Kazakh (39.7%); Russian (37.8%); German (5.8%); Ukrainian (5.4%)
Byelorussian SSR	10,151,806	Byelorussian (77.9%); Russian (13.2%); Polish (4.1%); Ukrainian (2.9%)
Azerbaijan SSR	7,021,178	Azerbaijani (82.7%); Russian (5.6%); Armenian (5.6%); Lezgins (2.4%)
Georgian SSR	5,400,841	Georgian (70.1%); Armenian (8.1%); Russian (6.3%); Azerbaijani (5.7%)
Tajik SSR	5,092,603	Tajik (62.3%); Uzbek (23.5%); Russian (7.6%); Tatar (1.4%)
Moldavian SSR	4,335,360	Moldavian (64.5%); Ukrainian (13.8%); Russian (13.0%); Gagauz (3.5%)
Kirghiz SSR	4,257,755	Kirghiz (52.4%); Russian (21.5%); Uzbek (12.9%); Ukrainian (2.5%)
Lithuanian SSR	3,674,802	Lithuanian (79.6%); Russian (9.4%); Polish (7.0%); Byelorussian (1.7%)
Turkmen SSR	3,522,717	Turkmen (72.0%); Russian (9.5%); Uzbek (9.0%); Kazakh (2.5%)
Armenian SSR	3,304,776	Armenian (93.3%); Azerbaijani (2.6%); Kurdish (1.7%); Russian (1.6%)
Latvian SSR	2,666,567	Latvian (52.0%); Russian (34.0%); Byelorussian (4.5%); Ukrainian (3.5%)
Estonian SSR	1,565,662	Estonian (61.5%); Russian (30.3%); Ukrainian (3.1%); Byelorussian (1.8%)

Table 5.1. Population Data for the Fifteen Soviet Republics Showing the Four Most Populous Ethnic Groups at the Time of the 1989 All-Union Population Census (in order by total population).

This book has demonstrated how Soviet civil religion, with its system of symbols, rituals, and myths, was used to create and reinforce a sense of Soviet identity amongst the citizens of the USSR. Chapter 3 examined the strategy through which symbols were used in schools as tools to politically socialise children and teach them about Marxism-Leninism. School lessons were supplemented by participation in the Pioneer organisation, through which children were expected to develop a strong sense of Soviet patriotism. Throughout the process of systematic political socialisation, a unified *Soviet* identity was meant to be forged amongst citizens who already maintained a diverse range of ethnic and cultural identities. Chapter 4 illustrated how banal nationalism, where Soviet symbols were distributed throughout the social environment, worked to remind citizens of their *Sovietness* and to reinforce that unified identity. Soviet identity, and its associated symbols, did not disappear when the flag of the USSR was lowered from the Kremlin for the final time. Today, decades after independence, lingering remnants of Soviet banal nationalism and civil religion can still be seen in different parts of the former Soviet Union.

The aim of this chapter is to briefly examine how Soviet symbols are viewed in different parts of the former USSR with the goal of learning more about the enduring effects of Soviet identity. In some countries there has been ambivalence about the communist era and the symbolic legacy of the USSR. For others, symbols of Soviet identity have become a focal point in conflicts over the nature of post-Soviet identity construction. An examination of countries where Soviet symbols have been devalued and rejected will demonstrate how symbolic purges have been used to reinforce revitalised national identities. There are also states where the symbols retain value as they illustrate significant historical narratives that continue to honour elements of the Soviet experience. Considering the commonalities where this is the case reveals patterns in how those countries view their Soviet pasts. The contrasts between where Soviet symbols have been completely rejected and where they are still valued offers striking examples of the lingering legacies of Soviet civil religion.

States in Transition: Making Public Spaces Their Own

The 1992 Winter and Summer Olympic Games were memorable by the absence of the Soviet flag and anthem. During this transitional period, most of the new states had not had time to build individual national teams. All except the three Baltic states participated that year under the name 'Unified Team' using the Olympic hymn and flag. These Olympics illustrate just how difficult it is to rebrand a country on many levels. As each republic set off on its own path governments chose new official names based upon their titular languages. Renaming in all regions occurred on variant levels – nationally, regionally, and locally. City names, street names, and those of institutions – all areas of the social space had to be reclaimed and customised for the new political reality. In Ukraine, the capital city is now Romanised as Kyïv or Kyiv reflecting the Ukrainian pronunciation, rather than Kiev which is based upon its spelling in Russian. The central square, once named 'October Revolution Square' has been renamed 'Independence Square'. Likewise, the former 'Lenin Square' in Yerevan, Armenia is now 'Republic Square'. Similar examples can be found in every former Soviet country. It is important to remember that in the Soviet Union, as in other countries that have experienced dramatic shifts in political orientation, the place names belonged to the victors. Likewise, when revolutions fall out of favour there is a tendency to again reclaim public spaces through naming practices.[315] The geopolitical map of the USSR was filled with reminders of Soviet ideology and values. While in the non-Russian republics place names related to the local culture and regional history had been retained, there were also numerous names that focused on Soviet culture or were clearly Russified. Typically, these were the names that were changed as each country sought to reemphasise their pre-Soviet historical narratives. While the focus of this study is on visual symbolism, it is important to remember that auditory and linguistic symbols are powerful and were part of the Soviet strategy of banal nationalism and its legacy.[316]

Government authorities and groups of citizens have actively pursued campaigns of anti-Soviet iconoclasm in some countries as part of efforts to cleanse public spaces of the symbols of the USSR. This process occurred to some extent in every republic with the removal of statues – especially those of Lenin – and other visual symbols from the social landscape. However, the degree to which iconoclasm was pursued has varied widely depending on the political environment in each new state. It is this aspect of symbols that reflects how the Soviet past is regarded in each country and demonstrates what legacies of Soviet civil religion remain in the new states. An examination of how the symbols of the USSR are perceived in the post-Soviet states shows that attitudes tend to differ based upon the history of the region and the new country's current relationship with the Russian Federation, the Soviet Union's successor state.

Living with Soviet Legacies: The Caucasus and Central Asia

The three former Soviet republics in the Caucasus – Armenia, Azerbaijan, and Georgia – enjoyed brief periods of independence before being incorporated into the original Transcaucasian SFSR of the Soviet Union in 1922. Therefore, each republic had pre-Soviet symbols available for use when they declared their independence.[317] In the last several years of Soviet rule, Armenia and Azerbaijan became embroiled in a conflict over the disputed region of Nagorno-Karabakh (*Artsakh* in Armenian) – an autonomous oblast of the AzSSR with a predominantly ethnic-Armenian population. Within post-Soviet Armenia, identity politics have focused on the dispute with Azerbaijan and the historic legacy of the Armenian Genocide of 1914-1923. Another significant factor has been the relationship between the Armenian state and diasporic Armenians, which has strengthened the reestablishment of a distinct Armenian nation state. In examining the coats of arms of pre-Soviet, Soviet, and post-Soviet Armenia there is one symbolic element in common – the portrayal of Mount Ararat. This sacred mountain of Biblical lore has long been considered the national symbol of the Armenian people. Having been historically held by Persia, Russia, the Ottoman Empire, and Armenia, Mount Ararat is now within the boundaries of Turkey – a result of the 1920 Turkish-Armenian war and the 1921 Treaty of Kars. The symbolic connection of the three emblems also reflects how modern Armenia views the Soviet era as the *second* Armenian republic, allowing for historical continuity between the pre-Soviet and post-Soviet periods of independence. For this reason, there has been little effort on the part of the Armenian government or people to purge reminders of their Soviet past. It is simply regarded as another epoch in the history of the country.[318]

In addition to the conflict with Armenia, the experience in Azerbaijan has focused on the reestablishment of a national culture rooted in Islam and promotion of state-building efforts in that country.[319] While independence resulted in the removal of Soviet symbols, some monuments, and replacement of overtly communist place names, like in neighbouring Armenia there has been little concern in Azerbaijan about lingering Soviet identity. Neither nation has taken action to discourage or outlaw the use of Soviet symbols within their territories. Three factors have likely contributed to this level of tolerance: 1) significantly high proportions of the population belong to the titular majority, 2) the Russophone populations in each country are quite small, and 3) neither country has had a direct conflict with the Russian Federation.[320] The experience in neighbouring Georgia, however, has differed significantly, causing Soviet symbols to fall out of favour there. This will be discussed later in the chapter.

As a contrast to the Caucasus, the five former-Soviet republics of central Asia gained their distinctive territorial identities as part of their Soviet history. Thus, there were no convenient pre-Soviet symbols available to represent these new states. Therefore, these five republics continued to use their Soviet-era flags until new ones were designed. However, Tajikistan's transitional flag retained only the stripes from the flag of the Tajik SSR, removing the combined hammer and sickle emblem as well as the red star. As each country adopted their new symbols they sought to represent the cultural and religious heritage of their majority populations. Uzbekistan was the first to adopt a new flag on 18 November 1991, retaining the sky blue and white colours from the Soviet-era flag, but identifying sky blue as the traditional colour of the Turkic people. Islam was represented by the addition of the traditional colour green, a crescent moon, and stars. Turkmenistan's new flag, adopted on 19 February 1992, was also based upon traditional culture and Islamic symbolism. The flag features *guls* from traditional rug patterns, a crescent moon, and stars on a green field. Kyrgyzstan chose a red field for its new flag, adopted on 3 March 1992, but ascribed its origins not to the red banner of revolution, but instead to the pennant of a Kyrgyz folk hero. The emblem on the flag is a sun, the centre of which depicts a *tunduk* – the opening in the top of a traditional yurt. Kazakhstan's new flag was also based upon the sky-blue colour of Turkic peoples with a sun, eagle, and traditional ornament of the Kazakhs. The last of the countries to retire its Soviet-era flag was Tajikistan, which adopted its new flag on 24 November 1992. While the flag preserved the colours of the Soviet-era flag, it assigned them to three equal-sized horizontal stripes, emblazoned with a crown and seven stars. Each of the five countries also adopted new state emblems, the basic layouts of which show the clear influence of Soviet-era heraldic practices. In particular, the coat of arms for Tajikistan and Uzbekistan are reflective of previous emblems of the Soviet SSRs in style and layout.[321]

Figures 5.1-5.2. National emblems of Tajikistan (*left*) and Uzbekistan (*right*) showing the influence of the socialist style of heraldry. Both coats of arms retain sun imagery and Soviet-style agricultural wreaths, replacing the red colour of the ribbon with stripes from their flags of independence. A new distinctly Uzbek star, bearing Islamic symbols, has replaced the red star crest. *See colour on plate C-15.*

Avenging the Past: Rejecting Soviet Symbols in the Baltics

It should be no surprise that the governments of Latvia, Lithuania, and Estonia readopted their pre-Soviet symbols and made efforts early on to strengthen the distinct national identities in their states.[322] Multiple factors made this part of the transition to independence relatively easy. These republics were sovereign states prior to their annexation by the Soviet Union in 1940 – a result of the 1939 Molotov-Ribbentrop Pact signed by the USSR and National Socialist Germany. When each of the Baltic republics declared independence in 1990, the era of pre-Soviet sovereignty was still within living memory of many individuals in the new states. In addition, there were some nations, such as Canada and the United States, that never formally recognised the annexation, considered the Baltic states to be 'occupied territories', and had special diplomatic relationships with governments in exile. This status of state continuity gave the Baltic countries a level of international recognition that made the transition to full independence smoother, at least in terms of global politics. All three countries have worked to align themselves to the West, culminating in their admission to the North Atlantic Treaty Organisation in March 2004 and to the European Union in May 2004.[323]

Symbolically, living memory also provided a key weapon in the fight for independence. The pre-Soviet symbols were well known and readily accepted by ethnic Estonians, Latvians, and Lithuanians. Images of pro-independence demonstrations from 1989 and 1990 show people in the streets carrying pre-Soviet flags.[324] When protestors used these symbols they were clearly rejecting their Soviet identities and asserting their ethnicities. As protests grew, even individuals who had never lived under the pre-Soviet regimes connected the symbols to their desire for independence. Therefore, in the Baltic states there was no need to create a new symbolic identity for those who belonged to the three titular groups. The primary issue facing the Baltic states, at least in terms of identity politics, has revolved around the status of ethnic minorities living in the countries. In their nation-building efforts each of the Baltic countries has focused on reinforcing the dominant culture of the titular majority.[325]

Early efforts to promote national identities in the Baltic region focused on language and national identity. Even prior to their declarations of independence, the Supreme Soviets of the Baltic republics adopted legislation that declared the titular languages as 'official state languages'. This movement began with a new language law in Latvia on 6 October 1988, one in Estonia on 18 January 1989, followed by a decree in Lithuania on 25 January 1989. The new constitutions in Latvia and Estonia granted citizenship only to those who had been citizens at the time of annexation and to their descendants. All others were required to acquire citizenship through the process of naturalisation, which included requirements for proficiency in the state language. The strategy in all three countries, in terms of socialisation of the population, has focused on the assimilation and integration of ethnic minorities through the language used in education, commerce, and society in general.[326]

Each of these nations have faced challenges with integrating their Russophone populations. For ethnic Russians, the shift from their Soviet majority status to that of an ethnic minority has been a challenge, especially in countries where they were not granted automatic citizenship. Those who chose to stay in the Baltic countries have had to adapt to new social realities.[327] While Soviet symbols were targeted by activists in the early stages of the struggle for independence, formal symbol bans took some time to develop and have been stimulated by conflicts that emerged related to the commemoration of the end of World War II. Ethnic Russians have continued to observe Victory Day as a celebration of the Soviet victory over National Socialist Germany. However, to the majority populations of the Baltic region this day is viewed as a reminder of Soviet occupation. In addition to Soviet flags, another contested symbol related to Victory Day is the St. George's ribbon, discussed in Chapter 4. The ribbon has become not just a reminder of Soviet military decorations, but also a symbol of Russian military might. Therefore, the governments of the Baltic region consider it an inappropriate symbol for commemorating the end of the war. To further reinforce their new historical narratives and reduce symbolic conflict, all three governments have pursued actions to systematically remove Soviet-era symbols. Lithuania and Latvia have adopted formal laws banning their use in public.[328]

Bans on Soviet symbols in the Baltic states have served as a form of civil religious lustration. In cleansing public spaces of the symbols of the old regime, the governments of these countries are signifying a break with Marxist-Leninist values and a complete rejection of Soviet identity. Apart from veterans of World War II, ethnic Russians, and others who still ascribe significance to these symbols, these actions have been welcomed by residents who desire to see the Soviet era consigned to history. In removing the final remains of Soviet visual identity from public spaces, governments send a clear message to their residents about the appropriate form of national identity in their new civil religious contexts. These actions also serve as external messages to both western democracies and to the Russian Federation that these nations are looking westward for the future.

Conflicting Identities in Moldova: Bessarabia and Transnistria

While the establishment of the Moldavian SSR (MSSR), like that of the Baltic SSRs, was the result of the forceful annexation of territory, the history of identity in the republic was more complex. The MSSR was created through the consolidation of two regions with different historical relationships to the Soviet Union. Western Moldova, historically referred to as Bessarabia, was taken from Romania in 1940. Therefore, the people in this region had a strong connection to Romanian language and culture. The newly occupied territory was merged with the Moldavian Autonomous Soviet Socialist Republic (MASSR), which was transferred from the Ukrainian SSR to the new Moldavian SSR. In the MASSR the population was more ethnically diverse, with significant numbers of Moldovans, Ukrainians, and Russians in addition to various minority groups. Due to the lack of an ethnic majority and the region's prolonged history as part of the USSR, Russian was the dominant language and few people in the region were fluent in the Moldovan language. For this reason, people in this part of the country had a stronger attachment to their Soviet identity when the Soviet Union broke apart, than those in Bessarabia.[329]

The transition to independence for Moldova included multiple acts that signalled that the country would promote and emphasise Romanian identity. Among these were the name change from Moldavia to Moldova, aligning with the Romanian name for the region. New state symbols, adopted in 1990, clearly reflect a pan-Romanian outlook. The flag is a vertical tricolour (blue, yellow, and red) derived from that of Romania, and defaced with an eagle bearing the shield from the Moldovan coat of arms. Those arms were based upon the second quarter of the Romanian coat of arms which historically represented the region. Perhaps the most important change in terms of identity, though, was linguistic. Language laws passed by the Moldovan Supreme Soviet in August 1989 established Moldovan as the official state language and specified that the language be written with Latin script. This final act was significant, both in practicality and symbolically, as the Cyrillisation of the language had been a key factor in the Soviet case for defining Moldovan as a separate language rather than a dialect of Romanian. In addition, the language laws included a provision requiring all citizens to learn the official language, and to prove their fluency, through official testing, by 1996.[330] In response to the Romanianisation of the country, two regions of Moldova declared their independence in 1990: Gagauzia a territory in the southern part of the country where the inhabitants are predominantly Orthodox Christian Turks, and Transnistria – the territory along the Dniester River that was once the MASSR. While Gagauzia has been reintegrated into Moldova, with constitutional provisions for some self-determination, the story of Transnistria has been quite different and is more significant in terms of the analysis of Soviet civil religion.[331]

Transnistria, officially the Pridnestrovian Moldavian Republic (*Pridnestrovskaia Moldavskaia Respublika*, in Russian), has retained its status as an unrecognised *de facto* independent republic for three decades. In practicality, this is because it has benefitted from military assistance from the Russian Federation, both during an armed conflict with Moldova in 1992 and after a ceasefire later the same year. More significant for this study, the continued existence of Transnistria as a self-proclaimed country offers a fascinating example of the legacies of Soviet civil religion and the transnational identity that it created in many Soviet citizens. This pseudo-Soviet identity is reflected in the official symbols of the republic. The official flag is, essentially, the same flag used by the Moldavian Soviet Socialist Republic from 1952-1990, and the coat of arms are derived from that of the MSSR with a few significant differences.[332]

Figure 5.3. Red/green/red flag of the Pridnestrovian Moldavian Republic. *See colour on plate C-16.*

Many elements from the MSSR coat of arms have been retained, but in place of 'Workers of the world, unite!' the new arms display the full name of the republic in three languages – Russian (left), Moldavian using Cyrillic script (centre), and Ukrainian (right). On the lesser arms, the full name was replaced by the abbreviation in the same languages. An additional symbol representing the Dniester River has been added in-between the rising sun and the red ribbon. The inclusion of prominent communist symbols, such as the red star and the combined hammer and sickle emblem, may seem surprising as Transnistria is not socialist. However, when the demographics of the republic are considered in terms of identity politics, it can be understood how these symbols are still seen as tools for unity and the creation of Transnistrian identity. In the region there is no ethnic majority, meaning that *Soviet* identity was the common identity shared by the citizenry at the time of the declaration of independence. As a result, the Soviet past is valued and the three prominent holidays of Soviet civil religion are still observed and celebrated – May Day, Victory Day, and the Anniversary of the Great October Revolution. Of these three holidays, the most significant in terms of reinforcing a separate Transnistrian identity, is Victory Day. This is due to the history of the region during World War II. A primary message conveyed by this observance in the Pridnestrovian Moldavian Republic reminds the residents that Romania collaborated with National Socialist Germany, not only to retake Bessarabia, but also to occupy Transnistria and part of Ukraine. This message helps to reinforce the shared identity of Transnistrians and to remind them of the dangers of the Romanianisation in neighbouring Moldova. It is also significant to note that, following a Soviet educational model, the government of Transnistria has been actively working to construct a distinct identity amongst the youngest residents of the region.[333]

Figures 5.4-5.5. Greater arms (*left*) and lesser arms (*right*) of the Pridnestrovian Moldavian Republic. *See colour on plate C-16.*

While the multinational people of Transnistria seem trapped in limbo in their internationally unrecognised pseudo-state, the government of Moldova has continued to look westward for a post-Soviet Moldovan identity. It has continued to strengthen the country's relationship with Romania, and through that association has developed closer relations with the European Union as a whole. In 2009 the government passed a law effectively banning Soviet symbols in public spaces in Moldova. While the law went into effect in 2012, the Constitutional Court of Moldova later found it to be unconstitutional. Despite that setback, outside of Transnistria there is little appreciation for the Soviet past and the symbols of the USSR in today's Republic of Moldova.[334]

Rejecting Soviet Symbols and Russian Influence: Georgia and Ukraine

Like Moldova, the Republic of Georgia has also experienced armed conflict with the Russian Federation regarding breakaway regions in the country. Two regions in the northern part of the country, bordering Russia, declared their independence from Georgia – South Ossetia in 1991 and Abkhazia in 1992. While neither has truly achieved statehood, they have attained autonomy from Georgia thanks to military support from Russia. The Rose Revolution of 2003 installed a pro-Western government, and later led to a change in the Georgian flag. After the breakup of the Soviet Union the country used the post-revolutionary flag of the Democratic Republic of Georgia (1918-1921), but the new 'Five Cross Flag' (adopted in 2004) has more ancient roots, dating back to the medieval Kingdom of Georgia.[335] In 2008, increased tensions and sporadic fighting resulted in a Russian invasion of Georgia and the occupation of the contested regions by Russian troops. An increase in anti-Russian sentiments in Georgia after the conflict also produced a lustration effort to decommunise Georgia. As part of the Freedom Charter (or Liberty Charter) adopted in October 2010, a ban on Soviet symbols was put in place in the country.[336] However, in a study conducted by political scientist Peter Kabachnik, interviews conducted in Georgia following the passage of the Freedom Charter revealed hybrid attitudes about Soviet symbols in the country. Kabachnik found that, while residents generally wanted Soviet-related street names to be changed, they did not always see the need to remove all symbols of the USSR from social spaces. Many of his interviewees were content with leaving symbolic elements that were integrated into architecture or construction from the Soviet era but preferred the removal of large Soviet monuments from central squares and prominent spaces. Interestingly, while many of the Georgians interviewed agreed that statues of Lenin should be removed, they did not always agree on those related to Stalin because he was Georgian.[337]

Of all the former Soviet republics, it seems that Ukraine is paying the highest price over conflicting views of history. Current troubles in Ukraine are deeply rooted in Soviet policies related to the region. Like Moldova, the country can be separated into distinct regions based upon their historical relationship to the USSR. Western Ukraine was annexed in the 1940s, while the central and eastern regions comprised the original Ukrainian SSR when it became a charter republic of the Soviet Union.[338] The historical difficulties for Ukraine, though, predate the communist era by centuries, as both Ukraine and Russia have sought to monopolise the historical legacy of Kyivan Rus'/Kievan Rus' (*Kyïvs'ka Rus'* in Ukrainian; *Kievskaia Rus'* in Russian) in their national foundation mythology. In addition, Ukraine has the largest Russophone minority population (nearly 30%[339]) of all the former Soviet countries — a group comprised of ethnic Ukrainians, Russians, and other nationalities. The situation is complicated further by the fact that the Russophone speakers are concentrated in the eastern and southern parts of the country and enjoy majority status in eight Ukrainian oblasts, out of a total of 27 regional subdivisions.

Conflicts over Soviet symbols have become a focal point of contested identity in Ukraine, particularly related to commemorations of World War II. This has been especially notable in the western region where Ukrainian nationalists have marched under the red and black flag of the

Ukrainian Insurgent Army (*Ukraïns'ka povstans'ka armiia*, or *UPA*). The *UPA* was a paramilitary group that, during the war, fought against foreign occupation (both Soviet and German) in the hope of achieving Ukrainian independence. However, because at times they collaborated with fascist forces against the Red Army, they were branded as traitors by Soviet authorities after the war. Therefore, a flag that serves as a symbol of Ukrainian freedom fighters for one group also symbolises fascist collaboration for non-Ukrainians in the region. An incident from the 2011 Victory Day observation in Lviv, Western Ukraine, illustrated how disagreements over contested symbols can escalate. Young Ukrainian nationalists confronted a mix of people who were using Soviet symbols during memorial events. They snatched flowers and Ribbons of St. George from elderly veterans, burned replicas of the Soviet Banner of Victory, and participated in violent confrontations with Russian nationalists. Incidents such as this were typical in portions of the country during this period, largely because Ukrainian nationalists considered Soviet symbols as reminders of occupation, and as a reminder of Russian interference in the country.[340]

Soviet and Russian symbols were also prominent targets during the Euromaidan protests of 2013-2014 which led to the ouster of pro-Russian president Viktor Yanukovych. One particularly significant phenomenon of the revolution was *Leninopad* – the toppling of Lenin statues which protestors staged in various Ukrainian cities. When mapped, the locations for these statues revealed three distinct regions: 1) the west, where presumably most Lenin statues had already been removed; 2) the central portion of the country; and 3) the eastern region. Most of the *Leninopad* statue removals were concentrated in the central region, an original part of the Ukrainian SSR where ethnic Ukrainians are in the majority.[341] Ukrainian historian Vladimir Vyatrovich, head of the country's National Memory Institute, estimated that of the 5,500 Lenin statues that were in place in Ukraine when the Soviet Union broke up, there were only about 1,300 remaining when the Euromaidan protests began. By October 2015, at least 500 more had been removed.[342]

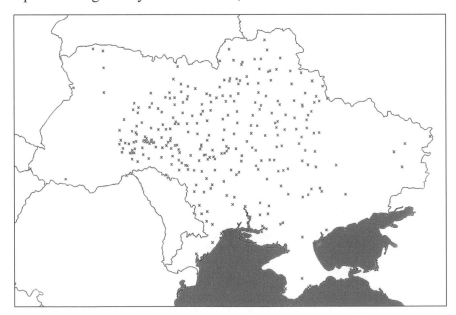

Figure 5.6. Map of Ukraine showing locations where Lenin statues were toppled during the Euromaidan protests and revolution (2013-2014).

The continued assault on the remaining symbols of the Soviet Union in Ukraine has escalated as a direct response to Russian interference in the country's affairs. Following the ouster of

Yanukovych, Russia lent its assistance to pro-Russian agitators in Crimea where it leased former Soviet naval facilities in Sevastopol as a base for their Black Sea fleet. After a contested referendum in Crimea where residents voted to leave Ukraine and join the Russian Federation, Russia formally annexed the region in March 2014.[343] In addition, the Russian government has also supported separatist rebels in the eastern regions of Donetsk and Luhansk since they declared independence from Ukraine in 2014. In Ukraine, the change in leadership and continued conflict with Russia has stimulated renewed efforts to remove Soviet symbols and prevent their use in public. In the spring of 2014, four 'memory laws' were passed including one that required changing place names and the removal of symbols that were connected to either the fascist or communist history of the country.[344] However, there are still those in Ukraine who believe that removing Soviet symbols is counterproductive. Historian Georgiy V. Kasyanov likened the lustration of decommunisation to the removal of tsarist symbols after the revolution:

> They behave like Bolsheviks: 'We have to wipe out the past!'

> They think the Soviet legacy can be destroyed by destroying statues of Lenin or by renaming streets, which is false. They are wrestling with ghosts.[345]

It is likely that the debate in Ukraine about its Soviet past will continue as long as there are still those alive who retain positive memories of their life in the USSR or who value that era as part of the country's history. Additionally, ethnic Russians and the Russophone population in Ukraine will likely continue to value the Soviet era as part of their heritage.

Respecting the Soviet Past: Belarus and the Russian Federation

One country in which Soviet-influenced state symbols have been readopted is Belarus. During the initial transition to independence, the country pursued nation-building policies like those of the Baltic states. The pre-Soviet flag and arms of the Grand Duchy of Lithuania were adopted as national symbols, the official name of the country was changed from Byelorussia to Belarus in accordance with the practice in the Belarusian language, and the local language was emphasised as the state language. However, multiple factors made this last strategy counterproductive. While over 80% of the population are ethnic Belarusians, the Russian language is the home language for nearly 70% of the population of the country. At the time of independence, Belarusian identity was closely tied to Soviet identity and to the experiences of World War II. In addition, the vision of Belarusian identity which was linked to the pre-Soviet era was promoted by a relatively small group of intellectuals and not widely accepted by the populace. For these reasons, it was quite easy for President Aliaksandr Ryhoravich Lukashènka (Alexander Grigorevich Lukashenko in Russian) to exploit these factors when he assumed office in July 1994. He initiated a national referendum held in May 1995 that essentially changed the branding of Belarus. The referendum contained several questions central to national identity – the status of Russian as an official language, adoption of new state symbols, and more integration with Russia. New symbols, which were officially adopted in July 1995, resurrected the basic design of the old Soviet BSSR flag with a few changes. The red star, hammer, and sickle were omitted, and the national ornament at the hoist was modified slightly. While the new arms are not derived from the Soviet-era emblem, they are clearly reflective of the socialist style of heraldry and include Soviet elements such as the red star crest, the rising sun, the globe, and the agricultural wreath wrapped in a ribbon of the flag. Interestingly, the pre-Soviet symbols have now found new meaning: they have been used by those opposing Lukashenka's autocratic rule.[346]

Figures 5.7-5.8. Soviet-inspired state symbols of Belarus adopted after the 1995 referendum. *See colour on plate C-16.*

In the Russian Federation, the Soviet era is viewed as part of the continuum of centuries of Russian history. Modern textbooks designed to teach children about the symbols of Russia begin with the symbols of *Kievskaia Rus'*, cover centuries of symbols from Imperial Russia, the RSFSR and the Soviet Union, and then culminate with the modern symbols of the Russian Federation. In the standard historical narrative as it is presented in modern Russia, Soviet symbols are as much a part of the historical landscape as statues of the tsars of bygone eras.[347]

Soviet symbols are prominently used in an official context in Russia for the celebration of Victory Day, honouring remaining World War II veterans, and memorialising the war dead. This has also been a primary rationale for outrage professed by the Russian government in response to symbol bans in other former Soviet republics, as many of the new laws have outlawed *both* Soviet and Nazi symbols. In the eyes of Russian officials equating the symbols of those regimes is an insult not just to Russia, but to all nations that fought alongside the USSR. From the Russian perspective, the legacy of victory and the liberation of Eastern Europe from fascist occupation clearly belongs to Russia and her people.[348]

It is also important to note that early attempts at symbolic decommunisation during the tenure of Russian President Boris Yeltsin met with little success. One initiative directly tied to the war was an attempt to change the design of the Banner of Victory that is often used in celebrations of Victory Day. The original flag is a war relic that was raised over the Reichstag in Berlin by Soviet forces, now held in a military museum. The flag was an improvised Soviet flag, upon which text was later added to commemorate the regiment responsible for its placement. Yeltsin issued a decree in 1996 to replace the Banner of Victory with a flag bearing a single star in the canton of a simple red banner. However, the new design was never widely accepted, and President Vladimir Putin signed a law in 2007 which restored the status of the original design and affirmed the status of the original flag as a war relic.[349]

Figure 5.9. The Soviet Banner of Victory on display in Moscow's Central Museum of the Armed Forces. Text on the flag translates as '150th Rifle, Order of Kutuzov 2nd class, Idritskaia Division, 79th Rifle Corps, 3rd Attack Army, 1st Byelorussian Front.'

There have also been discussions within the Russian Federation about removing Lenin from the mausoleum on Red Square and interring him in St. Petersburg. Despite much discussion and debate he remains at rest just outside the walls of the Kremlin.[350] And the original communist décor of the Moscow Metro is still in place, reminding thousands of commuters of the many advancements made in Russia as a direct result of Soviet power. For many Russians during the Soviet era, Russian identity *was* Soviet identity. There was no distinction between the two.[351] An enduring illustration of this duality of identity can still be found in the official state symbols of the Russian Federation. During the Soviet era, the RSFSR was the only republic which did not have its own official hymn. The pre-Soviet hymn was a tsarist anthem, making it unsuitable when the Soviet Union broke up. An instrumental anthem adopted by the Supreme Soviet of Russia in 1990 never gained popularity with the people. Shortly after Putin became president in 2000, the national hymn was changed to one that combined the music of the Soviet anthem with new lyrics specific to Russia. Through three sets of lyrics – those of the Stalin era, the post-Stalin version with his references removed, and finally the new distinctly Russian version – the familiar music heard at many Olympic gold medal ceremonies continues to remind Russians and non-Russians alike of the enduring legacy of Soviet civil religion.

Conclusion

Analysing the contrasts in post-Soviet countries it becomes clear that attitudes towards Soviet symbols are directly linked to the history of the regions and to identity politics in the post-Soviet era. In countries where symbols of the Soviet Union have been devalued and banned, the primary focus has been on delegitimising their Soviet history, often with the goal of characterising their inclusion in the USSR as an era of illegal occupation. This is certainly the case in the territories annexed in the 1940s – the Baltic states, western Ukraine, and Bessarabia in Moldova. In regions where Soviet symbols are tolerated within certain contexts, the Soviet era is viewed with more ambivalence and perhaps is seen as just another period in regional histories where shifting power structures and cultural influences have been the norm.

117

It is the regions where symbols of the Soviet era are still respected and valued that are the most significant for the study of the legacies of Soviet civil religion. In areas such as Transnistria or eastern Ukraine, the symbols represent a shared identity that both unifies the residents of those regions and differentiates them from the dominant ethnicity of their countries. In the Russian Federation, it is illustrative of how closely the identities of ethnic Russians were tied to their sense of Soviet identity. For Russians living in different parts of the Soviet Union, those identities were one and the same. It is for this reason that disrespectful treatment of Soviet symbols in other former Soviet countries is frequently viewed as an insult by ethnic Russians and by the Russian government. Most frequently these symbolic conflicts have related to symbol usage in commemorations related to World War II.

Finally, the legacies of Soviet civil religion demonstrate the relative success of forging Soviet identities amongst those who were content to live within the Soviet system. As generations of young people experience identity formation in educational systems focused on political socialisation toward new national identities and the associated political rhetoric of their new states, the percentage of the populations that value Soviet symbols will most likely decrease. Those symbols belong to their parents' or grandparents' generation and the associated baggage, both positive and negative, related to Soviet symbols will become less significant in their lives.

Chapter 6
Conclusion

In studies of national identity, it can be easy to understate the role of symbols in identity formation. However, when viewed within the context of civil religion it becomes apparent that symbols serve multiple functions in the modern state. While at first their primary function as representations of sovereignty and governmental authority may seem most important, the use of symbols in communication from those in power to their citizens is often ignored. Whitney Smith, in his numerous works, stressed the importance of national symbols, particularly flags, in communicating the common values of a society:

> To display a flag is to participate in a group or a philosophy that spans time and distances; it is to express one's own views to others in a concise but dramatic form. In a word the flag is a powerful instrument for social participation and communication.[352]

Because national symbols are adopted and deployed through the processes of governmental authority, they serve as a channel of communication from governments to their people. The concept of civil religion, as revived by Robert Bellah and further defined by Ellis West, suggests that it is through the combination of rituals, myths, and symbols that a nation's culture of patriotism contributes to the maintenance of national identity among the citizens.

This research has built upon earlier works on the civil religion of the Soviet Union in that it has examined in detail the role of symbols in the culture of patriotism in that society. In reviewing the development of the Soviet symbol set it has focused on the messages those symbols were meant to convey to the average Soviet citizen. It has analysed a range of material which was widely available in the USSR (*e.g.*: postcards, textbooks, songs, currency, and flags) and demonstrated how the meanings of the symbols deployed therein were defined for and communicated to Soviet citizens. When examined as a cohesive set, as demonstrated in Chapter 2, it is evident that the national symbol set of the USSR focused on the primary themes of union and unity at multiple levels in the society. This unity was meant to reinforce a primary concept from the teachings of Marxism-Leninism, namely that the most basic form of unity was that of the working class. Class consciousness was intended to transcend national borders and unite people from a diverse range of cultures for the common goal of advancing socialism and building a communist society. The promotion of socialist internationalism also served a practical need of the Communist Party and the Soviet government, as it was intended as the binding force that united citizens from fifteen constituent republics and over 100 ethnic groups. Socialist internationalism was described in state propaganda as both internal and external, meaning that it was intended to extend beyond the borders of the USSR to all working people of the world who were aspiring to the same goals.

In Chapter 3, an examination of the Soviet education system and the official children's organisations of the CPSU has demonstrated that symbols were a vital tool used to teach the values of Soviet patriotism and the lessons of Marxism-Leninism to new generations. Children were taught the meanings of the symbols and were reminded of their duties as citizens of the USSR. The badges, scarves, and banners of the Little Octobrists and Young Pioneers incorporated major elements of the national symbol set and were intended to give children a personal connection to the teachings of Lenin and the historical legacies of generations of Soviet citizens that preceded them. Party officials and Soviet educators hoped that the lessons of childhood would not only instil in the students a sense of Soviet identity, but would also encourage them to become active participants in the work of the Party later in life.

While not all Soviet citizens were fervent communists or Party members, the political lessons of their childhood were meant to be reinforced through frequent exposure to Soviet symbols and civil religious rituals. Drawing upon Michael Billig's concept of banal nationalism, the analysis of the material culture of the country in Chapter 4 demonstrated that Soviet symbols were frequently encountered through a variety of channels in public and private spaces. Although citizens may have passed by these symbols without consciously acknowledging them, subliminally they were intended to remind them of the basic principles of Marxism-Leninism and to reinforce a sense of Soviet identity.

The eventual breakup of the Soviet Union was caused by multiple factors including a resurgence of ethnic nationalism, particularly in regions that were annexed just prior to World War II. As Chapter 5 established, an examination of Soviet symbol valuation or devaluation in each of the post-Soviet states suggests a close linkage between the way the Soviet era was viewed by the majority ethnic group and the relationship the country has had with the Russian Federation, the USSR's successor state, since gaining independence. In instances where there have been lustration efforts to cleanse public spaces of Soviet symbols, the majority have been in countries where at least part of the territory was annexed by the USSR within living memory of the older generations. Where Soviet symbols are still respected as part of history, it is often indicative of populations where Soviet identity was more compatible with the ethnic identities of the residents. These regions typically have predominantly Russophone populations, even if non-Russians comprise a majority of the population. In places where ethnic Russians are the majority, this trend is a reminder that, for many, their Russian and Soviet identities were often one in the same.

As the examples given throughout the work clearly demonstrate, there was a civil religion in the Union of Soviet Socialist Republics and national symbols were a vital component of civil religious practice in the country. The analysis has revealed the many messages conveyed by Soviet *simvolika* and how the Party used symbols to teach and reinforce the values inherent to Marxism-Leninism. It has also validated the case that national symbols are more than just totems of sovereignty and governmental authority. They are valuable tools for the formation and maintenance of national identities, especially in multi-ethnic states. In addition, symbols have become so ingrained in the machinery of the modern state that it might be inconceivable that any state could function without them. This clearly indicates that national symbols are worthy of further study by scholars in a variety of fields.

Historically, the Soviet Union offers a useful example of both an experiment with large-scale state socialism and state-sponsored efforts to synthesise a shared identity in a multinational state. While there were many factors that led to the downfall of the Soviet system, it is fascinating how quickly the identity politics changed in the fifteen independent countries that emerged from it. The results of this research suggest multiple topics for future study. For example, it would be interesting to examine attitudes in post-Soviet countries after living memory ceases to be a factor in symbol valuation. Will attitudes change in areas where Soviet symbols are now considered offensive? Will those symbols still be valued in the Russian Federation after the last survivors of the Great Patriotic War have passed on? Additionally, studies which compare the intended messages of national symbols with the way the messages were received by the people (using memoirs, diaries, and oral histories) could help illuminate the gaps between governmental expectations and public perception. These are just a few examples of additional work that could be done in the post-Soviet space.

Other topics of research could include cross-cultural comparative studies with other multi-national states where populations are concentrated in their own distinct homelands. An example from the socialist experiment would be the former Yugoslavia and the states that emerged from its breakup. Such a study would require an analysis of the Yugoslav symbol set and its intended messages, an examination of state-led efforts to forge a unified Yugoslav identity, an investigation of banal nationalism in Yugoslavia, and an analysis of how Yugoslav symbols are regarded in the independent countries. What could be learned from a cross-cultural study of three societies, each distinctly different in political philosophy, but clearly similar in terms of the civil religious use of symbols? Perhaps a comparison of symbol usage and identity between National Socialist Germany, the Soviet Union, and the United States could reveal some interesting observations about the role of symbols in the political cultures of the twentieth century. Similarly, a longitudinal study of national symbol usage in countries that have been members of the European Union would yield interesting insights into the relationship between symbols and identities. In European countries where integration with the Union is seen as highly successful and desirable, will national symbols eventually be considered equal to, or even valued less than, those of the EU? In countries where membership has not been popular and in those that choose to leave the Union, will there be a notable increase or resurgence in the use of distinct national symbols?

The intent of this study has not simply been to provide insights into the connections between national symbols, civil religion, identity politics, and banal nationalism in the Soviet Union, although that has been one aim. It has also attempted to provide a model for the future study of these phenomena in modern nations. Clearly the Soviet case provides an extreme example of symbol usage within a civil religious cultural model to cultivate a state-designed identity amongst citizens. Other modern states have adopted different strategies: some governments allow national identity to develop organically, some direct the crafting of national identity from above, and others pursue a hybrid of both the organic and cultivated models. National symbols have become firmly entrenched in the process of nation building in the modern world. Across the globe, peoples, aspiring to have their own states, adopt distinctive national symbols to use in their cause. In some cases, those symbols have ancient lineage, while in others they are designed and promoted specifically to project an image of statehood. It is doubtful that the role of symbols in identity formation, civil religion, and state-building will be diminished any time soon. State symbols and their role in identity formation and political messaging have become a standard part of the portfolio of the modern state.

Appendix
Republic Symbols and Soviet National Hymn
Symbols of the Soviet Republics

The most distinctive symbols of the republics were their state arms. Each republic state emblem featured symbolic elements related to the geography, economy, or culture of the republic represented, along with the motto from the *Communist Manifesto* written in the titular language and Russian. However, visual unity with the Soviet Union was clearly shown in the republic arms through their conformity to the socialist style of heraldry and their resemblance to the State Emblem of the USSR. Common elements found on all the republic emblems were the red star, the hammer and sickle, the rays of the rising sun, representation of agricultural products, and the bilingual presentation of the *Manifesto* slogan.[353]

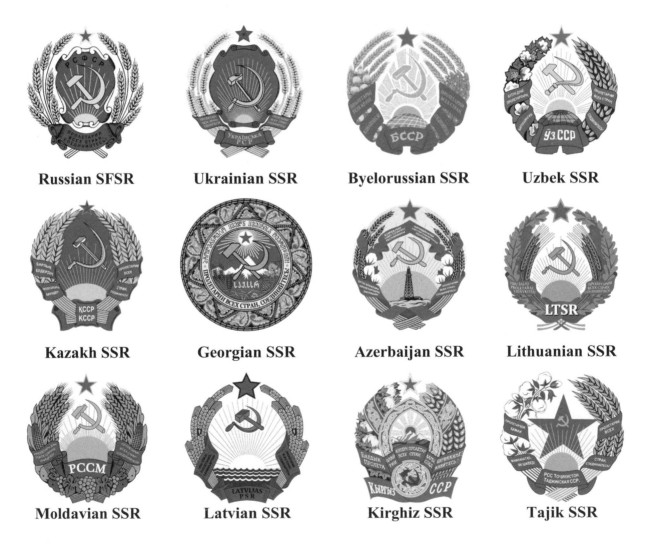

| Russian SFSR | Ukrainian SSR | Byelorussian SSR | Uzbek SSR |

| Kazakh SSR | Georgian SSR | Azerbaijan SSR | Lithuanian SSR |

| Moldavian SSR | Latvian SSR | Kirghiz SSR | Tajik SSR |

Figures A1-A12. State Arms of the fifteen Soviet Republics in Soviet order of precedence ('Constitutional order'). *See colour on plates C2-C3.*

122

Armenian SSR   **Turkmen SSR**   **Estonian SSR**

Figures A3-A15. State Arms of the fifteen Soviet Republics in Soviet order of precedence (continued). *See colour on plate C-3.*

Unlike the state arms of the republics, the flags were much less distinctive. Early flags for the union republics and autonomous republics were based upon the red banner of revolution. Some simply added the republic name, others used abbreviations, and a few used a combination of proletarian and local symbols. However, in the 1930s the designs were standardised so that they were clearly derivatives of the Soviet flag, defaced with the abbreviation of the Republic's name.[354]

Figures A16-A17. Flags of the Ukrainian Soviet Socialist Republic based upon the red banner of the revolution and the Soviet national flag. *Left:* Flag used 1919-1929, ***Right:*** Flag used 1937-1950. *See colour on plate C-3.*

During the period 1949-1954, new flags were introduced for each of the union republics. All flags used the field of the red banner of revolution and the star, hammer, and sickle from the national flag. Simple coloured stripes were used on most flags to distinguish between the different republics. An examination of Soviet flag books has yielded very little data about the symbolism used in the designs. Most descriptions emphasised the commonalities already noted, and described the variations in the blue, white, and green stripes which distinguished one flag from another. When symbolism was mentioned it was general in nature and details were not included for every flag. Differences in the flags were described as representative of the 'national, economic, or geographical uniqueness of the republic'. Blue was typically said to be symbolic of water, whether it was the waterways of the Russian SFSR, the waves of the Baltic Sea on the flags of the Latvian SSR and Estonian SSR, or the colour of mountain lakes in the Armenian SSR. Interestingly, the blue in the flag of the Ukrainian SSR was said to be symbolic of the long-standing friendship between the Russian and Ukrainian peoples, rather than of the waters of the Neva River or Black Sea. White in the flags of the Kirghiz SSR, Uzbek SSR, and Tajik SSR was said to represent cotton, the 'white gold' of the region, while the green in the flag of the Moldavian SSR was reminiscent of the vineyards in the republic. In describing the flag of the Byelorussian SSR, the pattern at the hoist was a 'national ornament' – a traditional Byelorussian embroidery pattern.

However, the reader was left to wonder about the solar ray design in the canton of the flag of the Georgian SSR, as no explanation was included.[355]

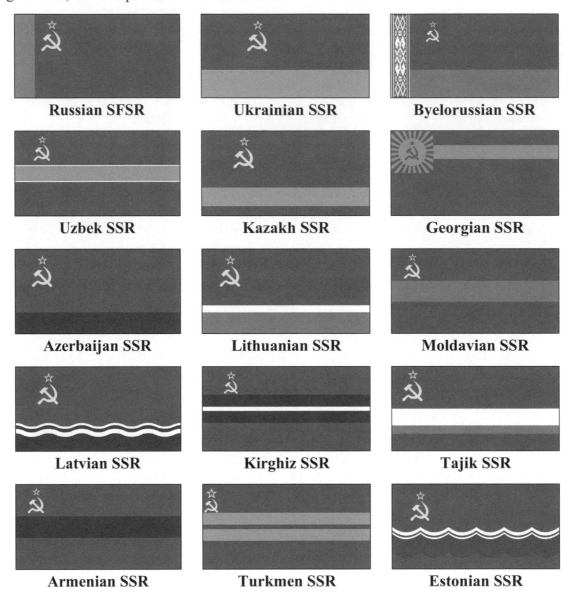

Figures A18-A32. State Flags of the Soviet Republics in Soviet order of precedence ('Constitutional order'). *See colour on inside back cover.*

As previously discussed in Chapter 4, it was common practice in the later Soviet period to portray the unity of the republics using these symbol sets. In individual republics, the symbols of the republic would typically have been displayed in combination with the equivalent symbol of the USSR. In this way, it was possible to represent a unique identity for an individual republic while still emphasising that the territory was an integral part of the larger Soviet state. A Ukrainian agitation manual for artists, published in 1959, provided guidance on how symbols of the republic should be combined with those of the Soviet Union for this type of display.

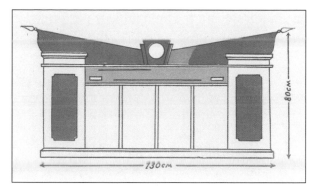

Figures A33-A34. Recommended arrangements for patriotic displays using flags of the Soviet Union and the Ukrainian SSR from a manual for artists.

State Hymn of the Soviet Union

The state anthem introduced on 15 March 1944 was the first written specifically for use in the Soviet Union. While officially titled the *State Anthem of the Soviet Union*, it was also known as *Slav'sya, Otechestvo nashe svobodnoe!*, meaning '*Be Glorious, Our Free Homeland!*'. Translations by the author with the assistance of Larry McLellan.

Original Lyrics of the State Hymn of the Soviet Union - 1944

Russian Lyrics	**Conceptual Literal Translation**
Soiuz nerushimyi respublic svobodnykh Splotila naveki Velikaia Rus'. Da zdravstvuet sozdannyi volei narodov Edinyi, moguchii Sovetskii Soiuz!	Great Russia has united forever the unbreakable union of free republics. Long live the united, mighty Soviet Union created by the will of the peoples!
[Refrain:] Slav'sia, Otechestvo nashi svobodnoe, Druzhby narodov nadezhnyi oplot! Znamia Sovetskoe, znamia narodnoe Pust' ot pobedy k pobede vedet!	[Refrain:] Be glorious, our free homeland, Reliable stronghold of friendship of the peoples! The Soviet banner, the people's banner, May it lead from victory to victory!
Skvoz' grozy siialo nam solntse svobody, I Lenin velikii nam pust' ozaril; Nas vyrastil Stalin — na vernost' narody, Na trud i na podvigi nas vdokhnovil!	Through storms the sun of freedom shone to us, And the great Lenin illuminated the way for us; Stalin raised us — he inspired us to faith in the people, to labour, and to great feats!
[Refrain:]	[Refrain:]
My armiiu nashu rastili v srazhen'iakh. Zakhvatchikov podlykh s dorogi smetem! My v bitvakh reshaem sud'bu pokolenii, My k slave Otchiznu svoiu povedem!	We raised our army in battles. We will sweep away the vile invaders! In battles we decide the fate of generations, We will lead our homeland to glory.

After Stalin's death the anthem was performed as an instrumental piece without lyrics. It was not until 1971 that one of the original lyricists was commissioned to revise the words, with his revisions officially adopted in October 1977.

Revised Lyrics of the State Hymn of the Soviet Union – 1977

Russian Lyrics	Conceptual Literal Translation
Soiuz nerushimyi respublic svobodnykh Splotila naveki Velikaia Rus'. Da zdravstvuet sozdannyi volei narodov Edinyi, moguchii Sovetskii Soiuz!	Great Russia has united forever the unbreakable union of free republics. Long live the united, mighty Soviet Union created by the will of the peoples!
[Refrain:] Slav'sia, Otechestvo nashi svobodnoe, Druzhby narodov nadezhnyi oplot! Partiia Lenina – sila narodnaia Nas k torzhestvu Kommunizma vedet!	[Refrain:] Be glorious, our free homeland, Reliable stronghold of friendship of the peoples! The Party of Lenin, the people's strength, leads us to the triumph of communism!
Skvoz' grozy siialo nam solntse svobody, I Lenin velikii nam pust' ozaril; Na pravoe delo on podnial narody, Na trud i na podvigi nas vdokhnovil!	Through storms the sun of freedom shone to us, And the great Lenin illuminated the way for us, He raised up our peoples to the righteous cause, He inspired us to labour and great feats!
[Refrain]	[Refrain]
V pobede bessmertnykh idei kommunizma My vidim griadushchee nashei strany, I Krasnomu znameni slavnoi Otchizny My budem vsegda bezzavetno verny!	In the victory of the immortal ideas of communism We see the future of our country, And to the red banner of our glorious homeland, We will always be selflessly faithful.

126

Endnotes

Chapter 1. Icons of Identity: Civil Religion and Symbols

[1] Ellis M. West, 'A Proposed Neutral Definition of Civil Religion', *Journal of Church and State* 22, no. 1 (1980), p. 39.

[2] For example, Sun-tsu described the use of flags as tools for military maneuvers centuries before the common era. Sun-tsu, *The Art of Warfare: The First English Translation Incorporating the Recently Discovered Yin-ch'üeh-shan Texts*, trans. Roger T. Ames (New York: Ballantine Books, 1993), pp. 131, 240, 247.

[3] Whitney Smith, 'Arab Flags', *The Arab World*, vol. 5, no. 10 (October 1959): pp. 12-13.

[4] Whitney Smith, *The Bibliography of Flags of Foreign Nations* (Boston: G. K. Hall & Co., 1965), pp. v-vi; Whitney Smith, *The Flag Book of the United States*, rev. ed. (New York: William Morrow & Company, 1975), p. vi.

[5] Whitney Smith, *Flags Through the Ages and Across the World* (New York: McGraw-Hill Book Company, 1975), p. 12.

[6] Whitney Smith, *Flags and Arms Across the World* (New York: McGraw-Hill, 1980), p. 5.

[7] Whitney Smith, 'Prolegomena to the Study of Political Symbolism' (unpublished PhD dissertation, Boston University Graduate School, 1968).

[8] Guenter's PhD thesis was later published in book form. See Scot M. Guenter, *The American Flag, 1777-1924: Cultural Shifts from Creation to Codification* (Rutherford, NJ: Fairleigh Dickinson University Press, 1990).

[9] William George Crampton, 'Flags as Non-Verbal Symbols in the Management of National Identity' (unpublished PhD thesis, University of Manchester, 1994).

[10] Heimer's thesis was published in English translation as: Željko Heimer, *Exploring Vexillology Through Military Unit Flags: With an Analysis of Croatian Armed Forces Flags During and After the 1991-1995 Homeland War* (Zagreb: Hrvatsko grboslovno i zastavoslovno društvo, 2016). See also the section of the thesis published as: Željko Heimer, *Vexillology as a Social Science* (Danvers, MA: Flag Heritage Foundation, 2017).

[11] Whitney Smith, 'Prolegomena', pp. 247-263; Crampton, 'Flags as Non-Verbal Symbols', pp. 74-78.

[12] Whitney Smith noted that 'many political activities are based on the model of religious worship'. Whitney Smith, *Flags Through the Ages and Across the World*, p. 35. See also Guenter, pp. 18-22. For a discussion of this phenomena as presented in the works of Durkheim, see Ruth A. Wallace, 'The Secular Ethic and The Spirit of Patriotism', *Sociological Analysis* 34, no. 1 (Spring 1973): pp. 3-11.

[13] Thomas A. Sebeok, *Signs: An Introduction to Semiotics*, 2nd ed. (Toronto: University of Toronto Press, 2001), pp. 156. See also, pp. 8-11, 25-63. For a large collection of essays engaging with the concept of signs in semiotics, see Marshall Blonsky, ed., *On Signs* (Baltimore, MD: Johns Hopkins University Press, 1985).

[14] Sebeok, p. 157. See also, pp. 11, 55-59.

[15] *Ibid.*, p. 153. See also, pp. 50-53, 114.

[16] *Ibid.*, p. 156. See also, pp. 10, 50-53, 103-114.

[17] Erwin Panofsky, 'Iconography and Iconology: An Introduction to the Study of Renaissance Art', in *Meaning in the Visual Arts: Papers in and on Art History* (Garden City, NY: Doubleday, 1955), p. 28. Emphasis in the original. See also, Christine Hasenmueller, 'Panofsky, Iconography, and Semiotics', *The Journal of Aesthetics and Art Criticism* 36, no. 3 (1978): pp. 289-301.

[18] Panofsky, p. 41.

[19] *Ibid.*, pp. 28-30, 41. Emphasis in the original.

[20] *Ibid.*, pp. 38-40. Emphasis in the original.

[21] *Ibid.*, p. 41. Emphasis in the original.

[22] Peter Kenez, *A History of the Soviet Union from the Beginning to the End*, 2nd ed (New York: Cambridge University Press, 2006). The third edition extended the period covered, as reflected in the new title. Peter Kenez, *A History of the Soviet Union from the Beginning to Its Legacy*, 3rd ed. (New York: Cambridge University Press, 2017).

[23] 'Communism', in Aleksandr Mikhailovich Prokhorov, ed., *Great Soviet Encyclopedia*, 31 vols. (New York: Macmillan, 1973), vol. 12, p. 230. Hereafter cited as *GSE*. See also, 'Socialism', in *GSE*, vol. 24, pp. 231-235.

[24] In Russian, the name of the party was *Kommunisticheskaia Partiia Sovetskogo Soiuza* (*KPSS*).

[25] Leonid Brezhnev, 'The 24th Congress of the Communist Party of the Soviet Union: The Report of the C.P.S.U. Central Committee to the 24th Congress of the Communist Party of the Soviet Union. – Report by Comrade L. I. Brezhnev, General Secretary of the Central Committee, on March 30, 1971 [Part 2]', *The Current Digest of the Soviet Press* 23, no. 13 (27 April 1971): pp. 4-5. The Russian version was published in *Pravda*, no. 90 (31 March 1971), p. 5 and *Izvestiia*, no. 75 (31 March 1971), p. 4.

[26] 'USSR: History', in *GSE*, vol. 31, p. 163.

[27] A discussion of *developed socialism* from the Soviet perspective can be found in V. S. Semenov, 'The Theory of Developed Socialism and Its Growth into Communism', *Soviet Studies in Philosophy* 19, no. 4 (April 1981): pp. 3-32. For a detailed analysis of the concept, see the works of Alfred B. Evans, including 'Developed Socialism in Soviet Ideology', *Soviet Studies* 29, no. 3 (July 1977): pp. 409-28, and 'The Decline of Developed Socialism? Some Trends in Recent Soviet Ideology', *Soviet Studies* 38, no. 1 (January 1986): pp. 1-23. Footnote 2 of the former includes a discussion of the Russian terms used in Soviet texts, and an explanation of how the translation of those terms into English has sometimes inadvertently lost some of the meaning. For example, when Soviet sources used the phrase 'developed socialism' they were evoking an image of the USSR as technologically advanced and part of the 'developed world'. For additional discussions of this period in Soviet history, see Mark Edele, *The Soviet Union: A Short History* (Hoboken, NJ: Wiley-Blackwell, 2019), pp. 167-187; and Mark Sandle, 'Brezhnev and Developed Socialism: The Ideology of Zastoi?', in *Brezhnev Reconsidered*, ed. Edwin Bacon and Mark Sandle (Basingstoke: Palgrave Macmillan Limited, 2002), pp. 165-87.

[28] The author witnessed this type of intensified patriotic behaviour in the United States following the terrorist attacks of 11 September 2001. Overnight, the level of flag display and the tone of patriotic rhetoric dramatically changed across the country.

[29] Jean-Jacques Rousseau, 'On Civil Religion', in *On the Social Contract with Geneva Manuscript and Political Economy*, ed. Roger D. Masters, trans. Judith R. Masters (New York: St. Martin's Press, 1978), pp. 124-33.

[30] Robert N. Bellah, 'Civil Religion in America', *Daedalus* 96, no. 1 (1967), pp. 3-4.

[31] *Ibid.*, pp. 1-21.

[32] Russell E. Richey and Donald G. Jones, 'The Civil Religion Debate', in *American Civil Religion*, (New York: Harper & Row, 1974), p. 15. Emphasis in the original.

[33] *Ibid.*, pp. 3-18. Emphasis in the original.

[34] West, 'A Proposed Neutral Definition of Civil Religion', p. 39. Emphasis in the original.

[35] *Ibid.*, pp. 39-40. West quoting John A. Coleman, 'Civil Religion', *Sociological Analysis* 31, no. 2 (Summer 1970), pp. 67-77.

[36] Peter Gardella, *American Civil Religion: What Americans Hold Sacred* (New York: Oxford University Press, 2014); Scot M. Guenter, 'Majulah Singapura: National Day and Flag Culture in a Southeast Asian City-State', *Raven: A Journal of Vexillology* 6 (1999): pp. 9-18; Scot M. Guenter, 'Micronesian Flag Cultures: An Exercise in Comparative Vexillology', *Raven: A Journal of Vexillology* 11 (2004): pp. 61-71.

[37] Emilio Gentile, 'Fascism, Totalitarianism and Political Religion: Definitions and Critical Reflections on Criticism of an Interpretation', *Totalitarian Movements and Political Religions* 5, no. 3 (Winter 2004): p. 364. Emphasis in the original.

[38] *Ibid.*, p. 329.

[39] For more on the debate about *political religion* as it has unfolded in the fields of fascism studies and totalitarian studies, see: Emilio Gentile, 'Political Religion: A Concept and Its Critics – a Critical Survey', *Totalitarian Movements and Political Religions* 6, no. 1 (June 2005): pp. 19-32; David D. Roberts, '"Political Religion" and the Totalitarian Departures of Inter-War Europe: On the Uses and Disadvantages of an Analytical Category', *Contemporary European History* 18, no. 4 (November 2009): pp. 381-414; Roger Griffin, 'Introduction: God's Counterfeiters? Investigating the Triad of Fascism, Totalitarianism and (Political) Religion', *Totalitarian Movements and Political Religions* 5, no. 3 (Winter 2004): pp. 291-325; and Michael Burleigh, 'National Socialism as a Political Religion', *Totalitarian Movements and Political Religions* 1, no. 2 (Autumn 2000): pp. 1-26. For a critique of the use of *political religion* in the study of Stalinism, see Erik van Ree, 'Stalinist Ritual and Belief System: Reflections on "Political Religion,"' *Politics, Religion & Ideology* 17, no. 2-3 (July 2016): pp. 143-61.

[40] For examples see Robert W. Strayer, *Why Did the Soviet Union Collapse?: Understanding Historical Change* (Armonk, NY: M. E. Sharpe, 1998); or any edition of Kenez's book.

[41] West, pp. 38-40.

Chapter 2. Communicating Soviet Values: The Role of Symbols

[42] 'State Coat of Arms of the Union of Soviet Socialist Republics', in *GSE*, vol. 6, p. 745.

[43] Moisei Filippovich Grin, S. V. Kalesnik, and V. F. Pavlenko, eds., *Soviet Union: A Geographical Survey* (Moscow: Progress Publishers, 1976), p. 162. Note the emphasis on the centuries-long shared heritage of the Soviet peoples as part of the Russian Empire.

[44] Vladimir Il'ich Lenin, 'On the Question of National Policy', in *Collected Works.*, vol. 20 (Moscow: Progress Publishers, 1964), p. 224.

[45] *Ibid.*, 223. Emphasis in the original. Lenin's notion of a voluntary union was reflected in the Soviet Constitution. According to Chapter 8, Article 72, 'Each Union Republic shall retain the right freely to secede from the USSR.' 'Constitution and Government', in *GSE*, pp. 5, 13.

[46] Vladimir Il'ich Lenin, 'The Working Class and the National Question', in *Marxism & Nationalism*, ed. Doug Lorimer (Chippendale, NSW: Resistance Books, 2002), 32-33.

[47] 'Soviet People', in *GSE*, vol. 24, p. 363. Emphasis in the original. While the English translation had the phrase 'growing together' the original Russian used *sblizhenie*, which translates as 'rapprochement'. The emphasis in the passage was on how all the different ethnicities of the Soviet Union had willingly come together to form a new distinct community that was unified in the goal of constructing a communist society. 'Sovetskii narod' in Aleksandr Mikhailovich Prokhorov, ed., *Bol'shaia sovetskaia entsiklopediia*, 3rd edition, (Moscow: Izdatel'stvo 'Sovetskaia entsiklopediia,' 1970), vol. 24, p. 25.

[48] *Ibid.* This portion of the article cited Lenin's essay 'Polozhenie i zadachi sotsialisticheskogo internatsionala', in V. I. Lenin, *Polnoe sobranie sochinenii*, 5th ed. (Moscow: Izdatel'stvo Politicheskoi literatury, 1967), vol. 26, pp. 39-40. The title translates as 'Position and tasks of the socialist international'. Originally published in *Socialist-Democrat*, no. 33 (1 November 1914).

[49] For the official Soviet perspective on how state languages were used in bourgeois countries, in contrast to how socialist countries guaranteed complete linguistic equality, see 'State Language, Official', in *GSE*, vol. 7, pp. 672-673.

[50] 'Soviet People', in *GSE*, vol. 24, p. 363. The work cited in the article is the essay 'K evreiskim rabochim', in Lenin, *Polnoe sobranie sochinenii*, vol. 10, pp. 266-269. The title translates as 'To the Jewish Workers'. This text was originally a preface to a pamphlet titled 'Report on the Third Congress of the R.S.D.L.P.' published in the Yiddish language. In the text Lenin was alluding to two different adjectives in the Russian language – *russkii*, which means ethnically Russian, and *rossiiskii*, which means 'of Russia' with no specific ethnic group inferred. All ethnic Russians, regardless of their place of citizenship are *russkii*, while all *rossiiskii* people are citizens of Russia regardless of their ethnicity. It is also important to note that, in the Russian Empire, Soviet Union, and in the modern Russian Federation, the word *evreiskii* (Jewish) was/is considered to be an ethnicity, as well as an adjective for those who practice Judaism.

[51] 'People', in *GSE*, vol. 17, p. 605; excerpted with emphasis in the original.

[52] *Ibid.*; excerpted with emphasis in the original.

[53] *Ibid.*; excerpted with emphasis in the original.

[54] 'Soviet People', in *GSE*, vol. 24, p. 363; See also Maxim Kim, *The Soviet People: A New Historical Community* (Moscow: Progress Publishers, 1974), pp. 31-54, 121-130.

[55] 'Soviet People', in *GSE*, vol. 24, p. 363.

[56] For a brief discussion on various religious groups in the USSR, see Felix Corley, ed., *Religion in the Soviet Union: An Archival Reader* (New York: New York University Press, 1996), pp. 4-12.

[57] Victoria Smolkin, *A Sacred Space Is Never Empty: A History of Soviet Atheism* (Princeton: Princeton University Press, 2018); Sabrina P. Ramet, ed., *Religious Policy in the Soviet Union* (Cambridge: Cambridge University Press, 1993). Primary source material on Soviet policy can be found in Corley, *Religion in the Soviet Union*.

[58] Timothy E. O'Connor, 'Lunacharskii's Vision of the New Soviet Citizen', *The Historian* 53, no. 3 (Spring 1991): 443-54; Roland Boer, 'Religion and Socialism: A. V. Lunacharsky and the God-Builders', *Political Theology* 15, no. 2 (March 2014): 188-209; Nina Tumarkin, 'Religion, Bolshevism, and the Origins of the Lenin Cult', *The Russian Review* 40, no. 1 (January 1981): 35-46; James Thrower, *Marxism-Leninism as the Civil Religion of Soviet Society: God's Commissar* (Lewiston, NY: Edwin Mellen Press, 1992), p. 34-38.

[59] Thrower, Lenin quote from p. 39.

[60] Tumarkin, 'Religion, Bolshevism, and the Origins of the Lenin Cult', pp. 35-46.

[61] Thrower, p. 41.

[62] Joseph A. Schumpeter, *Capitalism, Socialism, and Democracy* (New York: Harper & Brothers, 1942), p. 5. Emphasis in the original.

[63] Thrower, p. 169.

[64] See Christel Lane, *The Rites of Rulers: Ritual in Industrial Society - the Soviet Case* (Cambridge: Cambridge University Press, 1981) and Nina Tumarkin, *Lenin Lives!: The Lenin Cult in Soviet Russia* (Cambridge, MA: Harvard University Press, 1983).

[65] West, 'A Proposed Neutral Definition of Civil Religion', p. 38.

[66] Whitney Smith, 'Prolegomena', pp. 15-16. Emphasis in the original.

[67] *Ibid.*

[68] *Ibid.*, p. 16.

[69] *Ibid.*, pp. 1-23; quote from p. 18. For an excellent discussion of the nature of political symbolism, see chapter 2 of Crampton, 'Flags as Non-Verbal Symbols', pp. 13-65. For a discussion from the perspective of semiotics, see Sebeok.

[70] Karen A. Cerulo, *Identity Designs: The Sights and Sounds of a Nation* (New Brunswick, NJ: Rutgers University Press, 1995), p. 3.

[71] *Ibid.*, p. 17.

[72] *Ibid.*, pp. 16-17, emphasis in the original. See Émile Durkheim, *The Elementary Forms of Religious Life*, trans. Carol Cosman, (New York: Oxford University Press, 2001), p. 175.

[73] Durkheim, p. 175.

[74] Lane, p. 25. Lane's primary discussion of the symbols can be found in Chapter 11, 'Analysis of Soviet ritual symbolism'. Of interest are her discussions of the red banner (pp. 196), the colour red (p. 200-1), verbal and musical symbolism (pp. 201-6), personification and heroes (pp. 204-220), and Lenin (pp, 210-220).

[75] 'Propaganda', in *GSE*, vol. 21, pp. 269-70.

[76] 'Agitation', in *GSE*, vol. 1, pp. 137-8.

[77] *Ibid.* Plekhanov quote from p. 137 with emphasis in the original. See further: Georgii Valentinovich Plekhanov, 'O zadachakh sotsialistov v bor'be s golodom v Rossii (Pis'ma k molodym tovarishcham). Pis'mo tret'e. Nashi zadachi', in *Sochineniia*, ed. D. B. Riazanov, vol. 3 (Moscow: Gosudartstvennoe izdatel'stvo, 1923), p. 397.

[78] Orlando Figes and B. I. Kolonitskii, *Interpreting the Russian Revolution: The Language and Symbols of 1917* (New Haven: Yale University Press, 1999), p. 187.

[79] For more discussion on the use of symbols in 1917, see: N. A. Soboleva, 'K voprosu o simvolike Rossii v pervoi chetverti XX stoletiia: Novye podkhody k issledovaniiu', in *Rossiia v XIX-XX vekakh: Materialy II nauchnykh chtenii pamiati professora Valeriia Ivanovicha Bovykina, Moskva, MGU im. M. V. Lomonosova, 22 ianvaria 2002 g*, ed. V. I. Bovykin, A. G. Golikov, and A. P. Korelin (Moscow: ROSSPEN, 2002), 337-57; P. K. Kornakov, 'Simvolika i rituinaly revoliutsii 1917 g.', in *Anatomiia revoliutsii: 1917 god v Rossii: Massy, partii, vlast'*, ed. V. Iu. Cherniaev (Saint Petersburg: Glagol, 1994), 356-65; and Mark Ferro, 'Simvolika i politika vo vremiia revoliutsii 1917 g.', in *Anatomiia revoliutsii: 1917 god v Rossii: Massy, partii, vlast'*, 366-71; Figes and Kolonitskii, pp. 30-70.

[80] Paul Gabel, *And God Created Lenin: Marxism vs. Religion in Russia, 1917-1929* (Amherst, NY: Prometheus Books, 2005), p. 350.

[81] James H. Billington, *The Icon and the Axe: An Interpretive History of Russian Culture* (New York: Knopf, 1966), pp. 36-37.

[82] Gloria Calhoun, 'Saints Into Soviets: Russian Orthodox Symbolism and Soviet Political Posters', (unpublished master's thesis, Georgia State University, 2014), p. 25.

[83] *Ibid.*, p. 150.

[84] *Ibid.*

[85] For more discussion of the role of icons in Russian Orthodoxy and their influence on Soviet culture, see: Elena A. Avdyusheva and Irina V. Egorova, 'Communicative Value of the Russian Orthodox Icon', *Procedia - Social and Behavioral Sciences* 236 (2016): 305-9; Nikos Kokosalakis, 'Icons and Non-Verbal Religion in the Orthodox Tradition', *Social Compass* 42, no. 4 (December 1995): 433-49; and Ulf Abel, 'Icons and Soviet Art', in *Symbols of Power: The Esthetics of Political Legitimation in the Soviet Union and Eastern Europe* (Stockholm, Sweden: Almqvist & Wiksell International, 1987), pp. 141-62.

[86] Anastasiia Petrovna Evgen'eva, ed., 'Simvolika', in *Slovar' russkogo iazyka* (Moscow: Izdatel'stvo 'Russkii iazyk', 1981), v. 4, p. 94.

[87] Sovetskii Soiuz, 'Gerb, flag, gimn i stolitsa SSSR', in *Konstitutsiia (Osnovnoi zakon) Soiuza Sovetskikh Sotsialisticheskikh Respublik: Priniata na vneocherednoi sed'moi sessii Verkhovnogo Soveta SSSR deviatogo sozyva 7 oktiabria 1977 goda*, Chapter 21, Article 8 (Moscow: Izdatel'stvo 'Iuridicheskaia literatura', 1979), pp. 44-45.

[88] Nadezhda Aleksandrovna Soboleva, 'From the History of Soviet Political Symbolism', *Russian Studies in History* 47, no. 2 (Fall 2008): 59-91. For the Russian-language version, see Nadezhda Aleksandrovna Soboleva, 'Iz istorii sovetskoi politicheskoi simvoliki', *Otechestvennaia istoriia*, no. 2 (April 2006): 89-109.

[89] Whitney Smith, 'Soviet State Symbolism', in William E. Butler, ed., *Soviet State Symbolism: Flags and Arms of the USSR and Its Constituent Parts, 1917-1971*, published as *The Flag Bulletin*, 11 no. 1 (Winchester, MA: Flag Research Center, Winter 1972), pp. 26-42.

[90] See Soboleva, 'From the History of Soviet Political Symbolism', pp. 64-72 for more on the use of symbols during this period.

[91] G. F. Kiselev and N. N. Speransov, *Emblemy mira i truda: Gosudarstvennye gerby i flagi Sovetskogo Soiuza i soiuznykh respublik* (Moscow: Politicheskoi literatury, 1968), pp. 9-10.

[92] This story was also repeated in Vladimir A. Potseluev, *Gerby Soiuza SSR: Iz istorii razrabotki* (Moscow: Izdatel'stvo politicheskoi literatury, 1987), pp. 35-41; V. Karpenko, 'Nashi slavnye simvoly', *Vospitanie shkol'nikov*, no. 4 (1986): 59-63; and L. Mysova, 'Ispol'zovanie gosudarstvennoi simvolika v vospitatel'noi rabote', *Vospitanie shkol'nikov*, no. 6 (1986): 13-16. For a historical analysis of the story, see G. F. Kiselev and V. A. Liubesheva, 'V. I. Lenin i sozdanie gosudarstvennoi pechati i gerba RSFSR', *Istoriia SSSR*, no. 5 (October 1966): 21-26.

[93] 'State Coat of Arms of the Union of Soviet Socialist Republics', in *GSE*, vol. 6, p. 745. For a description of the arms in Russian see Sovetskii Soiuz, 'Gerb, flag, gimn i stolitsa SSSR', in *Konstitutsiia*, pp. 44-45, and in English see 'Constitution', in *GSE*, vol. 31, p. 19.

[94] For historical discussions of the state emblem, see: Kiselev and Liubesheva, 'V. I. Lenin i sozdanie gosudarstvennoi pechati i gerba RSFSR', pp. 21-26; S. Bolotina, 'Kak sozdavalsia nash gerb', *Nauka i zhizn'*, no. 11 (November 1983): 20-24; Lev V. Roshchin, *Nashi voinskie simvoly* (Moscow: Izdatel'stvo DOSAAF SSSR, 1989), pp. 8-16; A. V. Ivanchenko, *Soiuz serpa i molota: Gosudarstvennye simvoly RSFSR* (Moscow, Sovetskaia Rossiia, 1987); Kiselev and Speransov, *Emblemy mira i truda*, pp. 7-26, 41-43; Soboleva, 'From the History of Soviet Political Symbolism', pp. 59-91; and Whitney Smith, 'Soviet State Symbolism', pp. 26-42. Suggestions for Soviet teachers on how to teach about the Soviet coat of arms can be found in V. Stepanenko, 'Gerb Sovetskogo Soiuza', *Vospitanie shkol'nikov*, no. 1 (1978), pp. 16-17 and Karpenko, pp. 59-63.

[95] Valentin Karamanchev, *Proletarskaia simvolika* (Moscow: Geral'dika trudovoi, 1978), pp. 73-77; Nikolai Dmitrievich Chernikov, ed., *Nasha krasnaia zvezda* (Moscow: Detskaia literatura, 1987), p. 5.

[96] 'Znachek Krasnogvardeitsev', *Pravda*, Issue #75 (19 April 1918), p. 4. The basic description of the insignia in *Izvestiia* was the same, but without the disparaging reference to the White Guards (the 'flour party'). See also, 'Znachek Krasnoarmeitsa', *Izvestiia*, Issue #77 (19 April 1918), p. 5.

[97] O. V. Kharitonov, *Soviet Military Uniform and Insignia, 1918-1958* (St. Petersburg: Alga-Fund, 1993), pp. 8-16; O. V. Kharitonov, *Illiustrirovannoe opisanie obmundirovaniia i znakov razlichiia Krasnoi i Sovetskoi Armii (1918-1945 gg.)* (Leningrad: Artilleriiskii istoricheskii muzei, 1960).

[98] RRMC is an abbreviation for Republic's Revolutionary Military Council. In Russian this would be *Revoliutsionnyi Voennyi Sovet Respubliki* (*RVSR*). For a discussion of the history of Soviet military insignia, see Kharitonov.

[99] Sovetskii Soiuz, 'Gerb, flag, gimn i stolitsa SSSR', in *Konstitutsiia*, pp. 44-45; 'The Emblem, Flag, Anthem, and Capital of the USSR', in *GSE*, vol. 31, p. 19; Soboleva, 'From the History of Soviet Political Symbolism', pp. 74-77; Karpenko, p. 60; Karamanchev, pp. 73-77; Potseluev, pp. 16-21. For discussions of the Soviet arms and flag, see: Whitney Smith, *Flags Through the Ages and Across the World*, pp. 174-179, 130-131; William G. Crampton, *Flags of the World: A Pictorial History* (New York: Dorset Press, 1990), pp. 99-100; Alfred Znamierowski, *The World Encyclopedia of Flags: The Definitive Guide to International Flags, Banners, Standards and Ensigns* (London: Lorenz, 1999), pp. 126-127, 242-243. To see how this symbol was explained in children's books, see Chernikov, *Nasha krasnaia zvezda*.

[100] Mikhail Aleksandrovich Topolin, *Kremlevskie zvezdy* (Moscow: Moskovskii rabochii, 1980), p. 3.

[101] Topolin, pp. 3-61; 'Kremlin Stars', in *GSE*, vol. 13, p. 499; A. S. Chernyak, 'Kremlin Ruby Stars Are 30 Years Old (Development of Ruby Glass)', *Glass and Ceramics* 24, no. 11 (November 1967): pp. 650-51; Julia Bekman Chadaga, 'Light in Captivity: Spectacular Glass and Soviet Power in the 1920s and 1930s', *Slavic Review* 66, no. 1 (Spring 2007): pp. 82-105.

[102] The documentary *My Perestroika* offers an excellent glimpse of the 'peace' theme in action. Historical footage shows Soviet children mailing letters for peace and discussing what they would say if they met US President Ronald Reagan. One of the interview subjects reflects that, while now it seems silly, Soviet children took the 'peace' message very seriously. 'It all sounds like a joke now… but it was a fundamental part of my everyday life. I go to school, I eat my dinner, and I also sing songs for peace!' Robin Hessman, *My Perestroika*, video recording (Red Square Productions, 2011).

[103] G. Calhoun, p. 73-74.

[104] *Ibid.*, p. 74.

[105] *Ibid.*, pp. 71-77.

[106] Vladimir Pavlovich Lapshin, *Khudozhestvennaia zhizn' Moskvy i Petrograda v 1917 godu* (Moscow: Sovetskii khudozhnik, 1983), pp. 120-22. Translation from Soboleva, 'From the History of Soviet Political Symbolism', pp. 83-84.

[107] Aleksei Fedorovich Losev, *Problema simvola i realisticheskoe iskusstvo* (Moscow: Iskusstvo, 1976), p. 315. Translation from Soboleva, 'From the History of Soviet Political Symbolism', p. 86.

[108] While the intelligentsia was considered part of the working class, this group was not depicted in this important symbol. In North Korean symbolism, the emblem of the Worker's Party of Korea illustrates all three groups using a 'a combination of three tools: a hammer, a long-handled sickle, and a calligraphy brush: representing the country's workers, the country's farmers, and the country's intellectuals'. Dean Thomas, 'Flags and Emblems of the Democratic People's Republic of Korea: Vexillidolatry in Its Purest Form', *Raven: A Journal of Vexillology* 21 (2014): 95-115.

[109] 'Hammer and Sickle', in *GSE*, vol. 23, p. 101-102.

[110] Figes and Kolonitskii, pp. 61-62; Ivanchenko, *Soiuz serpa i molota*; Soboleva, 'From the History of Soviet Political Symbolism', pp. 74-77, 83-86; Konstantin A. Ivanov, 'Soviet Russian Flags', trans. Whitney Smith, *The Flag Bulletin* 6, no. 1-2 (Winter 1966-1967), pp. 45-51; Karpenko, pp. 60-61; Karamanchev, pp. 83-88; Potseluev, pp.23-26.

[111] Karamanchev, pp. 83-88. For a brief discussion of the abundance theme in action see Diana Kurkovsky, 'Monumentalizing Wheat: Soviet Dreams of Abundance', *Gastronomica* 7, no. 1 (Winter 2007): 15-17.

[112] Karl Marx and Friedrich Engels, *Manifesto of the Communist Party* (New York: International Publishers, 1948), p. 44; and the Russian version – Karl Marks and Fridrikh Engel's, *Manifest Kommunisticheskoi partii* (Moscow: Izdatel'stvo Politicheskoi literatury, 1980), p. 61. For a discussion of the importance of slogans as proletarian symbols, see Karamanchev, pp. 45-70.

[113] 'Constitution (Fundamental Law) of the Union of Soviet Socialist Republics' [1977], in *GSE*, vol. 31, p. 19.

[114] 'Constitution (Fundamental Law) of the Union of Soviet Socialist Republics' [1924], in *Soviet State Symbolism*, p. 44; 'Fundamental Law (Constitution) of the Union of Soviet Socialist Republics' [1936], in *Soviet State Symbolism*, pp. 54-56; 'On changing the design of the state arms of the USSR in connection with the increase of the number of Union Republics, Edict of June 26, 1946, *Verdomosti SSSR* (1946), No. 25', in *Soviet State Symbolism*, p. 57; 'On Changing the Design of the State Arms of the USSR, Edict of September 12, 1956, *Verdomosti SSSR* (1956), No. 18, item 395', in *Soviet State Symbolism*, pp. 61-62.

[115] Population numbers for 1940 were found in 'Population', in *GSE*, vol. 31, p. 20. Statistics for 1939 were found in Sovetskii Soiuz, Tsentral'noe statisticheskoe upravlenie, *Chislennost' i sostav naseleniia SSSR: Po dannym Vsesoiuznoi perepisi naseleniia 1979 goda* (Moscow: Finansy i statistika, 1984), p. 10-14.

[116] Vladislav Aleksandrovich Sokolov, *Flagi Rossiiskoi Imperii i SSSR v dokumentakh* (Moscow. MGIU, 2001), p. 201. Russian text of the treaty is available at http://www.libussr.ru/doc_ussr/ussr_1468.htm.

[117] 'Postanovlenie Pravitel'stvo SSSR ot 12 noiabria 1923 g. O gosudarstvennoi flage Soiuza SSR', in Sokolov, p. 203; K. Ivanov, 'Soviet Russian Flags', pp. 42-51. In the fields of vexillology and heraldry, the strip of contrasting colour such as the gold 'edge' that delineates the red star from the red field of the flag is called a fimbriation. In Russian sources, the word used for this element is typically *krai*, which means 'edge' or 'rim'.

[118] 'Treaty Concerning the Formation of the Union of Soviet Socialist Republics', excerpt in *Soviet State Symbolism*, pp. 43-44. Note that it is common for the colour yellow to be used in place of gold in Soviet flags and portrayals thereof. See also: Kiselev and Speransov, *Emblemy mira i truda*, pp. 49-53.

[119] 'On a Detailed Description of the State Flag of the USSR', 18 April 1924, in *Soviet State Symbolism*, pp. 44-45. Russian text available at http://www.libussr.ru/doc_ussr/ussr_1999.htm.

[120] Soviet Union, *The Soviet Socialist Constitution* (Moscow: Russia To-day Society, 1941), p. 26.

[121] 'On Confirming the Statute on the State Flag of the USSR', Edict of 19 August 1955, in *Soviet State Symbolism*, pp. 58-61. The accompanying image was included in the edict, and in the translated source.

[122] *Ibid.* For more discussion of the history of Soviet flags and their usage, see Kiselev and Speransov, *Emblemy mira i truda*, pp. 49-55.

[123] 'Flag', in *GSE*. See also: A. Signev, 'Kak sozdavalsia gosudarstvennyi flag nashei rodiny', *Voprosy istorii*, no. 11 (November 1964): 211-15. The Russian word *kolkhoz* is a portmanteau formed from the words *kollektivnoe*, meaning 'collective', and *khoziastvo*, meaning 'enterprise'. In the combined form, the meaning is 'collective farm'.

[124] 'Red Banner', in *GSE*, vol. 14, pp. 707-8. See also, the discussion of red banners as revolutionary symbols in Kiselev and Speransov, *Emblemy mira i truda*, pp. 46-49.

[125] P. F. Maksiashev, 'Kogda vpervye v Rossii bylo podniato Krasnoe znamia', *Voprosy istorii*, no. 3 (March 1965): 206-7; Figes and Kolonitskii, pp. 41-43; Lane, *The Rites of Rulers*, pp. 200-201; Soboleva, 'From the History of Soviet Political Symbolism', pp. 59-91; K. Ivanov, 'Soviet Russian Flags', pp. 42-51; John Cartledge, 'Though Cowards Flinch: The Story of the Red Flag as a Symbol of Rebellion', paper presented to the Sydney Flag Congress / International Congress of Vexillology – ICV 26 (Sydney, New South Wales, Australia, 2015), publication pending in the conference proceedings; Karpenko, pp. 59-61; Konstantin Konstantinovich Mamaev, *Flagi rasskazyvaiut* (Leningrad: Avrora, 1972), pp. 8-21; Potseluev, pp. 26-35. For a fascinating photo essay on the red banner of socialism, see Pierre Znamensky and Guy Gallice, *Sous les plis du drapeau rouge* (Rodez: Rouergue, 2010). This book is rich in historical photographs showing the wide-spread use of red banners in revolutionary Russia and the Soviet Union.

[126] Numerous examples of military banners bearing images of Lenin, Stalin, or both leaders were observed by the author during a visit to the Military Historical Museum of Artillery, Engineers and Signal Corps (the Artillery Museum) in Saint Petersburg in 2007. The banners were on display in the gallery dedicated to the Siege of Leningrad during World War II. More research on the linkage between icon-based military banners and Soviet military banners bearing Lenin and/or Stalin is needed. See Znamensky and Gallice, *Sous les plis du drapeau rouge* for images of military banners from the Soviet Union. More research is also needed on the military traditions related to Soviet banners and any possible linkage to the veneration of icons.

[127] Lane, p. 37.

[128] 'Red Banners (challenge red banners)' in *GSE*, vol. 14, p. 708.

[129] *Ibid.*

[130] See Znamensky and Gallice for photographs of military and civilian banners from the Soviet Union. Numerous examples of challenge red banners are held in the collection of the Wende Museum, a museum of the Cold War in Culver City, California. The author also holds multiple examples in her personal collection.

[131] Wolfgang G. Jilek, 'Nazi and Communist Flags: Semiotic Aspects and Psychophysiological Dynamics of Totalitarian Symbols', *The Flag Bulletin*, #197, v. 40, no. 1 (February 2001), pp. 24. For more on the colour red in Russian culture, see: Iozef Kiblitskii, 'Nemnogo o tsvete, o krasnom tsvete...', in *Krasnyi tsvet v russkom iskusstve*, Evgeniia N. Petrova (ed.), (Saint Petersburg: Gosudarstvennyi russkii muzei, 1997), pp. 6-7; Alexander Pronin and Barbara Pronin, *Russian Folk Arts* (South Brunswick: A. S. Barnes and Company, 1975), p. 153; N. M. Shanskii, *Russian Word Formation*, (Oxford: Pergamon Press, 1968), p. 39; Lev Vasil'evich Uspenskii, '*Krasá*', in *Pochemu ne inache?: Etomologicheskii slovarik shkol'nika* (Moscow: Izdatel'stvo Detskaia literatura, 1967), p. 150; Kiselev and Speransov, *Emblemy mira i truda*, pp. 46.

[132] G. Calhoun, p. 80.

[133] *Ibid.*, pp. 77-83.

[134] For a discussion of *The Internationale* as a proletarian symbol, see Karamanchev, pp. 27-41. For more on the Soviet anthem, see Sovetskii Soiuz, 'Gerb, flag, gimn i stolitsa SSSR', in *Konstitutsiia*, pp. 44-45; Caroline Brooke, 'Changing Identities: The Russian and Soviet National Anthems', *Slavonica*, 13, no. 1 (April 2007), pp. 27-38. See further: Joseph Zikmund II, 'National Anthems as Political Symbols', *Australian Journal of Politics & History*, 15, no. 3 (December 1969), pp. 73-80; Karen A. Cerulo, 'Sociopolitical Control and the Structure of National Symbols: An Empirical Analysis of National Anthems', *Social Forces*, 68, no. 1 (September 1989), pp. 76-99; Karen A. Cerulo, 'Symbols and the World System: National Anthems and Flags', *Sociological Forum*, 8, no. 2 (June 1993), pp. 243-71; Karen Petrone and Kenneth Slepyan, *The Soviet Union and Russia, 1939-2015: A History in Documents* (New York, 2017), pp. xxv-xxviii; Figes and Kolonitskii, pp. 62-68; Roshchin, pp. 16-18; Xing Hang, *Encyclopedia of National Anthems*, 2nd ed., vol. 2 (Lanham, MD: Scarecrow Press, 2011), pp. 1016-1021; N. A. Soboleva, 'The Composition of State Anthems of the Russian Empire and the Soviet Union', *Russian Social Science Review* 50, no. 2 (April 2009): 67-94.

[135] For more on destalinization, see Kenez, *A History of the Soviet Union From the Beginning to the End*, pp. 190-194; and Edward Taborsky, 'The Destalinized Stalinism', *Southwestern Social Science Quarterly* 37, no. 4 (March 1957): 311-29.

[136] Hang, pp. 1016-1021; Brooke, pp. 27-38; Petrone and Slepyan, pp. xxv-xxviii; 'Lyrics for Soviet Anthem Revised, So People No Longer Have to Hum', *New York Times* (1 September 1977), p. 2.

[137] Figes and Kolonitskii, pp. 60-61. See further: Karamanchev, pp. 101-108.

[138] Alexei Yurchak, 'Bodies of Lenin. The Hidden Science of Communist Sovereignty', *Representations* 129, no. 1 (February 2015): 116-57; Alexei Yurchak, 'Form Versus Matter: Miraculous Relics and Lenin's Scientific Body', in *Death and Mortality: From Individual to Communal Perspectives*, ed. Outi Hakola, Sara Heinämaa, and Sami Pihlström, (Helsinki: Helsinki Collegium for Advanced Studies, 2015), 61-81; Tumarkin, *Lenin Lives!*, p. 183.

[139] Olga Velikanova, *Making of an Idol: On Uses of Lenin* (Göttingen: Muster-Schmidt, 1996); Lane, *The Rites of Rulers*, pp. 210-220; Thrower, *Marxism-Leninism as the Civil Religion of Soviet Society*, pp. 85-92; Tumarkin, *Lenin Lives!*. For a discussion of the sacredness of Red Square, see David A. Weber, 'Changing Sacredness and Historical Memory of Moscow's Red Square', *Studies in Slavic Cultures* 8 (August 2009): pp. 43-64.

[140] Hedrick Smith, *The Russians* (New York: Quadrangle/New York Times Book Co., 1976), pp. 273-276.

[141] Hedrick Smith quotes a dispatch from TASS (the Soviet news agency) dated November 1974 that demonstrates that the Soviet author recognised the religious nature of the pilgrimage to Lenin's mausoleum:

> From early dawn an endless line of people formed up across Red Square from the granite sepulchre held sacred by the working people throughout the world. Over the half-century, 77 million people [have] passed in a mournful and stern march by the sarcophagus where the genius of humanity lies in state. From this day onwards new thousands and millions of people will be bringing worship to Lenin from all over the world.

Hedrick Smith, p. 279. See also, Thrower, pp. 89-90.

[142] Tumarkin, *Lenin Lives!*, pp. 3-6, 126-127, 131, 217, 221-232, 239-245, 259; Figes and Kolonitskii, pp. 101-103; Thrower, pp. 77-92; E. Tiazhel'nikov, 'Bring Up Young Leninists', *Soviet Education*, 15, no. 3 (January 1973), pp. 23-46; Velikanova, pp. 123-126; Nina Tumarkin, 'Political Ritual and the Cult of Lenin', *Human Rights Quarterly*, 5, no. 2 (May 1983), pp. 203-6.

[143] G. Calhoun, p. 15.

[144] G. Calhoun, p. 16. Calhoun is citing Matthew Cullerne Bown, *Art Under Stalin* (New York: Holmes & Meier, 1991), p. 87. See also G. Calhoun, pp. 67-77.

[145] For extensive discussions of this use of Lenin, see Tumarkin, pp. 207-251; Thrower, pp. 77-92; Lane, pp. 204-219; and Gill, *Symbols and Legitimacy in Soviet Politics*.

[146] Lane, *The Rites of Rulers*, pp. 204-220.

[147] Charles Edward Merriam, *Political Power* (New York: Collier Books, 1964), pp. 51-52.

[148] 'Patriotism', in *GSE*, vol. 19, p. 343. The in-text citation refers to the programme of the Communist Party of the Soviet Union from 1974.

[149] Friedrich Kuebart, 'The Political Socialisation of Schoolchildren', in *Soviet Youth Culture*, Jim Riordan (ed.) (Bloomington, IN: Indiana University Press, 1989), pp. 112.

Chapter 3. Little Leninists: Symbols and the Political Socialisation of Soviet Children

[150] Nadezhda Konstantinovna Krupskaia, 'Pomen'she barabannogo boia', in *Pedagogicheskie sochineniia*, vol. 5, (Moscow: Izdatel'stvo Akademii Pedagogicheskikh Hauk, 1957), p. 103.

[151] A. F. Davies, 'The Child's Discovery of Nationality', *The Australian and New Zealand Journal of Sociology*, 4, no. 2 (September 1968), pp. 107-25.

[152] Eugene L. Horowitz, 'Some Aspects of the Development of Patriotism in Children', *Sociometry*, 3, no. 4 (1940), pp. 329-41; Eugene A. Weinstein, 'Development of the Concept of Flag and the Sense of National Identity', *Child Development*, 28, no. 2 (June 1957), pp. 167-74; Edwin D. Lawson, 'Development of Patriotism in Children – A Second Look', *The Journal of Psychology*, 55 (January 1963), pp. 279-286; Davies, pp. 107-25.

[153] Weinstein, pp. 167-74.

[154] David Easton and Robert D. Hess, 'The Child's Political World', *Midwest Journal of Political Science*, 6, no. 3 (1962), pp. 229-46. For a more detailed sociological analysis of American civil religion in schools, see Adam Gamoran, 'Civil Religion in American Schools', *Sociological Analysis*, 51, no. 3 (Autumn 1990), pp. 235-56.

[155] David Statt, 'Flag Choices of Elite American and Canadian Children', *Psychological Reports*, 32, no. 1 (February 1973), pp. 85-86; Gustav Jahoda, 'The Development of Children's Ideas About Country and Nationality: Part 1: The Conceptual Framework', *British Journal of Educational Psychology*, 33, no. 1 (February 1963), pp. 47-60; Gustav Jahoda, 'The Development of Children's Ideas About Country and Nationality: Part II: National Symbols and Themes', *British Journal of Educational Psychology*, 33, no. 2 (June 1963), pp. 143-53; R. Jackson, 'The Development of Political Concepts in Young Children', *Educational Research*, 14, no. 1 (November 1971), pp. 51-55; György Csepeli, 'Sense of National Belonging as a Result of Socialisation', *International Journal of Political Education*, 5, no. 4 (1982), pp. 377-87.

[156] Csepeli, pp. 377-87. Quote from p. 382.

[157] For a more detailed discussion of political socialisation, see Richard E. Dawson, Kenneth Prewitt, and Karen S. Dawson, *Political Socialization: An Analytic Study* (Boston: Little, Brown, 1977); Gamoran, pp. 235-256.

[158] Nadezhda Konstantinovna Krupskaya, 'The Young Pioneer Movement as a Pedagogical Problem', in *On Education: Selected Articles and Speeches*, trans. G. P. Ivanov-Mumjiev (Moscow: Foreign Languages Publishing House, 1957), pp. 119-120.

[159] Albert Hughes, *Political Socialization of Soviet Youth* (Lewiston, NY: Edwin Mellen Press, 1992), pp. 27-40; Krupskaia, 'The Young Pioneer Movement as a Pedagogical Problem', pp. 118-122.

[160] Miriam Morton, *Growing Up in the Soviet Union: From the Cradle to Coming of Age* (Moscow: Progress Publishers, 1982), pp. 15-25; Aleksandr Andreevich Didusenko, *Soviet Children* (Moscow: Progress Publishers, 1965), pp. 17-36; Urie Bronfenbrenner and John C. Condry, *Two Worlds of Childhood: U.S. and U.S.S.R.* (New York: Simon and Schuster, 1970), pp. 17-25; Robert W. Clawson, 'Political Socialization of Children in the USSR', *Political Science Quarterly*, 88, no. 4 (1973), pp. 703-709; Jean MacIntyre, 'Political Socialization of Youth in the Soviet Union: Its Theory, Use, and Results', (unpublished master's thesis, US Naval Postgraduate School, 1993), pp. 11-15.

[161] Fedar Filippovich Korolev, *Education in the U.S.S.R.* (London: Soviet News, 1957), p. 12; MacIntyre, pp. 11-15.

[162] Kitty D. Weaver, *Lenin's Grandchildren: Preschool Education in the Soviet Union* (New York: Simon and Schuster, 1971), pp. 36.

[163] *Ibid.*, p. 37.

[164] Bronfenbrenner and Condry, pp. 17-25; Weaver, *Lenin's Grandchildren*, pp. 24-42. See also Lisa A. Kirschenbaum's description of political education in the kindergartens. Lisa A. Kirschenbaum, *Small Comrades: Revolutionizing Childhood in Soviet Russia, 1917-1932* (New York: RoutledgeFalmer, 2000), pp. 123-132.

[165] In the 'Guidelines for the Economic and Social Development of the USSR', plans were made to transition to universal kindergarten preparation for all Soviet students by 1990. This transition was in process during the final years of the Soviet Union, when the combination of increased nationalism in the republics and relaxation of control by the central authorities led to more variation in the curricula of schools in different parts of the country. N. Vishneva-Sarafanova, *The Privileged Generation: Children in the Soviet Union* (Moscow: Progress Publishers, 1984), pp. 178-180, 183-188.

[166] A description of the welcoming ceremony as seen from the perspective of visiting kindergartners is found in Miriam Morton's book. Morton, p. 24. Bronfenbrenner and Lane also describe the celebrations related to the first day of school. Bronfenbrenner and Condry, pp. 17-25; Lane, *The Rites of Rulers*, pp. 94-96. See also, *My Perestroika* [film], and *Semiletnie. Rozhdennye v SSSR / Age 7 in the USSR* [film], directed by Sergei Miroshnichenko (New York, NY: Films for the Humanities & Sciences, 2013).

[167] Miroshnichenko's films have inadvertently became a poignant portrayal of how individuals were affected by the breakup of the Soviet Union. 7 Up series were designed to follow the lives of children in different countries beginning at age 7, updated every 7 years thereafter. The first installment of the Russian version was filmed in the late 1980s. By the time his subjects had reached the age of 14, the Soviet Union had dissolved, and the children were living in different countries. Two more installments have since been competed, showing how the individuals have changed since they reached adulthood. Sophia Kishkovsky, 'A '7 Up' Series for Russia, With Soviet Roots', *New York Times* (4 October 2013), https://artsbeat.blogs.nytimes.com/2013/10/04/a-7-up-series-for-russia-with-soviet-roots/ [accessed 27 May 2017].

[168] Korolev, *Education in the U.S.S.R.*, p. 6.

[169] Korolev, *Education in the U.S.S.R.*; Bronfenbrenner and Condry, pp. 28-69; MacIntyre, pp. 18-29; Ina Schlesinger, 'The Pioneer Organization: The Evolution of Citizenship Education in the Soviet Union' (unpublished PhD dissertation, Columbia University, 1967), pp. 67-99.

[170] Hermann Rajamaa, *The Moulding of Soviet Citizens: A Glance at Soviet Educational Theory and Practice* (London: Boreas Publishing Co., 1948); Bronfenbrenner and Condry, pp. 28-69; MacIntyre, pp. 18-29; Hughes, pp. 151-160.

[171] Alexander M. Chabe, 'Star Badges and Red Scarves', *The Educational Forum*, 34, no. 4 (May 1970), pp. 485-93; Jim Riordan, 'The Role of Youth Organizations in Communist Upbringing in the Soviet School', in *The Making of the Soviet Citizen: Character Formation and Civic Training in Soviet Education*, George Avis (ed.), (London: Croom Helm, 1987), pp. 136-160; MacIntyre, pp. 42-49.

[172] Krupskaia, 'Pomen'she barabannogo boia'.

[173] Krupskaia, 'International Children's Week (*Pravda*, 1923)', in *On Education: Selected Articles and Speeches*, pp. 107-10.

[174] Deana Levin, *Children in Soviet Russia* (London: Faber and Faber, 1942), pp. 18-28; MacIntyre, pp. 42-49; Riordan, 'The Role of Youth Organizations in Communist Upbringing...', pp. 136-137; Nadezhda Konstantinovna Krupskaya, 'The School and the Pioneer Movement', in *Soviet Educators on Soviet Education*, Helen B. Redl (ed.), (New York: Free Press of Glencoe, 1964), pp 225-28. See further, other works by Krupskaya in *Soviet Educators on Soviet Education*, pp. 221-244.

[175] Chabe, p. 486; Riordan, 'The Role of Youth Organizations in Communist Upbringing...', pp. 138-142.

[176] Vitalii Solomonovich Khanchin, ed. *Tovarishch: Zapisnaia knizhka pionera na 1961/62 uchebnyi god* (Moscow: Izdatel'stvo TSK VLKSM Molodaia gvardiia, 1961), p. 124; Aleksandra S. Smirnova, *Oktiabriata – budushchie pionery: Rekomendatel'nyi ukazatel' literatury dlia vozhatykh oktiabriatskikh grupp i zvezdochek* (Leningrad: Ministerstvo kul'tury RSFSR, 1960), p. 6; MacIntyre, pp. 42-49.

[177] Descriptions of the induction ritual can be found in the manual for Pioneer leaders. See Vasilii Golyshkin and V. A. Taborko, *Kniga vozhatogo* (Moscow: Molodaia Gvardiia, 1965) pp. 19-20; A. A. Derkach, G. Chubarova, and L. Iashunina, *Kniga vozhatogo* (Moscow: Molodaia Gvardiia, 1982), pp. 50-51.

[178] Khanchin, *Tovarishch*, pp. 74-75.

[179] Samuel N. Harper, *Civic Training in Soviet Russia* (Chicago: University of Chicago Press, 1929), p. 72.

[180] MacIntyre, pp. 42-49; Harper, pp. 61-85; Riordan, 'The Role of Youth Organizations in Communist Upbringing...', pp. 142-149; S. Furin, *The World of Young Pioneers* (Moscow: Progress Publishers, 1982), pp. 8, 31.

[181] Kuebart, pp. 103-21; Scott E. Votey, 'Political Attitudes Reflected in Soviet Elementary Textbooks', *Social Education*, 42 (March 1978), pp. 228-30; MacIntyre, pp. 16-30.

[182] Vladimir Maiakovskii, '*Komsomol'skaia*', in *Sobranie sochinenii: v dvenadtsati tomakh*, vol. 3 (Moscow: Pravda, 1978), pp. 26-30.

[183] MacIntyre, pp. 16-30; Vseslav Gavrilovich Goretskii, Viktor Andreevich Kiriushkin, and Anatolii Filippovich Shan'ko, *Azbuka* (Moscow: Prosveshchenie, 1991), pp. 2-5, 100.

[184] Goretskii, Kiriushkin, and Shan'ko, *Azbuka*, pp. 162-163, 186-187; MacIntyre, pp. 16-30; Genevra Gerhart, *The Russian's World: Life and Language* (New York: Harcourt Brace Jovanovich, 1974), p. 21.

[185] Goretskii, Kiriushkin, and Shan'ko, *Azbuka*, pp. 171, 188-191. For a further discussion of the political content in the readers designed for Soviet children, see Joseph Zajda, 'The Moral Curriculum in the Soviet School', *Comparative Education*, 24, no. 3 (1988), pp. 389-404; MacIntyre, pp. 16-30.

[186] Vseslav Gavrilovich Goretskii, V. A. Kiriushkin, and A. F. Shan'ko, *Chitaem sami: Posobie dlia uchashchikhsia 1 klassa trekhletnei nachal'noi shkoly* (Moscow: Prosveshchenie, 1989), p. 69.

[187] Goretskii, Kiriushkin, and Shan'ko, *Chitaem sami*, entire book, quote from p. 53.

[188] Felicity Ann O'Dell, *Socialisation through Children's Literature: The Soviet Example* (Cambridge: Cambridge University Press, 1978), pp. 75-121. See also: Lev Abramovich Kassil', *Flazhok: Kniga dlia chteniia vo vtorom klasse*, (Moscow: Prosveshchenie, 1972).

[189] Riordan, 'The Role of Youth Organizations in Communist Upbringing…', pp. 138-142.

[190] 'Oktiabriatskaia zvezdochka', *Vozhatyi* (1958), p. 45; Smirnova, p. 7; MacIntyre, pp. 42-46; Riordan, 'The Role of Youth Organizations in Communist Upbringing…', pp. 138-142.

[191] S. V. Orleanskaia, *Nashe imia – oktiabriata: Sbornik rasskazov, stikhov, stsenok, pesen, igr, zagadok, skorogovorok dlia oktiabriat* (Moscow: Detgiz, 1959), pp. 9-10.

[192] Vseslav Gavrilovich Goretskii, *Rodnoe slovo: Uchebnik po chteniiu dlia uchashchikhsia 2 klassa chetyrekhletnei nachal'noi shkoly* (Moscow: Prosveshchenie, 1989); MacIntyre, pp. 42-46.

[193] Riordan, 'The Role of Youth Organizations in Communist Upbringing…', pp. 136-142. An excellent account illustrating the anticipation that children felt about their induction into the Young Pioneers can be found in the children's historical novel, *Breaking Stalin's Nose*, by Russian-American author Eugene Yelchin. In the story, 10-year-old Sasha Zaichik anxiously prepares himself on the eve of his promotion to the Young Pioneers. Unfortunately, his happy Soviet childhood is disrupted by the realities of life during the Stalinist purges. Eugene Yelchin, *Breaking Stalin's Nose* (New York: Henry Holt, 2011).

[194] Khanchin, *Tovarishch*, pp. 29-30.

[195] Furin, pp. 30-31, 176-177; V. Nikolaev, 'Tvoi pionerskii znachok', *Iunyi tekhnik*, no. 5 (May 1972), pp. 18-19, back cover; E. Vainshtein, 'Pervyi pionerskii znachok', *Sovetskii kollektsioner*, no. 2 (1964), p. 117. A photograph of this badge style can be found on the *Muzei SSSR* website at https://u-ssr.ru/icon/545-istorija-detskih-organizacij-v-sssr.html.

[196] Furin, pp. 30-31, 176-177; Nikolaev, pp. 19, back cover.

[197] The Scouting Movement, founded by Robert Baden-Powell, began in the UK in 1907. It quickly spread throughout the British Empire and, by 1910, became established in ten countries beyond the Empire including Russia.

[198] Furin, pp. 30-31. Furin's account matches Krupskaia's letter to the Pioneers, '*Bud' gotov*', which was published in the children's magazine *Pioneer* in 1924. Nadezhda Konstantinovna Krupskaia and Nikolai Ivanovich Monakhov, *O vozhatom i ego rabote s pionerami* (Moscow: Molodaia Gvardiia, 1961), pp. 173-175; Vladimir Il'ich Lenin, *What Is to Be Done?: Burning Questions of Our Movement* (New York: International Publishers, 1969), pp. 171-172.

[199] Tiazhel'nikov, pp. 27-28; Krupskaia and Monakhov, pp. 173-175; Lenin, *What Is to Be Done?*, pp. 171-172; Jim Riordan, '"Be Prepared": Russian Boy Scouts and Soviet Pioneers', *Stadion: Internationale Zeitschrift für Geschichte des Sports/International Journal of the History of Sports*, 11, no. 1 (January 1985), pp. 93-106; Jim Riordan, 'The Russian Boy Scouts', *History Today*, 38, no. 10 (October 1988), pp. 48-52; Kuebart, pp. 110-113; Harper, pp. 61-85.

[200] Furin, pp. 30-31, 176-177; Nikolaev, pp. 19, 76, back cover.

[201] Nikolaev, p. 76, back cover; Khanchin, *Tovarishch*, p. 79.

[202] Nikolaev, pp. 76, back cover; Furin, pp. 30-31, 176-177. This author has been unable to determine the exact usage dates for each of these designs. Furin's book from 1982 states that the Lenin-portrait design had been in use since 1962, but in the Young Pioneer leader's manual published in 1965 the illustrations and text all describe the earlier version with the hammer and the sickle. This discrepancy could have occurred because the transition of the emblem was a gradual process and took several years to implement across the country. See Furin, pp. 30-31; Golyshkin and Taborko, *Kniga vozhatogo* (1965).

[203] The use of military terms such as troop, detachment, and unit were likely derived from the heritage of Scouting. They also connected the Young Pioneers to elements of paramilitary instruction in Soviet secondary education.

[204] Furin, pp. 26-28, 33; Khanchin, *Tovarishch*, p. 78; Golyshkin and Taborko, *Kniga vozhatogo* (1965), pp. 17-18; Derkach, Chubarova, and Iashunina, *Kniga vozhatogo* (1982), pp. 14-17, plate [8] following 64.

[205] Furin, p. 40; Khanchin, *Tovarishch*, p. 78; Golyshkin and Taborko, *Kniga vozhatogo* (1965), facing page 64.

[206] Khanchin, *Tovarishch*, p. 79.

[207] Lane, *The Rites of Rulers*, pp. 91-92.

[208] Julie K. deGraffenried, *Sacrificing Childhood: Children and the Soviet State in the Great Patriotic War*, (Lawrence, KS: University Press of Kansas, 2014), pp. 96-97. The English version of the Galia Dotsenko story is deGraffenried's translation, but a similar account of this story in Russian can be found in the Young Pioneer leaders' handbook from 1954. A. Stroev and T. Matveeva, *Kniga vozhatogo* (Moscow: Izdatel'stvo TSK VLKSM 'Molodaia gvardiia', 1954), pp. 32-33.

[209] Stroev and Matveeva, *Kniga vozhatogo* (1954), pp. 9-23; Derkach, Chubarova, and Iashunina, *Kniga vozhatogo* (1982), pp. 48-54; deGraffenried, *Sacrificing Childhood*; Svetlana Maslinskaya, 'A Child Hero: Heroic Biographies in Children's Literature', lecture delivered at the University of California, Santa Barbara, (27 April 2017); Svetlana G. Leont'eva, 'Zhizneopisanie pionera-geroia: Tekstovaia traditsiia i ritual'nyi kontekst', in *Sovremennaia rossiiskaia mifologiia*, M. V. Akhmetova (ed.), (Moscow: Rossiiskii gosudartsvennyi gumanitarnyi universitet, 2005), pp. 89-123; Svetlana G. Leont'eva, 'Pioner: Vsem primer', *Otechest'vennye zapiski*, no. 3 (18) (2004), pp.249-59; Kirill A. Maslinsky, personal communication (27 April 2017); Furin, pp. 64-69, 164-165; Tiazhel'nikov, pp. 30-31. For an excellent historical assessment of the story of Pavlik Morozov, see Catriona Kelly, *Comrade Pavlik: The Rise and Fall of a Soviet Boy Hero* (London: Granta Books, 2005).

[210] Murray J. Edelman, *The Symbolic Uses of Politics* (Urbana: University of Illinois Press, 1964), p. 16.

[211] O'Dell, pp. 114-118.

[212] Lane, *The Rites of Rulers*, pp. 130-188; Thrower, pp. 61-63; Kuebart, pp. 110-113; John Dunstan, 'Atheistic Education in the USSR', in *The Making of the Soviet Citizen: Character Formation and Civic Training in Soviet Education*, George Avis (ed.), (London: Croom Helm, 1987), pp. 50-79; Iu. I. Bokan', V. V. Zaikin, and V. G. Sinitsyn (eds.), *Nashi prazdniki (Sovetskie obshchegosudarstvennye, trudovye, voinskie, molodezhnye i semeino-bytovye prazdniki, obriady, rituraly)* (Moscow: Izdatel'stvo Politicheskoi literatury, 1977).

[213] Anatolii Vasil'evich Mitiaev and Iurii Kopeiko, *Segodnia prazdnik: Rasskazy* (Moscow: Detskaia literatura, 1981), p. 29.

[214] Mitiaev and Kopeiko; Goretskii, Kiriushkin, and Shan'ko, *Chitaem sami*; Goretskii, *Rodnoe slovo*; Kuebart, pp. 103-21; Bokan', Zaikin, and Sinitsyn, *Nashi prazdniki*.

[215] Anne M. Platoff, 'Soviet Children's Flags', *Raven: A Journal of Vexillology*, 17 (November 2010), pp. 63-84 and individual emails cited in that work; Samantha Smith, *Journey to the Soviet Union* (Boston: Little, Brown, 1986), p. 38. For a historical analysis of Smith's trip, see Matthias Neumann, 'Children Diplomacy During the Late Cold War: Samantha Smith's Visit of the "Evil Empire"', *History* 104, no. 360 (2019): pp. 275-308.

[216] Platoff, 'Soviet Children's Flags'.

[217] Platoff, 'Soviet Children's Flags', p. 73.

[218] Platoff, 'Soviet Children's Flags'.

[219] Tiazhel'nikov, pp. 27-28; Riordan, '"Be Prepared"', pp. 93-106; Golyshkin and Taborko, *Kniga vozhatogo* (1965), pp. 49-55; Derkach, Chubarova, and Iashunina, *Kniga vozhatogo* (1982), pp. 14-27.

[220] Golyshkin and Taborko, *Kniga vozhatogo* (1965), pp. 50-52, 55; Derkach, Chubarova, and Iashunina, *Kniga vozhatogo* (1982), pp. 19-21.

[221] Furin, pp. 37-38; Golyshkin and Taborko, *Kniga vozhatogo* (1965), pp. 52-54; Derkach, Chubarova, and Iashunina, *Kniga vozhatogo* (1982), pp. 21-25.

[222] Derkach, Chubarova, and Iashunina, *Kniga vozhatogo* (1982), p. 15.

[223] Derkach, Chubarova, and Iashunina, *Kniga vozhatogo* (1982), pp. 14-19; Furin, p. 30. One of Robin Hessman's subjects recalled a time from her childhood when she heard the national anthem playing from the television. She described how she immediately stood at attention and gave the Pioneer salute until the anthem finished. This is an excellent example of civil religious ritual having become ingrained into everyday behavior. *My Perestroika* [film].

[224] Golyshkin and Taborko, *Kniga vozhatogo* (1965), p. 54.

[225] *Ibid.*

[226] Anton Semionovich Makarenko (1888-1939) was one of the founders of Soviet pedagogy and one of the early architects of the Soviet educational system.

[227] S. A. Shmakov, 'To Inspire Children (A Pioneer Leader's Notebook)', in *Soviet Educators on Soviet Education*, p. 246.

[228] Derkach, Chubarova, and Iashunina, *Kniga vozhatogo* (1982), p. 27.

[229] Jill Dubisch, 'Pilgrimage', in Mark Juergensmeyer and Wade Clark Roof (eds), *Encyclopedia of Global Religion* (Thousand Oaks, CA: SAGE Publications, 2012), pp. 992-996; 'Pilgrimage, N.', *OED Online*, http://www.oed.com.proxy.library.ucsb.edu:2048/view/Entry/143868 [accessed June 18, 2017].

[230] Furin, p. 39; Derkach, Chubarova, and Iashunina, *Kniga vozhatogo* (1982), p. 25.

[231] Golyshkin and Taborko, *Kniga vozhatogo* (1965), p. 39.

[232] Hedrick Smith, *The Russians*, p. 371; Thrower, p. 75.

[233] For more discussion about Soviet propaganda and the portrayal of a 'happy Soviet childhood', see Catriona Kelly, *Children's World: Growing Up in Russia, 1890-1991* (New Haven, CT: Yale University Press, 2007). Chapter 4 of Kelly's book discussed the post-Stalin era in the USSR. See also, Catriona Kelly, 'A Joyful Soviet Childhood: Licensed Happiness for Little Ones', in *Petrified Utopia: Happiness Soviet Style*, ed. Marina Balina and E. A. Dobrenko (London: Anthem Press, 2009), 3-18. Other essays in the latter work examine happiness in the Soviet Union.

Chapter 4. Banal Nationalism in the USSR: State Symbols in the Daily Lives of Soviet Citizens

[234] Michael Billig, *Banal Nationalism* (London: SAGE Publications, 1995), p. 8.

[235] For a thorough discussion of the competing definitions of 'nationalism', see Jonathan Hearn, *Rethinking Nationalism: A Critical Introduction* (Houndmills: Palgrave Macmillan, 2006). For a discussion of the diverse forms of nationalism, see Craig J. Calhoun, *Nationalism* (Minneapolis: University of Minnesota Press, 1997).

[236] Raymond Pearson, *National Minorities in Eastern Europe, 1848-1945* (New York: St. Martin's Press, 1983), pp. 13-43; Michael Keating, 'Nations Without States: The Accommodation of Nationalism in the New State Order', in *Minority Nationalism and the Changing International Order*, ed. Michael Keating and John McGarry (Oxford: Oxford University Press, 2001), pp. 19-43.

[237] David D. Laitin, 'National Identities in the Emerging European State', in *Minority Nationalism and the Changing International Order*, ed. Keating and McGarry, pp. 84-113.

[238] Erika Harris, *Nationalism: Theories and Cases* (Edinburgh: Edinburgh University Press, 2009), pp. 144-160. For a historical discussion of the role of ethnicity in the evolution of the nation-state, see Anthony D. Smith, *The Ethnic Origins of Nations* (Oxford: Basil Blackwell, 1987) and C. Calhoun, *Nationalism*.

[239] Harris, pp. 128-143; Amartya Sen, *Identity and Violence: The Illusion of Destiny* (New York: W. W. Norton & Co, 2007).

[240] Billig, *Banal Nationalism*.

[241] *Ibid.*, p. 6. Emphasis in the original.

[242] *Ibid.*, p. 7.

[243] As a sample exercise in how the language of banal nationalism could be studied, Billig conducted a survey of language usage in British national newspapers on 28 June 1993. See Billig, *Banal Nationalism*, pp. 93-127.

[244] It is important to acknowledge that Billig's book is not without its critics. Some have noted that he did not provide enough examples in his analysis, that he limited his study to western states, or that his focus on the banal was an oversimplification of the phenomenon of nationalism. However, the impact of his work has been to renew an interest in the study of national identity and nationalism when some scholars were suggesting that globalism would render the concept obsolete. As Koch and Paasi noted, 'Billig's book was significant in turning the attention of nationalism scholars to the everyday and the mundane routines and discourses where nationalism is reproduced.' His work is now considered a classic and has influenced scholars working in many different fields. Most importantly, from the perspective of the study of civil religion and symbols, Billig has inspired many works focused on everyday nationhood. *Banal Nationalism* demonstrated that a focus on everyday life, material culture, and communication can lead to a better understanding of the processes through which individuals develop a sense of national identity and a connection to the society in which they live. For critical analyses of Billig's work, see: Natalie Koch and Anssi Paasi, 'Banal Nationalism 20 Years On: Re-Thinking, Re-Formulating and Re-Contextualizing the Concept', *Political Geography*, 54 (September 2016), pp. 1-6; Michael Skey, 'The National in Everyday Life: A Critical Engagement with Michael Billig's Thesis of *Banal Nationalism*', *The Sociological Review* 57, no. 2 (May 2009), pp. 331-46; Sophie Duchesne, 'Who's Afraid of Banal Nationalism?', *Nations and Nationalism* 24, no. 4 (October 2018), pp. 841-56; and Michael Skey and Marco Antonsich, eds., *Everyday Nationhood: Theorising Culture, Identity and Belonging after* Banal Nationalism (London: Palgrave Macmillan, 2017).

[245] Billig, *Banal Nationalism*, p. 8.

[246] *Ibid.*, p. 38.

[247] *Ibid.*, p. 175.

[248] 'Nationalism', in *GSE*, v. 17, p. 365.

[249] Vladimir Il'ich Lenin, 'The Right of Nations to Self-Determination', in *Collected Works*, vol. 20 (Moscow: Progress Publishers, 1964), p. 396.

[250] *Ibid.*, p. 400, 410. Emphasis in the original.

[251] *Ibid.*, p. 411. Emphasis in the original.

[252] *Ibid.*, pp. 393-454.

[253] *Ibid.*, p. 424.

[254] A search on the phrase *banal'nyi natsionalizm* in *Google Scholar* found no works by Russian scholars on banal nationalism in the USSR. However, they are using this concept to investigate Russian nationalism in the post-Soviet era. See M. Iu. Martynov, L. A. Fadeeva, and A. I. Gaberkorn, 'Patriotizm kak politicheskii diskurs v sovremennoi Rossii', *Polis: Politicheskie issledovaniia* no. 2 (2020), pp. 109-121.

[255] David G. Wagner, 'Flag Usage in the Soviet Union', *The Flag Bulletin* #122, v. 26, no. 5 (October 1987), p. 240.

[256] For a discussion of Red Square as a site of historical memory, see Weber, pp. 43-64.

[257] GUM is an acronym for the full name of the shopping centre in Russian. In the Soviet era the name was *Gosudarstvennyi universal'nyi magazin*, meaning 'State Department Store'. In today's Russia the 'G' stands for *Glavnyi*, meaning 'Main'.

[258] Vladimir Chernov, *Moscow: A Short Guide* (Moscow: Progress Publishers, 1979), pp. 13-66; 'Kremlin Stars', in *GSE*, vol. 13, p. 499; Topolin, *Kremlevskie zvezdy*.

259 'Sovetskie prazdniki' in Nataliia B. Lebina, *Entsiklopediia banal'nostei: Sovetskaiia povsednevnost'–kontury, simvoly, znaki* (Saint Petersburg: Dmitrii Bulanin, 2008), pp. 330-32.

260 Whitney Smith, *Flags Through the Ages and Across the World*, p. 7.

261 Billig, *Banal Nationalism*, p. 40.

262 Sergei Kruk, 'Semiotics of Visual Iconicity in Leninist "Monumental" Propaganda', *Visual Communication* 7, no. 1 (February 2008), p. 35.

263 Michael Ignatieff, 'Soviet War Memorials', *History Workshop Journal* 17, no. 1 (Spring 1984), pp. 157-63. For an in-depth analysis of a Soviet war memorial as part of an 'officially sanctioned cult dedicated to the Great Patriotic War', see Scott W. Palmer, 'How Memory Was Made: The Construction of the Memorial to the Heroes of the Battle of Stalingrad', *The Russian Review* 68, no. 3 (July 2009), pp. 373-407.

264 *Leniniana* is the term Bonnell used to describe imagery and items related to the life of Lenin. In the Soviet Union, such items would have been found in both public and personal spaces. Victoria E. Bonnell, *Iconography of Power: Soviet Political Posters Under Lenin and Stalin* (Berkeley: University of California Press, 1997), pp. 153-155.

265 Victoria E. Bonnell, 'The Leader's Two Bodies: A Study in the Iconography of the "Vozhd"', *Russian History* 23, no. 1-4 (Spring-Winter 1996), pp. 116-7. Translation in parentheses is from the original, those in square brackets have been added by the author; Bonnell, *Iconography of Power*, pp. 139-155.

266 *Ibid.*, pp. 113-124; Bonnell, *Iconography of Power*, pp. 139-155; Alan Cienki and Cornelia Müller, 'Metaphor, Gesture, and Thought', in *The Cambridge Handbook of Metaphor and Thought*, ed. Raymond W. Gibbs, Jr. (Cambridge: Cambridge University Press, 2008), pp. 483-501.

267 'Socialist Realism', in *GSE*, vol. 5, pp. 244-6.

268 Vera Ignatevna Mukhina, *A Sculptor's Thoughts* (Moscow: Foreign Languages Publishing House, 1952), pp. 34-44. For more on socialist realist art at the Paris exhibition, see Sarah Wilson, 'The Soviet Pavilion in Paris', in *Art of the Soviets: Painting, Sculpture, and Architecture in a One-Party State, 1917-1992*, ed. Matthew Cullerne Bown and Brandon Taylor (Manchester: Manchester University Press, 1993), pp. 106-20.

269 'World's Fairs', in *GSE*, vol. 5, pp. 731-2; Mukhina, pp. 34-44; Bonnell, *Iconography of Power*, pp. 42-43.

270 Olga Kostina, 'The Moscow Metro: "Ode to Joy"', trans. Albina Ozieva and Jeremy Howard, *Art in Translation* 8, no. 2 (April 2016), pp. 242-58, quote from p. 244; Andrew Jenks, 'A Metro on the Mount: The Underground as a Church of Soviet Civilization', *Technology and Culture* 41, no. 4 (October 2000), pp. 697-724; V. M. Pavlov, et al., *Moskovskoe metro = Moscow Metro: [fotoal'bom]*, 2nd ed. (Moscow: Moskovskii rabochii, 1980). The articles by Kostina and Jenks offer excellent discussions of the themes and architypes portrayed in the artwork of the Moscow Metro, while the book by Pavlov, et al. is a photo album of the Metro system.

271 Billig, *Banal Nationalism*, pp. 41-42.

272 Eric Helleiner, 'National Currencies and National Identities', *American Behavioral Scientist* 41, no. 10 (August 1998), pp. 1412-13.

273 Josh Lauer, 'Money as Mass Communication: U.S. Paper Currency and the Iconography of Nationalism', *The Communication Review* 11, no. 2 (May 2008), p. 127. For a discussion of the relationship between national iconography on currency and the representation of the state's authority, see Georgios Papadopoulos, 'Currency and the Collective Representations of Authority, Nationality, and Value', *Journal of Cultural Economy* 8, no. 4 (2015), pp. 521-34. See also, Ellen R. Feingold, 'The Messages of Money', *Financial History*, no. 116 (Winter 2016), p. 20.

274 Feingold, p. 20; 'Coins from the Empire of Russia', *Numista*, accessed 16 February 2019, https://en.numista.com/catalogue/russia-empire-1.html; 'Coins from Soviet Union (USSR)', *Numista*, accessed 16 February 2019, https://en.numista.com/catalogue/ancienne_urss-1.html; Chester L. Krause, Clifford Mishler, and Colin R. Bruce, *Collecting World Coins: A Century of Circulating Issues, 1901-Present* (Iola, WI: Krause Publications, 2001), pp. 574-576. See also the historical survey of the use of national symbols on currency in Lauer.

275 *Ibid.*; 'List of Commemorative Coins of the Soviet Union', *Wikipedia*, accessed 18 February 2019, https://en.wikipedia.org/wiki/List_of_commemorative_coins_of_the_Soviet_Union.

[276] V. B. Zagorskii, *Bumazhnye denezhnye znaki Rossii: Gosudarstvennye vypuski s 1769 goda: Katalog = Paper Money of Russia: State Issues From 1769: Catalogue* (Saint Petersburg: Standart-Kollektsiia, 2010).

[277] Mark Sebba, 'The Visual Construction of Language Hierarchy: The Case of Banknotes, Coins and Stamps', *Journal of Language and Politics* 12, no. 1 (January 2013), pp. 109-112.

[278] Bonnell, *Iconography of Power*; Anita Pisch, *The Personality Cult of Stalin in Soviet Posters, 1929-1953: Archetypes, Inventions & Fabrications* (Acton, ACT: Australian National University Press, 2016); Stephen White, *The Bolshevik Poster* (New Haven: Yale University Press, 1988); Nina I. Baburina, *The Soviet Political Poster: 1917-1980: From the USSR Lenin Library Collection*, trans. Boris Rubalsky (London: Penguin Books, 1988); Victor Litvinov and Alexander Yegorov, *The Posters of Glasnost and Perestroika*, trans. John Crowfoot (London: Penguin Books, 1989). See also Gary Yanker, 'The Political Poster: A Worldwide Phenomenon', *World Affairs* 133, no. 3 (December 1970), pp. 215-23; and *'Toward the Bright Future of Communism': Soviet Propaganda Posters from Brezhnev to Gorbachev* [Exhibit Guide] ([Clinton, NY]: Emerson Gallery, Hamilton College, 1995).

[279] For discussions of the colour red in Russian Orthodoxy and Soviet posters, see Bonnell, p. 32; Abel, 'pp. 152-3; G. Calhoun, pp. 30-31, 48, 79-83, 102.

[280] G. Calhoun, pp. 15-16, 67-77, 77-95.

[281] Posters are reproduced from Baburina: Viktor Ivanov, 'Lenin lived, Lenin lives, Lenin will live forever' (Moscow: Sovietsky Khudozhnik, 1967), poster 149 in Baburina; Iuri Tupitsyn, 'Fulfil the 10th Five-year plan with shock work' (Moscow: Plakat, 1976), poster 157 in Baburina; Reino Yussikainen, 'The Union of the Republics is invincible', (Moscow: Izobrazitelnoye Iskusstvo, 1972), poster 152 in Baburina. Information about the posters is from pp. 196-9.

[282] Donald M. Reid, 'The Symbolism of Postage Stamps: A Source for the Historian', *Journal of Contemporary History* 19, no. 2 (April 1984), pp. 223-49; Stanley D. Brunn, 'Stamps as Iconography: Celebrating the Independence of New European and Central Asian States', *GeoJournal* 52, no. 4 (December 2000), pp. 315-23.

[283] Reid, p. 224.

[284] *Ibid.*, p. 225.

[285] *Ibid.*, p. 226. Emphasis in the original.

[286] *Ibid.*, pp. 224-226, 246. Emphasis in the original.

[287] Jonathan Grant, 'The Socialist Construction of Philately in the Early Soviet Era', *Comparative Studies in Society and History* 37, no. 3 (July 1995), p. 484.

[288] Rowley has used the gender neutral 'New Soviet Person' when most sources use 'New Soviet Man'. Alison Rowley, 'Miniature Propaganda: Self-Definition and Soviet Postage Stamps, 1917-41', *Slavonica* 8, no. 2 (November 2002), pp. 140.

[289] Rowley, pp. 135-57; Stanley D. Brunn, 'Stamps as Messengers of Political Transition', *Geographical Review* 101, no. 1 (January 2011), pp. 19-36. Other sources that are useful for the study of symbols and postage stamps include Henio Hoyo, 'Posting Nationalism: Postage Stamps as Carriers of Nationalist Messages', in *Beyond Imagined Uniqueness: Nationalisms in Contemporary Perspectives*, ed. Joan Burbick and William Glass (Cambridge: Cambridge Scholars Publishing, 2010), pp. 67-92; Alexander Kolchinsky, 'Stalin on Stamps: Design, Propaganda, and Politics', in *The Winton M. Blount Postal History Symposia: Select Papers, 2010-2011*, ed. Thomas Lera, vol. 56, Smithsonian Contributions to History and Technology (Washington, DC: Smithsonian Institution Scholarly Press, 2012), pp. 45-67; Vida Zei, 'Stamps and the Politics of National Representation', *Javnost-The Public* 4, no. 1 (1997), pp. 65-84; Brunn, 'Stamps as Iconography', pp. 315-23; 'The Philatelist's Corner: New Money, New Stamps', *The Current Digest of the Soviet Press* 12, no. 49 (4 January 1961), pp. 26-27, translation of an article from *Sovetskaia kultura* (8 December 1961), p. 4; Sebba, pp. 109-112.

[290] V. Iu. Solov'ev, *Pochtovye marki Rossii i SSSR (1857-1991 gg.): Spetsializirovannyi katalog-spravochnik* (Moscow: Izdatel'stvo po atomnoi nauke i tekhnike IzdAT, 1998).

143

[291] L. Voronkova, 'From the Courtroom: Businessman in Stamp Collecting', *The Current Digest of the Soviet Press* 14, no. 22 (27 June 1962): p. 24, translation of an article published in *Trud*, 13 May 1962; N. Dolenko, 'On Moral Themes: Downhill', *The Current Digest of the Soviet Press* 15, no. 6 (6 March 1963): pp. 32-33, translation of an article from *Izvestiia*, 6 February 1963; A. Nikitin, 'Spectrum of Avocations', *The Current Digest of the Soviet Press* 23, no. 46 (14 December 1971): pp. 31, 40, translation of an article from *Izvestiia*, 14 November 1971.

[292] Grant, pp. 476-484.

[293] I. I. Likhitskiy, *Art of Russian Metal Miniature: Catalogue of Badges, 1917-1991* (Lvov: Udacha, 1995), p. 5.

[294] *Ibid.*

[295] *Ibid.*, p. 9. Images of over a thousand examples of badges from the first four categories identified by Likhitskiy can be found in V. D. Krivtsov, *Sovetskie znaki i zhetony: Katalog dlia kollektsionerov = Soviet Badges and Jetons: Catalogue for Collectors: Price Guide* (Moscow: Avers, 1996). For a thorough collection of imagery covering the badges of the *Komsomol* and Young Pioneer organisations, see I. A. Zhukov, Iu. V. Pogodaev, and A. I. Cherepov, *Znaki i znachki Komsomola: Ocnovnye znaki Komsomola (KIM, RLKSM, RKSM i VLKSM): (1920-1991 gg.)* (Moscow: Izdatel'stvo 'Lukomor'e', 2014).

[296] Jessie L. Miller and James G. Miller, 'Behavioral Scientists Visit the Soviet Union', *Behavioral Science* 7, no. 3 (July 1962), p. 353; Hedrick Smith, 'Pin Hobby, Soviet Fad, Is Criticized', *New York Times*, 22 September 1974, p. 6.

[297] Matteo Bertelé, 'The Soviet Picture Postcard as a Transmedial Object of Mass Culture and Ideological Practice', in *Ästhetiken des Sozialismus: Populäre Bildmedien im späten Sozialismus / Socialist Aesthetics: Visual Cultures of Late Socialism*, ed. Alexandra Köhring and Monica Rüthers (Köln: Böhlau Verlag, 2018), pp. 38-60; quotes from p. 45 and p. 59.

[298] A. L. Rubinchik, *Zhivopis' sotsrealizma v sovetskikh otkrytkakh / Socialist Realism Paintings in Soviet Postcards*, trans. A. B. Klionsky (Moscow Izdatel'stvo OOO 'Magma', 2008), p. 8.

[299] This is like Americans celebrating 'the 4th of July', without referring to the holiday by its official name – Independence Day.

[300] E. G. Imanakova, 'Simvoly 9 Maia v Sovetskoi filokartii: Kul'turologicheskii aspekt', in *70-letie Velikoi Pobedy: Istoricheskii opyt i problemy sovremennosti. Sbornik nauchnykh statei*, ed. A. V. Speranskii, Chast' 2 (Ekaterinburg: Institut istorii i arkheologii UrO RAN, 2015), pp. 30-37; Gerhart, pp. 104-110. For more information on Soviet holidays, see Bokan', Zaikin, and Sinitsyn, *Nashi prazdniki*.

[301] Bokan', Zaikin, and Sinitsyn, *Nashi prazdniki*, pp. 21-26; Gerhart, pp. 108-109.

[302] 'Union of Soviet Socialist Republics', in *GSE*, vol. 31, p. 12.

[303] Karen Petrone, *Life Has Become More Joyous, Comrades: Celebrations in the Time of Stalin*, (Bloomington: Indiana University Press, 2000), pp. 85-109; Alla Salnikova, 'Not Yuletide? Fir Tree Ornaments as an Integral Part of Soviet Socialization Practices (1920s-1960s)', *History of Education & Children's Literature* 5, no. 1 (2010), pp. 355-74; Elena Vladimirovna Dushechkina, *Russkaia Elka: Istoriia, mifologiia, literatura* (Saint Petersburg: Norint, 2002); Gerhart, pp. 104-107; Bokan', Zaikin, and Sinitsyn, *Nashi Prazdniki*, pp. 147-152.

[304] Pavel Postyshev, 'Davaite organizuem k novomu godu detiam khoroshuiu elku', *Pravda*, 28 December 1935, p. 3.

[305] Petrone, pp. 85-100.

[306] Salnikova, p. 366.

[307] *Ibid.*, p. 371.

[308] *Ibid.*, pp. 367-374.

[309] Michael Billig, 'Banal Nationalism and the Imagining of Politics', in Skey and Antonsich, p. 309. Billig is referencing nationalism scholar Craig Calhoun, the author of another chapter in Skey and Antonsich's anthology. See Craig Calhoun, 'The Rhetoric of Nationalism', in Skey and Antonsich, pp. 17-30.

[310] Billig, *Banal Nationalism*, p. 7.

[311] *Ibid.*, p. 175.

Chapter 5. Symbolic Afterlife: Legacies of Soviet Civil Religion

[312] Marx and Engels, *Manifesto of the Communist Party*, p. 1.

[313] With independence, the preferred name of what was Soviet Moldavia is now Moldova. The standard English names of multiple territories changed when the Soviet Union broke up. While in previous chapters the English versions of the Soviet names were used, this chapter will use the English versions of the post-Soviet names unless specifically referring to the territory during the Soviet era.

[314] For a discussion of ethnic migration resulting from the breakup of the Soviet Union, see Timothy Heleniak, 'The End of an Empire: Migration and the Changing Nationality Composition of the Soviet Successor States', in *Diasporas and Ethnic Migrants: German, Israel, and Post-Soviet Successor States in Comparative Perspective*, ed. Rainer Münz and Rainer Ohliger (London: Frank Cass, 2003), pp. 115-40.

[315] For further discussion of commemorative place names, see Maoz Azaryahu, 'The Power of Commemorative Street Names', *Environment and Planning D: Society and Space* 14, no. 3 (June 1996): pp. 311-30.

[316] For analyses of Soviet place names and the transitions after the breakup of the USSR, see Graeme J. Gill, 'Changing Symbols: The Renovation of Moscow Place Names', *The Russian Review* 64, no. 3 (July 2005): pp. 480-503; John Murray, *Politics and Place-Names: Changing Names in the Late Soviet Period*, Birmingham Slavonic Monographs, No. 32 (Birmingham: Dept. of Russian, University of Birmingham, 2000); Arseny Saparov, 'The Alteration of Place Names and Construction of National Identity in Soviet Armenia', *Cahiers du monde russe* 44, no. 1 (January-March 2003): pp. 179-98; Charles B. Peterson, 'The Nature of Soviet Place-Names', *Names: A Journal of Onomastics* 25, no. 1 (March 1977): pp. 15-24.

[317] For more on the historic flags of the Caucasus, see Walter Trembicky, *Flags of Non-Russian Peoples Under Soviet Rule,* published as *The Flag Bulletin* 8 #3 (Lexington, Mass.: Flag Research Center, 1969), pp. 82-87, 98-102. For a comparative discussion of how Soviet heritage is viewed in the independent countries of the Caucasus, see A. A. Tokarev, 'Otritsanie, vstraivanie, postepennoe zabvenie: Gosudarstvennye strategii po otnosheniiu k sovetskomu naslediiu v Gruzii, Armenii i Azerbaidzhane', *Vestnik. MGIMO-Universiteta* 5, no. 56 (September 2017): pp. 60-80.

[318] For more on how Armenian identity is linked to memorialisation of the genocide, see Zigmas Vitkus, 'The Armenian Genocide - Not Forgotten', *Armenpress News Agency (Yerevan, Armenia)*, 9 May 2020, *Access World News* database. For a discussion of the conflict over Nagorno-Karabakh, the Armenian diaspora, and the early years of Armenian independence, see Ronald Grigor Suny, *Looking Toward Ararat: Armenia in Modern History* (Bloomington: Indiana University Press, 1993), pp. 192-246. Analysis of symbols in modern Armenia can be found in Diana K. Ter-Ghazaryan, '"Civilizing the City Center": Symbolic Spaces and Narratives of the Nation in Yerevan's Post-Soviet Landscape', *Nationalities Papers* 41, no. 4 (July 2013): pp. 570-89; Diana Ter-Ghazaryan, 'Re-Imagining Yerevan in the Post-Soviet Era: Urban Symbolism and Narratives of the Nation in the Landscape of Armenia's Capital' (unpublished PhD thesis, Florida International University, 2010).

[319] Sabuhi Ahmadov, 'National Flag of the Republic of Azerbaijan', *IRS Heritage*, no. 33-34 (Spring 2018): pp. 76-83; Tokarev, pp. 60-80; Ceylan Tokluoglu, 'Definitions of National Identity, Nationalism and Ethnicity in Post-Soviet Azerbaijan in the 1990s', *Ethnic and Racial Studies* 28, no. 4 (July 2005): pp. 722-58.

[320] Tokarev, pp. 60-80.

[321] Sergei Matjunin, 'The New State Flags as the Iconographic Symbols of the Post-Soviet Space', *GeoJournal* 52, no. 4 (December 2000): pp. 311-13. For further analysis of how Soviet symbols are perceived in the Central Asian countries, see Ayşegül Aydıngün, 'State Symbols and National Identity Construction in Kazakhstan', in *The Past as Resource in the Turkic Speaking World*, ed. Ildikó Bellér-Hann (Würzburg: Ergon, 2008), pp. 139-58; Sally N. Cummings, 'Inscapes, Landscapes and Greyscapes: The Politics of Signification in Central Asia', *Europe-Asia Studies* 61, no. 7 (September 2009): pp. 1083-93; Sally N. Cummings, 'Leaving Lenin: Elites, Official Ideology and Monuments in the Kyrgyz Republic', *Nationalities Papers* 41, no. 4 (July 2013): pp. 606-21; William O. Beeman, 'The Struggle for Identity in Post-Soviet Tajikistan', *MERIA: Middle East Review of International Affairs* 3, no. 4 (December 1999): pp. 100-105; Michael Denison, 'The Art of the Impossible: Political Symbolism, and the Creation

of National Identity and Collective Memory in Post-Soviet Turkmenistan', *Europe-Asia Studies* 61, no. 7 (September 2009): pp. 1167-87; James Bell, 'Redefining National Identity in Uzbekistan: Symbolic Tensions in Tashkent's Official Public Landscape', *Ecumene* 6, no. 2 (April 1999): pp. 183-213.

[322] Matjunin, p. 311. For more on the historic flags of the Baltic nations, see Trembicky, pp. 96-98, 102-110.

[323] For an analysis of living memory and nationalism in the Baltic republics, and the role it played in the breakup of the Soviet Union, see Mark A. Jubulis, 'The Persistence of the Baltic Nations Under Soviet Rule: An Ethno-Symbolist Critique of Modernist Perspectives on the Breakup of the USSR', in *Nationalism in a Global Era: The Persistence of Nations*, ed. Mitchell Young, Eric G. E. Zuelow, and Andreas Sturm (London: Routledge, 2007), pp. 161-77. A discussion of identity in post-Soviet Estonia can be found in Triin Vihalemm and Anu Masso, '(Re)Construction of Collective Identities after the Dissolution of the Soviet Union: The Case of Estonia', *Nationalities Papers* 35, no. 1 (March 2007): pp. 71-91.

[324] Images found in the *Associated Press Images Collection*, database access via Ebsco subscription services, accessed 25 July 2020 [subscription required]; and through general web searching. For examples, see: https://commons.wikimedia.org/wiki/File:Baltic_Way_in_Moteris_magazine.jpeg, https://commons.wikimedia.org/wiki/File:Balti_kett_22.jpg, https://commons.wikimedia.org/wiki/File:Baltic_Way_in_Latvia_near_Krekava.jpeg, and https://commons.wikimedia.org/wiki/File:1989_08_23_Baltijoskelias14.jpg.

[325] For more discussion on identity politics in the Baltic republics, see Ralph Tuchtenhagen, 'The Problem of Identities in the Baltic Countries', in *The Fall of an Empire, the Birth of a Nation: National Identities in Russia*, ed. Chris J. Chulos and Timo Piirainen (Aldershot, England: Ashgate, 2000), pp. 141-60.

[326] Further analysis can be found in Priit Järve, 'Two Waves of Language Laws in the Baltic States: Changes of Rationale?', *Journal of Baltic Studies* 33, no. 1 (Spring 2002): 78-110; Rogers Brubaker, 'Nationalizing States Revisited: Projects and Processes of Nationalization in Post-Soviet States', *Ethnic and Racial Studies* 34, no. 11 (November 2011): pp. 1785-1814; and David D. Laitin, 'Identity in Formation: The Russian-Speaking Nationality in the Post-Soviet Diaspora', *European Journal of Sociology / Archives Européennes de Sociologie / Europäisches Archiv Für Soziologie* 36, no. 2 (1995): pp. 281-316. For an explanation of the citizenship law and the status of ethnic minorities from the perspective of the Latvian government, see Embassy of Latvia in Georgia, 'Basic Facts About Latvia', 19 May 2020, https://www.mfa.gov.lv/en/georgia/basic-facts-about-latvia, accessed 1 August 2020.

[327] For more discussion of the Russian diaspora, see Heleniak, pp. 115-40; Wim van Meurs, 'Social Citizenship and Non-Migration: The Immobility of the Russian Diaspora in the Baltics', in *Diasporas and Ethnic Migrants: German, Israel, and Post-Soviet Successor States in Comparative Perspective*, ed. Rainer Münz and Rainer Ohliger (London: Frank Cass, 2003), pp. 174-90.

[328] 'Latvia to Toughen Ban on Use of Soviet Symbols', *Baltic News Service*, 4 April 4, 2013; 'Latvian Parlt to Toughen Ban on Use of Soviet Symbols Ahead of May 9', *Baltic News Service*, 11 April 2013; 'Latvia Bans Soviet and Nazi German Uniforms at Public Events', *Baltic News Service*, 23 April 2020; Liudas Dapkus, 'Lithuanian Parliament Passes Law Banning Symbols from Soviet, Nazi Regimes', *Associated Press International*, 18 June 2008; 'Ban on Soviet-Era Emblems May Spoil Moscow-Vilnius Relations', *ITAR-TASS News Agency*, 18 June 2008. All articles found in the *Nexis Uni* subscription database.

[329] Charles King, 'Moldovan Identity and the Politics of Pan-Romanianism', *Slavic Review* 53, no. 2 (Summer 1994): pp. 345-49.

[330] *Ibid.*, pp. 349-58.

[331] *Ibid.*, pp. 358-63.

[332] Monica Heintz, 'Republic of Moldova Versus Romania: The Cold War of National Identities', *Journal of Political Science and International Relations* 2, no. 1 (2005): pp. 71-81.

[333] Pål Kolstø and Andrei Malgin, 'The Transnistrian Republic: A Case of Politicized Regionalism', *Nationalities Papers* 26, no. 1 (March 1998): pp. 103-27; Rebecca Chamberlain-Creangă, 'The "Transnistrian People": Citizenship and Imaginings of "The State" in an Unrecognized Country', *Ab Imperio*, no. 4 (2006): pp. 371-99; Natalia Cojocaru, 'Nationalism and Identity in Transnistria', *Innovation: The European Journal of Social Science Research* 19, no. 3-4

146

(September 2006): pp. 261-72; Stefan Troebst, '"We Are Transnistrians!" Post-Soviet Identity Management in the Dniester Valley', *Ab Imperio*, no. 1 (2003): pp. 437-66; Ala Şveţ, 'Staging the Transnistrian Identity Within the Heritage of Soviet Holidays', *History and Anthropology* 24, no. 1 (March 2013): pp. 98-116.

[334] 'Moldova Condemns Soviet Hammer and Sickle Symbol', *RusData Dialine - Russian Press Digest*, 26 May 2010, in *Nexis Uni* database; The Canadian Press, 'Moldovan Parliament Outlaws Communist Hammer, Sickle to Honour Thousands Killed Under Soviets', 13 July 2012, in *Nexis Uni* database; 'Ban on Communist Symbols in Moldova is Mockery - Russian Foreign Ministry', *Russia & CIS Diplomatic Panorama, Interfax News Agency*, 30 July 2012, in *Nexis Uni* database; 'Moldovan Constitutional Court Finds Ban on Soviet Symbols Unconstitutional', *Russia & CIS General Newswire, Interfax News Agency*, 4 June 2013, in *Nexis Uni* database; 'Moldova's Dodon Explains Soviet Symbols "Blunder"', *BBC Worldwide Monitoring*, 26 June 2020, in *Nexis Uni* database.

[335] For more information on the historic flags of Georgia, see Trembicky, pp. 98-102.

[336] Thea Morrison, 'The Banning of Soviet Symbols in Georgia', *Georgia Today*, 10 May 2018, http://georgiatoday.ge/news/10215/The-Banning-of-Soviet-Symbols-in-Georgia; Giorgi Kldiashvili, 'Lustration', in *Memory of Nations: Democratic Transition Guide [The Georgian Experience]* ([Washington, DC]: National Endowment for Democracy, 2018), pp. 19-27.

[337] Peter Kabachnik, 'The Power of Place, or Powerless Places? Hybrid Attitudes Towards Soviet Symbols in Post-Soviet Georgia', *Central Asian Survey* 37, no. 2 (June 2018): pp. 265-85. See also Kabachnik's other works on attitudes about Stalin in Georgia: Alexi Gugushvili and Peter Kabachnik, 'Stalin Is Dead, Long Live Stalin? Testing Socialization, Structural, Ideological, Nationalist, and Gender Hypotheses', *Post-Soviet Affairs* 31, no. 1 (2014): pp. 1-36; Alexi Gugushvili and Peter Kabachnik, 'Stalin on Their Minds: A Comparative Analysis of Public Perceptions of the Soviet Dictator in Russia and Georgia', *International Journal of Sociology* 49, no. 5-6 (September 2019): pp. 317-41; Peter Kabachnik, Ana Kirvalidze, and Alexi Gugushvili, *Stalin Today: Contending with the Soviet Past in Georgia* (Tbilisi: Ilia State University, 2016).

[338] For more information on the historic flags of Ukraine, see Trembicky, pp. 126-136.

[339] This figure is according to the most-recent census conducted in Ukraine, which was held in 2001. State Statistics Committee of Ukraine, 'All-Ukrainian Population Census '2001: Linguistic Composition of the Population (English Edition)', accessed 3 September 2020, http://2001.ukrcensus.gov.ua/eng/results/general/language/.

[340] Tatyana Ivzhenko, 'Ukraine Integrity Said Threatened by Authorities' Populism Over Lviv Row', *Nezavisimaya Gazeta* (11 May 2011), *BBC Worldwide Monitoring*, from *LexisNexis Academic* database; 'Victory Day: Soviet Liberators or Occupiers?', *Voice of America* (13 May 2011), http://blogs.voanews.com/russia-watch/2011/05/13/victory-day-soviet-liberators-or-occupiers/, accessed 29 August 2012.

[341] Sasha Senderovich, 'Goodbye, Lenin?', *New York Times Online* (blog), 9 December 2013, *ProQuest New York Times* database; Charlotte Alfred, '*Leninopad*, Ukraine's Falling Lenin Statues, Celebrated As Soviet Symbols Toppled Nationwide', *Huffington Post* (blog), 24 February 2014, https://www.huffpost.com/entry/leninopad-falling-lenins-statues-ukraine_n_4847364; User 'iaruna', 'Good Bye Lenin!: Desovietyzatsiia Ukraïny. Kinets' 2013 - pochatok 2014 rokiv', interactive map, *Carto*, https://iaryna.carto.com/viz/b42d0d78-9b3b-11e3-9701-0ed66c7bc7f3/public_map, image contrast modified by Tom Brittnacher.

[342] Neil MacFarquhar, 'Ukraine Ban on Russian Symbols Fuels Fight Over National Identity', *New York Times Online* (blog), 27 October 2015, *ProQuest New York Times* database.

[343] The Republic of Crimea and City of Sevastopol were formally admitted as Federal Subjects of the Russian Federation on 21 March 2014. While some countries have since recognised Crimea as part of Russia, most United Nations members consider the region as illegally occupied territory.

[344] Nick Shchetko and Laura Mills, 'Ukraine Bans Soviet-Era Symbols', *Wall Street Journal (Online)*, 10 April 2015, *ProQuest Wall Street Journal* database; 'Ukraine "Attempting to Wipe Away Its Past," Russian Commentator Says', *BBC Worldwide Monitoring*, 17 April 2015, *Nexis Uni* database.

[345] Quoted in MacFarquhar, 'Ukraine Ban on Russian Symbols Fuels Fight Over National Identity'.

[346] For an analysis of identity politics in the Lukashenko era, see Vitali Silitski, 'Still Soviet?: Why Dictatorship Persists in Belarus', *Harvard International Review* 28, no. 1 (Spring 2006): pp. 46-53; Natalia Leshchenko, 'A Fine Instrument: Two Nation-Building Strategies in Post-Soviet Belarus', *Nations and Nationalism* 10, no. 3 (2004): pp. 333-52; Per Anders Rudling, 'Belarus in the Lukashenka Era: National Identity and Relations with Russia', in *Europe's Last Frontier? Belarus, Moldova, and Ukraine between Russia and the European Union*, ed. Oliver Schmidtke and Serhy Yekelchyk (New York: Palgrave Macmillan US, 2008), pp. 55-77; Nelly Bekus, 'Ideological Recycling of the Socialist Legacy: Reading Townscapes of Minsk and Astana', *Europe-Asia Studies* 69, no. 5 (May 2017): pp. 794-818; Astrid Sahm, 'Political Culture and National Symbols: Their Impact on the Belarusian Nation-Building Process', *Nationalities Papers* 27, no. 4 (December 1999): pp. 649-60; Natalia Leshchenko, 'The National Ideology and the Basis of the Lukashenka Regime in Belarus', *Europe-Asia Studies* 60, no. 8 (October 2008): pp. 1419-33. An examination of photos from demonstrations which occurred after the election of August 2020 showed protestors using the white/red/white flag as well as that flag emblazoned with the pre-Soviet arms. For more information on the historic flags of Belarus, see Trembicky, pp. 136-138.

[347] A thorough analysis of symbols and change in Russia following the breakup of the Soviet Union can be found in Graeme J. Gill, *Symbolism and Regime Change in Russia* (Cambridge: Cambridge University Press, 2013). The discussion on pp 183-191 addresses how the city of Moscow dealt with Soviet symbols. For examples of textbooks about Russian symbols, see: Evgenii Vladimirovich Pchelov, *Gosudarstvennye simvoly Rossii: Gerb, flag, gimn: Uchebnoe posobie dlia 5-9 klassov*, 2nd ed. (Moscow: Russkoe slovo, 2002) and Boris Nikolaevich Serov, *Pourochnye razrabotki po kursu 'Gosudarstvennaia simvolika': Gimn. Gerb. Flag* (Moscow: BAKO, 2005).

[348] 'Russian Formin Calls Planned Banning of Soviet Symbols in Estonia Amoral', *Baltic News Service*, 1 December 2006; ITAR-TASS, 'Russian Senators Respond to Lithuanian Law Banning Soviet Symbols', 18 June 2008; ITAR-TASS News Agency, 'Ban on Soviet-Era Emblems May Spoil Moscow-Vilnius Relations', 18 June 2008; Interfax News Agency, 'Ban on Communist Symbols in Moldova is Mockery - Russian Foreign Ministry', *Russia & CIS Diplomatic Panorama*, 30 July 2012; Piter Spinella, 'Russia Outraged at Latvian Ban of Soviet Symbols', *RIA Novesti*, 24 June 2013; LETA (Latvia National News Agency), 'Russian State Duma Dissatisfied With Ban on USSR Symbols at Public Events in Latvia', 24 June 2013. All articles from the *Nexis Uni* database.

[349] For a thorough discussion of the Soviet Banner of Victory, see Anne M. Platoff, 'Of Tablecloths and Soviet Relics: A Study of the Banner of Victory (*Znamia Pobedy*)', *Raven: A Journal of Vexillology* 20 (2013): pp. 55-84. A snapshot of the public's reaction to the restoration of the traditional form of the Banner of Victory can be found in 'Pobeda nad znamenem', *Ogonëk*, (7 May 2007), p. 8.

[350] 'Against Interring Lenin's Body', *Current Digest of the Post-Soviet Press* 49, no. 25 (23 July 1997): p. 20, translated from *Nezavisimaia gazeta*, (24 June 1997), p. 2; Chris Bryant, 'Remains of the Deity', *New Statesman* 126, no. 4346 (8 August 1997): p. 17.

[351] See Gill, *Symbolism and Regime Change in Russia*, pp. 134-177.

Chapter 6. Conclusion

[352] Whitney Smith, *Flags Through the Ages and Across the World*, pp. 36.

Appendix

[353] A. I. Denisov and M. G. Kirichenko, *Soviet State Law* (Moscow: Foreign Languages Publishing House, 1960), pp. 183-84.

[354] Whitney Smith, 'Soviet State Symbolism', pp. 21-22; K. Ivanov, 'Soviet Russian Flags', pp. 42-51; Denisov and Kirichenko, *Soviet State Law*, pp.184-87.

[355] Mamaev, *Flagi rasskazyvaiut*, pp. 10-11, 20-21; M. Liashenko, *Tvoe krasnokryloe znamia* (Moscow: Detskaia literatura, 1978), pp. 135-139; Denisov and Kirichenko, *Soviet State Law*, pp. 183-187; *Gosudarstvennye gerby i flagi SSSR, soiuznykh i avtonomnykh respublik* (Moscow: Izvestiia sovetov deputatov trudiashchikhsia SSSR, 1972), pp. 5-12; Kiselev and Speransov, *Emblemy mira i truda*, pp. 55-57.

List of Tables

List of Figures

Figure 2.11. Soviet State Emblem: version 3, 1946-1956 (16 republics). *Source:* Frédéric Michel, artist. *Wikimedia Commons*, https://commons.wikimedia.org/wiki/File:Coat_of_arms_of_the_Soviet_Union_ (1946-1956).svg. Public domain.

Figure 2.12. National Flag of the Soviet Union. *Source:* Various Artists. *Wikimedia Commons*, https://commons.wikimedia.org/wiki/File:Flag_of_the_Soviet_Union.svg. Public domain.

Figure 2.13. National Flag of the Soviet Union. *Source:* 'Ukaz Prezidiuma VS SSSR ot 19.08.1955 ob utverzhdenii Polozheniia o gosudartsvennom flage SSSR', 19 August 1955. Image file from *Vikiteka*, https://ru.wikisource.org/wiki/%D0%A4%D0%B0%D0%B9%D0%BB:Flag_the_USSR_schema_Sbornik_zakonov _1938-1956.svg. Creative Commons License: CC BY-SA 3.0.

Figure 2.14. Postal card: '1 May' (Saviour's Tower and flags). *Source:* V. Chmarov (Leningrad: Ministerstvo sviazi SSSR, 1985).

Figure 2.15. Postal card: 'With the holiday 1 May!' *Source:* A. Boikov (Leningrad: Ministerstvo sviazi SSSR, 1975).

Figure 2.16. Postal card: 'Peace. Labour. May' *Source:* V. Bochkarev (Leningrad: Ministerstvo sviazi SSSR, 1978).

Figure 2.17. Postal card: 'With the holiday 1 May!' *Source:* E. Kvavadze (Leningrad: Ministerstvo sviazi SSSR, 1983).

Chapter 3. Little Leninists: Symbols and the Political Socialisation of Soviet Children

Figure 3.1. Young Pioneers escort Little Octobrists. *Source:* N. Panova, *Oktiabriata* (Moscow: Molodaia gvardiia, 1959), p. 55.

Figure 3.2. Image of Red Square showing pilgrims waiting in the queue to pay their respects to Lenin. *Source:* Vseslav Gavrilovich Goretskii, Viktor Andreevich Kiriushkin, and Anatolii Filippovich Shanko, *Azbuka* (Moscow: Prosveshchenie, 1991), p. 4-5.

Figure 3.3. Explanation of the red banner from a Soviet alphabet book. *Source:* Vseslav Gavrilovich Goretskii, Viktor Andreevich Kiriushkin, and Anatolii Filippovich Shanko, *Azbuka* (Moscow: Prosveshchenie, 1990), p. 100.

Figure 3.4. Children marching with flags. *Source:* Vseslav Gavrilovich Goretskii, Viktor Andreevich Kiriushkin, and Anatolii Filippovich Shanko, *Azbuka* (Moscow: Prosveshchenie, 1990), p. 171.

Figure 3.5. Children celebrating the 'unbreakable union of free republics'. *Source:* Vseslav Gavrilovich Goretskii, Viktor Andreevich Kiriushkin, and Anatolii Filippovich Shanko, *Azbuka* (Moscow: Prosveshchenie, 1990), pp. 190-191.

Figure 3.6. Little Octobrist badge (late 1950s). *Source:* Collection of the author.

Figure 3.7. Little Octobrist badge (date unknown). *Source:* Collection of the author.

Figure 3.8. Little Octobrist badge (date unknown). *Source:* Collection of the author.

Figure 3.9. Little Octobrist flag (1986). *Source:* Collection of the author.

Figure 3.10. Young Pioneer badge, red banner design (1923-1927). *Source:* S. Furin, *The World of the Young Pioneers* (Moscow: Progress Publishers, 1982), p. 176.

Figure 3.11. Young Pioneer badge, tie-clip design (1929-ca. 1942). *Source:* S. Furin, *The World of the Young Pioneers* (Moscow: Progress Publishers, 1982), p. 176.

Figure 3.12. Young Pioneer badge, World War II red star design (ca. 1942-ca. 1946). *Source:* S. Furin, *The World of the Young Pioneers* (Moscow: Progress Publishers, 1982), p. 176.

Figure 3.13. Young Pioneer badge, hammer and sickle design (ca. 1946-1962). *Source:* Collection of the author.

Figure 3.14. Young Pioneer badge, Lenin design (1962-1991). *Source:* Collection of the author.

Figure 3.15. Banner of a Young Pioneer group (1962-1991). *Source:* Collection of the author.

Figure 3.16. Flag of a Young Pioneer detachment (1962-1991). *Source:* Collection of the author.

Figure 3.17. Reverse side of a Pioneer banner showing the honorary name of the detachment. *Source:* Vasilii Golyshkin and V. A. Taborko, *Kniga vozhatogo* (Moscow: Molodaia Gvardiia, 1965), facing page 64, modified by the author.

Figure 3.18. Induction ceremony for the Young Pioneers, School No. 54, Moskvoretskii District, Moscow (1 January 1984). *Source:* Viacheskav Runov, photographer. *RIA Novosti Archive*, image #761255, https://commons.wikimedia.org/wiki/File:RIAN_archive_761255_Pavilion-museum_Vladimir_Lenin%27s_Funeral_Train.jpg. Creative Commons License CC-BY-SA 3.0.

Figure 3.19. Postcard for May Day (2 Little Octobrists). *Source:* V. I. Zarubin and S. K. Rusakov, artists (Moscow: Ministerstvo sviazi SSSR, 1964). Collection of the author.

Figure 3.20. Postcard for May Day (4 Little Octobrists). *Source:* E. Ioffe, artist (Moscow: Sovetskii khudozhnik, 1968). Collection of the author.

Figure 3.21. Postcard for May Day (Young Pioneers). *Source:* A. A. Gorpenko, artist. Moscow: Ministerstvo sviazi SSSR, 1958. Collection of the author.

Figure 3.22. Holiday postcard (Red Square demonstration). *Source:* A. Kalashnikov, artist. Moscow: Ministerstvo sviazi SSSR, 1968. Collection of the author.

Figures 3.23-3.38. Little holiday flags. *Source:* Collection of the author.

Figure 3.39. Standard-bearers: *Smirno*! Translates as 'Quietly' (Attention). *Source:* A. A. Derkach, G. Chubarova, and L. Iashunina, *Kniga vozhatogo* (Moscow: Molodaia gvardiia, 1982), plate [11] following 64.

Figure 3.40. Standard-bearers: *Ravniais'*! Translates as 'Equal' (Present colours). *Source:* A. A. Derkach, G. Chubarova, and L. Iashunina, *Kniga vozhatogo* (Moscow: Molodaia gvardiia, 1982), plate [11] following 64.

Figure 3.41. Standard-bearers: *Vol'no*! Translates as 'Freely' (At ease). *Source:* A. A. Derkach, G. Chubarova, and L. Iashunina, *Kniga vozhatogo* (Moscow: Molodaia gvardiia, 1982), plate [11] following 64.

Figure 3.42. Young Pioneers in front of the Lenin Mausoleum. *Source:* Lev Polikashin, photographer. *RIA Novosti Archive*, image #640497, *Wikimedia Commons*, https://commons.wikimedia.org/wiki/File: RIAN_archive_640497_Young_Pioneers_at_Vladimir_Lenin%27s_Mausoleum.jpg. Creative Commons License CC-BY-SA 3.0.

Chapter 4. Banal Nationalism in the USSR: State Symbols in the Daily Lives of Soviet Citizens

Figures 4.1-4.2. Photo of the author and her companion on *Nevskii Prospekt* in Leningrad (December 1982). *Source:* Michael Platoff, personal collection.

Figure 4.3. Union flag display on Palace Square in front of the Winter Palace (Leningrad, December 1982). *Source:* Photo by the author, personal collection.

Figure 4.4. Diagram of Red Square from a Soviet-era guidebook of Moscow. *Source:* Vladimir Chernov, *Moscow: A Short Guide* (Moscow: Progress Publishers, 1979), pp. 36-37.

Figure 4.5. Photo of a red-glass star atop a tower of the Moscow Kremlin. *Source:* 'Kheres' and Fedor Gusliarov, photographers. *Wikimedia Commons*, https://commons.wikimedia.org/wiki/File:Kremlin_Star.jpg. Public domain.

Figure 4.6. View of Red Square during the celebration of the anniversary of the Great October Revolution (1981). *Source:* Still image from video found on *Wikipedia*, https://en.wikipedia.org/wiki/File:USSR_Anthem,_Revolution_Day_1981_%D0%93%D0%B8%D0%BC%D0%BD_%D0%A1%D0%A1%D0%A1%D0%A0.webm. URL no longer valid.

Figure 4.7. Lenin statue at the Finland Station in Saint Petersburg (18 June 2017). *Source:* Joao Paulo V Tinoco, photographer. *Shutterstock*, image #781305463, https://www.shutterstock.com/image-photo/saint-petersburg-russia-june-18-2017-781305463.

Figure 4.8. Portrait of Lenin surrounded by pictures of Soviet children on the Palace of the Pioneers in Leningrad (December 1982). *Source:* Photo by the author.

Figure 4.9. Building plaque reading 'V. I. Lenin was a regular reader of the Public Library in the years 1893-1895' (Saint Petersburg, July 2007). *Source:* Photo by the author.

Figure 4.10. Vera Mukhina, sculptor, 'The Worker and the *Kolkhoz* Woman'. *Source:* Vladimir Zhupanenko, photographer (1 August 2018). *Shutterstock*, image #1153708588, https://www.shutterstock.com/image-photo/ moscow-russia-august-01-2018-view-1153708588.

Figure 4.11. Mosfilm, studio logo, 1947-2005. *Source: Wikimedia Commons*, https://en.wikipedia.org/wiki/ File:Mosfilm_logo_old.jpg. Trademark Mosfil'm.

Figure 4.12. Chandelier at the *Kurskaia* station of the Moscow Metro (25 May 2018). *Source:* Wasilisa, photographer. *Shutterstock*, image #1098916190, https://www.shutterstock.com/image-photo/russia-moscow-may-25-2018-chandelier-1098916190.

Figure 4.13. Red star under the dome of a vestibule in the *Arbatskaia* metro station, Moscow (n.d.). *Source:* Arthur Lookyanov, photographer. *Shutterstock*, image #376408666, https://www.shutterstock.com/image-photo/ red-soviet-star-under-dome-ground-376408666.

Figure 4.14. Detail from the *Komsomolskaia* station of the Moscow Metro (6 July 2012). *Source:* Sirio Carnevalino, photographer. *Shutterstock*, image #1086751901, https://www.shutterstock.com/image-photo/ moscow-russia-6th-july-2012-local-1086751901.

Figure 4.15. Decorative element from the *Prospekt Mira* metro station, Moscow (30 December 2018). *Source:* Loretta Damska, photographer. *Shutterstock*, image #1349033183, https://www.shutterstock.com/image-photo/ moscow-russiadecember-30-2018moscow-metroprospekt-mira-1349033183.

Figures 4.16-4.17. One-ruble coin issued by the Russian Soviet Federative Socialist Republic (1922). *Source: Wikimedia Commons*, https://commons.wikimedia.org/wiki/File:1_rouble_of_1922.jpg. Public Domain.

Figures 4.18-4.19. One-ruble coin (1964). *Source: Wikimedia Commons*, https://commons.wikimedia.org/ wiki/File:USSR_One_Ruble_Coin_1961-67_Style.jpg. Public Domain.

Figure 4.20. Fifteen-kopek commemorative coin, obverse (1967). *Source: Wikimedia Commons*, https://commons.wikimedia.org/wiki/File:USSR-1967-15copecks-CuNi-SovietPower50-a.jpg. Public Domain.

Figure 4.21. Fifteen-kopek commemorative coin, reverse (1967). *Source: Wikimedia Commons*, https://commons.wikimedia.org/wiki/File:USSR-1967-15copecks-CuNi-SovietPower50-b.jpg. Public Domain.

Figure 4.22. Fifty-kopek commemorative coin, obverse (1967). *Source: Wikimedia Commons*, https://commons.wikimedia.org/wiki/File:USSR-1967-50copecks-CuNi-SovietPower50-a.jpg. Public Domain.

Figure 4.23. Fifty-kopek commemorative coin, reverse (1967). *Source: Wikimedia Commons*, https://commons.wikimedia.org/wiki/File:USSR-1967-50copecks-CuNi-SovietPower50-b.jpg. Public Domain.

Figure 4.24. Obverse of Soviet one-*chervonets* banknote, valued at ten rubles (1937). *Source:* Collection of Lawrence Kaplan.

Figure 4.25. Reverse side of Soviet five-ruble banknote (1961). *Source:* Collection of Lawrence Kaplan.

Figure 4.26. Soviet Poster: 'Lenin lived, Lenin lives, Lenin will live'. *Source:* Viktor Ivanov, artist (Moscow: Sovetskii khudozhnik, 1967). In Nina I. Baburina, *The Soviet Political Poster: 1917-1980: From the USSR Lenin Library Collection*, trans. Boris Rubalsky (London: Penguin Books, 1988), poster 149.

Figure 4.27. Soviet Poster: 'To the tenth five-year plan – high-powered labour!' *Source:* Iuri Tupitsyn, artist (Moscow: Plakat, 1976). In Nina I. Baburina, *The Soviet Political Poster: 1917-1980: From the USSR Lenin Library Collection*, trans. Boris Rubalsky (London: Penguin Books, 1988), poster 157.

Figure 4.28. Soviet Poster: 'The union of the republics is indestructible!' *Source:* Reino Yussikainen, artist (Moscow: Izobrazitel'noe iskusstvo, 1972). In Nina I. Baburina, *The Soviet Political Poster: 1917-1980: From the USSR Lenin Library Collection*, trans. Boris Rubalsky (London: Penguin Books, 1988), poster 152.

Figures 4.29-4.34. Set of six postage stamps: '60-years of the foundation of the USSR' *Source:* Yu. Ryakhovsky, artist (1982). Collection of the author.

Figure 4.35. Postage stamp: Marx and Lenin, 'Proletariat of all countries, unite!'. *Source:* E. Aniskin, artist (1976). Collection of the author.

Figure 4.36. Postage stamp: Marx, Engels, Lenin, and Stalin, '37th anniversary of the Great October Socialist Revolution'. *Source:* E. Gundobin, artist (1954). Collection of the author.

Figure 4.37. Postage stamp: 'Congress KPSS 1981'. *Source:* I. Krylkov and A. Smirnov, artists. Collection of the author.

Figure 4.38. Postage stamp: 'With the New Year'. *Source:* S. Gorlischev, artist (1982). Collection of the author.

Figure 4.39. Souvenir sheet: Centenary of May Day celebrations. *Source:* A. Shmidshtein, artist (1989). Collection of the author.

Figure 4.40. Postage stamp: 'Glory to Great October'. *Source:* S. Gorlischev, artist (1983). Collection of the author.

Figure 4.41. Postage stamp: National flag of the USSR. *Source:* A. Kalashnikov, artist (1980). Collection of the author.

Figure 4.42. Souvenir sheet: 60 years of the USSR. *Source:* Yu. Bronfenbrener, artist (1982). Collection of the author.

Figure 4.43. Postal cover: 'Transcaucasia '84 Philately Exhibition'. *Source:* V. Konovalov, artist (n.p.: Ministerstvo sviazi SSSR, 1984). Collection of David Phillips.

Figure 4.44. Postal cover: '40 Years of the Estonian SSR and the USSR' (n.p.: Ministerstvo sviazi SSSR, 1980). Postage stamp: '40 Years of the Estonian SSR'. *Source:* P. Veremenko, cachet artist; Yury Korosukov, stamp artist (1980). Collection of David Phillips.

Figure 4.45. Commemorative badge: International Workers' Day, 'Peace. Labour. May'. *Source:* Collection of the author.

Figure 4.46. Commemorative badge: 60th anniversary of the Soviet Union (1982). *Source:* Collection of the author.

Figure 4.47. Commemorative badge: '50 Years' (1972). *Source:* Collection of the author.

Figure 4.48. Commemorative badge: 'USSR / 60 Years / 1922-1982'. *Source:* Collection of the author.

Figure 4.49. Badge: Flag of the Ukrainian SSR. *Source:* Collection of the author.

Figure 4.50. Badge: Flag of the Armenian SSR. Text in Armenian is the abbreviation for the name of the republic. *Source:* Collection of the author.

Figure 4.51. Badge: Flag and arms of the Georgian SSR, 'Georgian SSR'. *Source:* Collection of the author.

Figure 4.52. Badge: Flag of the Latvian SSR, '60 Years of the USSR / Latvian SSR' (1982). *Source:* Collection of the author.

Figure 4.53. Badge: Flag and arms of the Turkmen SSR, 'Turkmen SSR'. *Source:* Collection of the author.

Figure 4.54. Postcard: 'Glory to the Soviet armed forces!'. *Source:* S. Gorlishchev, artist (Moscow: Izdatel'stvo 'Plakat', 1976). Collection of the author.

Figure 4.55. Postal card: 'Glory to the armed forces of the USSR!'. *Source:* L. Kuznetsov, artist (n.p.: Ministerstvo sviazi SSSR, 1987). Collection of the author.

Figure 4.56. Postal card: 'Glory to the armed forces of the USSR!'. *Source:* A. Shchedrin, artist (n.p.: Ministerstvo sviazi SSSR, 1983). Collection of the author.

Figure 4.57. Postcard: 'With the holiday 1 May!'. *Source:* I. Vasil'ev, artist (Moscow: Izdatel'stvo 'Plakat', 1981). Collection of the author.

Figure 4.58. Postcard: '1 May'. *Source:* G. Bodrova and M. Sapozhnikov, artists (Kalinin: IZOGIZ, 1962). Collection of the author.

Figure 4.59. Postcard: 'Long live 1 May'. *Source:* Z. Plaka, artist (Rīgā: Latvijas Valsts izdevniecība, 1963). Collection of the author.

Figure 4.60. Postcard: 'Peace / May / Labour / 1 May – Day of the International Solidarity of the Workers!' *Source:* N. Kutilov, artist (Moscow: 'Sovetskii khudozhnik', 1968). Collection of the author.

Figure 4.61. Postcard: 'Glory to Great October'. *Source:* V. Semenov, artist (Moscow: Izdatel'stvo 'Plakat', 1986). Collection of the author.

Figure 4.62. Postal card: '1917 October / With the holiday!'. *Source:* A. Shchedrin, artist (n.p.: Ministerstvo sviazi SSSR, 1982). Collection of the author.

Figure 4.63. Postcard: 'Peace / Labour / May'. *Source:* M. Sapozhnikov, artist (Moscow: 'Sovetskii khudozhnik', 1964). Collection of the author.

Figure 4.64. Postal card: '8 March / Glory to Soviet Women!'. *Source:* Iu. Artsimenev, artist (n.p.: Izdanie Ministerstva sviazi SSSR, 1972). Collection of the author.

Figure 4.65. Postcard: 'Be glorious, our free homeland'. *Source:* D. Zus'kov, artist (Moscow: 'Izobrazitel'noe iskusstvo' (IZOGIZ), 1972). Collection of the author.

Figure 4.66. Postal card: 'With the New Year!'. *Source:* S. Gorlishchev, artist (n.p.: Ministerstvo sviazi SSSR, 1979). Collection of the author.

Figure 4.67. Postal card: 'With the New Year!'. *Source:* B. Parmeev, artist (n.p.: Ministerstvo sviazi SSSR, 1975). Collection of the author.

Figure 4.68. Postal card: 'With the New Year!'. *Source:* B. Parmeev, artist (n.p.: Ministerstvo sviazi SSSR, 1970). Collection of the author.

Figure 4.69. Artefact: Red star New Year's fir tree topper. *Source:* Catalogue #2010.1055.012, Wende Museum of the Cold War (Culver City, CA). Photo by the author.

Figure 4.70. New Year's fir tree ornament. *Source: Soviet Art: USSR Culture* website, https://soviet-art.ru/wp-content/uploads/2016/11/Hammer-and-Sickle-%E2%98%AD-a-symbol-symbolizing-the-unity-of-the-workers-and-peasants.jpg.

Figure 4.71. New Year's fir tree ornament. *Source: Soviet Art: USSR Culture* website, https://soviet-art.ru/wp-content/uploads/2016/11/Hammer-and-Sickle-%E2%98%AD-the-state-emblem-of-the-Soviet-Union.jpg.

Figure 4.72. Postal card: 'Glory to the Union of Soviet Republics! / With the New Year!' *Source:* Iu. Artsimenev, artist (n.p.: Ministerstvo sviazi SSSR, 1972). Collection of the author.

Figure 4.73. Greeting card: *Ded Morozh* with Kremlin. *Source:* I. Lobova, artist (Moscow: 'Izobrazitel'noe iskusstvo', 1984). Collection of the author.

Figure 4.74. V. Ponomarev, artist, '1 May / With the holiday!', postal card (n.p.: Ministerstvo sviazi SSSR, 1973). *Source:* Collection of the author.

Figure 4.75. A. Antonchenko, artist, 'With the holiday Great October!', postcard (Kalinin: 'Izobrazitel'noe iskusstvo' (IZOGIZ), 1959). *Source:* Collection of the author.

Chapter 5. Symbolic Afterlife: Legacies of Soviet Civil Religion

Figure 5.1. National emblem of Tajikistan. *Source: Wikimedia Commons*, https://commons.wikimedia.org/wiki/File:Emblem_of_Tajikistan.svg. Public domain.

Figure 5.2. National emblem of Uzbekistan. *Source: Wikimedia Commons*, https://commons.wikimedia.org/wiki/File:Emblem_of_Uzbekistan.svg. Public domain.

Figure 5.3. Flag of the Pridnestrovian Moldavian Republic. *Source:* Ministry of Foreign Affairs, Pridnestrovian Moldavian Republic, http://mfa-pmr.org/en/about_republic. Public domain.

Figure 5.4. Greater arms of the Pridnestrovian Moldavian Republic. *Source:* Ministry of Foreign Affairs, Pridnestrovian Moldavian Republic, http://mfa-pmr.org/en/about_republic. Public domain.

Figure 5.5. Lesser arms of the Pridnestrovian Moldavian Republic. *Source:* Ministry of Foreign Affairs, Pridnestrovian Moldavian Republic, http://mfa-pmr.org/ru/republic_main. Public domain.

Figure 5.6. Map of Ukraine showing locations where Lenin statues were toppled during the Euromaidan protests and revolution (2013-2014). *Source:* User 'iaruna', 'Good Bye Lenin!: Desovietyzatsiia Ukraïny. Kinets' 2013 - pochatok 2014 rokiv', interactive map, *Carto*, https://iaryna.carto.com/viz/b42d0d78-9b3b-11e3-9701-0ed66c7bc7f3/public_map. Map contrast modified by Tom Brittnacher.

Figure 5.7. Soviet-inspired flag of Belarus adopted after the 1995 referendum. *Source:* User 'IDiamond', artist. *Wikimedia Commons*, https://commons.wikimedia.org/wiki/File:Flag_of_Belarus.svg. Public domain.

Figure 5.8. Soviet-inspired emblem of Belarus adopted after the 1995 referendum. *Source:* Kot Baiun, artist. Wikimedia Commons, https://commons.wikimedia.org/wiki/File:Coat_of_arms_of_Belarus_(2020).svg. Public domain.

Figure 5.9. The Soviet Banner of Victory. Central Museum of the Armed Forces (Moscow). *Source:* Photographed for the author by Ken Martinez in 2012.

Appendix

Figure A1. State Emblem of the Russian SFSR (1978-1991). *Source:* User 'Pianist', *Wikimedia Commons*, https://commons.wikimedia.org/wiki/File:Coat_of_arms_of_the_Russian_Soviet_Federative_Socialist_Republic.svg. Creative Commons License: CC BY-SA 3.0.

Figure A2. State Emblem of the Ukrainian SSR, 1949-1991. *Source:* User 'Gunnar.Forbrig', *Wikimedia Commons*, https://commons.wikimedia.org/wiki/File:Emblem_of_the_Ukrainian_SSR.svg. Public Domain.

Figure A3. State Emblem of the Byelorussian SSR, 1981-1991. *Source:* User 'Jam123', *Wikimedia Commons*, https://commons.wikimedia.org/wiki/File:Emblem_of_the_Byelorussian_SSR_(1981-1991).svg. Public Domain.

Figure A4. State Emblem of the Uzbek SSR, 1970s-1992. *Source:* User 'Jam123', *Wikimedia Commons*, https://commons.wikimedia.org/wiki/File:Emblem_of_the_Uzbek_SSR.svg. Public Domain.

Figure A5. State Emblem of the Kazakh SSR, 1978-1991. *Source:* User 'Jam123', *Wikimedia Commons*, https://commons.wikimedia.org/wiki/File:Emblem_of_Kazakh_SSR.svg. Public Domain.

Figure A6. State Emblem of the Georgian SSR, 1978-1990. *Source:* User 'TheSign 1998', *Wikimedia Commons*, https://commons.wikimedia.org/wiki/File:Emblem_of_the_Georgian_SSR.svg. Public Domain.

Figure A7. State Emblem of the Azerbaijan SSR, 1937-1992. *Source:* User 'TheSign 1998', *Wikimedia Commons*, https://commons.wikimedia.org/wiki/File:Emblem_of_the_Azerbaijan_SSR.svg. Public Domain.

Figure A8. State Emblem of the Lithuanian SSR, 1940-1991. *Source:* User 'TheSign 1998', *Wikimedia Commons*, https://commons.wikimedia.org/wiki/File:Emblem_of_the_Lithuanian_SSR.svg. Public Domain.

Figure A9. State Emblem of the Moldavian SSR, 1941-1990. *Source:* Users: 'Fry1989', 'Jam123', and 'TilmannR', *Wikimedia Commons*, https://commons.wikimedia.org/wiki/File:Emblem_of_the_Moldavian_SSR_(1981-1990).svg. Creative Commons License: CC BY-SA 3.0.

Figure A10. State Emblem of the Latvian SSR, 1940-1990. *Source:* User 'TheSign 1998', *Wikimedia Commons*, https://commons.wikimedia.org/wiki/File:Emblem_of_the_Latvian_SSR.svg. Public Domain.

Figure A11. State Emblem of the Kirghiz SSR, 1948-1994. *Source:* User 'TheSign 1998', *Wikimedia Commons*, https://commons.wikimedia.org/wiki/File:Emblem_of_the_Kirghiz_SSR.svg. Public Domain.

Figure A12. State Emblem of the Tajik SSR, 1940-1992. *Source:* User 'TheSign 1998', *Wikimedia Commons*, https://commons.wikimedia.org/wiki/File:Emblem_of_the_Tajik_SSR.svg. Public Domain.

Figure A13. State Emblem of the Armenian SSR, 1937-1992. *Source:* User 'TheSign 1998', *Wikimedia Commons*, https://commons.wikimedia.org/wiki/File:Emblem_of_the_Armenian_SSR.svg. Public Domain.

Figure A14. State Emblem of the Turkmen SSR, 1937-1992. *Source:* User 'TheSign 1998', *Wikimedia Commons*, https://commons.wikimedia.org/wiki/File:Emblem_of_the_Turkmen_SSR.svg. Public Domain.

Figure A15. State Emblem of the Estonian SSR, 1940-1990. *Source:* User 'Jam123', *Wikimedia Commons*, https://commons.wikimedia.org/wiki/File:Emblem_of_the_Estonian_SSR.svg. Public Domain.

Figure A16. Flag of the Ukrainian SSR, 1919-1929. *Source:* User 'Alex:D', *Wikimedia Commons*, https://commons.wikimedia.org/wiki/File:Flag_of_the_Ukrainian_Soviet_Socialist_Republic_(1919-1929).svg. Public Domain.

Figure A17. Flag of the Ukrainian SSR, 1937-1950. *Source:* User 'SeNeKa', *Wikimedia Commons*, https://commons.wikimedia.org/wiki/File:Flag_of_the_Ukrainian_Soviet_Socialist_Republic_(1937-1949).svg. Public Domain.

Figure A18. State Flag of the Russian SFSR, 1954-1991. *Source:* User 'Pianist', *Wikimedia Commons*, https://commons.wikimedia.org/wiki/File:Flag_of_the_Russian_Soviet_Federative_Socialist_Republic_(1954%E2%80%931991).svg. Public Domain.

Figure A19. State Flag of the Ukrainian SSR, 1950-1991. *Source:* User 'Zscout370', *Wikimedia Commons*, https://commons.wikimedia.org/wiki/File:Flag_of_the_Ukrainian_Soviet_Socialist_Republic.svg. Public Domain.

Figure A20. State Flag of the Byelorussian SSR, 1951-1991. *Source:* Users 'Zscout370' and 'Pianist', *Wikimedia Commons*, https://commons.wikimedia.org/wiki/File:Flag_of_the_Byelorussian_Soviet_Socialist_Republic_ (1951%E2%80%931991).svg. Public Domain.

Figure A21. State Flag of the Uzbek SSR, 1952-1991. *Source:* Users 'Denelson83', 'Urmas', and 'Nokka', *Wikimedia Commons*, https://commons.wikimedia.org/wiki/File:Flag_of_the_Uzbek_Soviet_Socialist_ Republic_(1952%E2%80%931991).svg. Public Domain.

Figure A22. State Flag of the Kazakh SSR, 1953-1990. *Source:* Users 'Urmas' and 'Nokka'. *Wikimedia Commons*, https://commons.wikimedia.org/wiki/File:Flag_of_the_Kazakh_Soviet_Socialist_Republic.svg. Public Domain.

Figure A23. State Flag of the Georgian SSR, 1951-1990. *Source:* Users 'Dbenbenn' and 'Nokka', *Wikimedia Commons*, https://commons.wikimedia.org/wiki/File:Flag_of_the_Georgian_Soviet_Socialist_Republic_ (1951%E2%80%931990).svg. Public Domain.

Figure A24. State Flag of the Azerbaijan SSR, 1956-1991. *Source:* Users 'Denelson83', 'Urmas', 'Nokka', *Wikimedia Commons*, https://commons.wikimedia.org/wiki/File:Flag_of_the_Azerbaijan_Soviet_Socialist_ Republic_(1956%E2%80%931991).svg. Public Domain.

Figure A25. State Flag of the Lithuanian SSR, 1953-1988. *Source:* User 'Denelson83', *Wikimedia Commons*, https://commons.wikimedia.org/wiki/File:Flag_of_the_Lithuanian_Soviet_Socialist_Republic_ (1953%E2%80%931988).svg. Public Domain.

Figure A26. State Flag of the Moldavian SSR, 1952-1990. *Source:* User 'Pianist', *Wikimedia Commons*, https://commons.wikimedia.org/wiki/File:Flag_of_the_Moldavian_Soviet_Socialist_Republic_(1952%E2%80%931 990).svg. Public Domain.

Figure A27. State Flag of the Latvian SSR, 1953-1990. *Source:* Users 'Denelson83', 'Urmas', and 'Nokka', *Wikimedia Commons*, https://commons.wikimedia.org/wiki/File:Flag_of_the_Latvian_Soviet_Socialist_Republic_ (1953%E2%80%931990).svg. Public Domain.

Figure A28. State Flag of the Kirghiz SSR, 1952-1992. *Source:* Users 'Urmas' and 'Nokka', *Wikimedia Commons*, https://commons.wikimedia.org/wiki/File:Flag_of_the_Kyrgyz_Soviet_Socialist_Republic.svg. Public Domain.

Figure A29. State Flag of the Tajik SSR, 1953-1991. *Source:* User 'Pianist', *Wikimedia Commons*, https://commons.wikimedia.org/wiki/File:Flag_of_the_Tajik_Soviet_Socialist_Republic.svg. Public Domain.

Figure A30. State Flag of the Armenian SSR, 1952-1990. *Source:* User 'Aivazovsky', *Wikimedia Commons*, https://commons.wikimedia.org/wiki/File:Flag_of_the_Armenian_Soviet_Socialist_Republic_ (1952%E2%80%931990).svg. Public Domain.

Figure A31. State Flag of the Turkmen SSR, 1973-1992. *Source:* Users 'Denelson83', 'Urmas', and 'Nokka', *Wikimedia Commons*, https://commons.wikimedia.org/wiki/File:Flag_of_the_Turkmen_Soviet_Socialist_ Republic.svg. Public Domain.

Figure A32. State Flag of the Estonian SSR, 1953-1990. *Source:* Users 'Urmas' and 'Nokka', *Wikimedia Commons*, https://commons.wikimedia.org/wiki/File:Flag_of_the_Estonian_Soviet_Socialist_Republic_ (1953%E2%80%931990).svg. Public Domain.

Figures A33-A34. Recommended arrangements for patriotic displays using flags of the Soviet Union and the Ukrainian SSR from a manual for artists. *Source:* I. Martoloha, *Na dopomohu kul'turno-osvitnim pratsivnykam ta samodiial'nym khudozhnykam v oformlenni naochnoï agitatsiï* (n.p.: Kirovohrads'ke oblasne upravlinnia kul'tury oblasnii budinok narodnoï tvorchosti, 1959), p. 10, 20.

Page 184. Map by the author, based upon Soviet Union map by User:Morwen, *Wikimedia Commons*, https://commons.wikimedia.org/wiki/File:Soviet_Union_Map.png, (CC BY-SA 3.0).

Selected Bibliography

Abel, Ulf. 'Icons and Soviet Art.' In *Symbols of Power: The Esthetics of Political Legitimation in the Soviet Union and Eastern Europe*, 141-62. Stockholm, Sweden: Almqvist & Wiksell International, 1987.

Access World News. NewsBank subscription database.

Ahmadov, Sabuhi. 'National Flag of the Republic of Azerbaijan.' *IRS Heritage*, no. 33-34 (Spring 2018): 76-83.

Al'bom flagov i vympelov Soiuza Sovetskikh Sotsialisticheskikh Respublik. Moscow: Litizdat N.K.I.D., 1925.

Aleev, R. G. *Simvolika: Katalog-spravochnik: nekotorye rekomendatsii khudozhnikam-oformiteliam po ispolzovaniiu simvolov, znakov i nachertanii*. Moscow: Plakat, 1986.

Alfred, Charlotte. 'Leninopad, Ukraine's Falling Lenin Statues, Celebrated as Soviet Symbols Toppled Nationwide.' *Huffington Post* (blog), 24 February 2014. https://www.huffpost.com/entry/leninopad-falling-lenins-statues-ukraine_n_4847364.

Arkhiv zhurnalov Filateliia. 1896-1991. http://philately.ru/archive.shtml.

Artimovich, Nicholas A., II. Personal Collection of Soviet Postage Stamps.

Arvidsson, Claes, and Lars Erik Blomqvist. *Symbols of Power: The Esthetics of Political Legitimation in the Soviet Union and Eastern Europe*. Stockholm: Almqvist and Wiksell International, 1987.

Associated Press Images Collection. Database access via Ebsco subscription services. Accessed 25 July 2020. [subscription required].

Avdyusheva, Elena A., and Irina V. Egorova. 'Communicative Value of the Russian Orthodox Icon.' International Conference on Communication in Multicultural Society, CMSC 2015, 6-8 December 2015, Moscow, Russian Federation. *Procedia - Social and Behavioral Sciences*, 236 (14 December 2016): 305-9.

Avis, George, ed. *The Making of the Soviet Citizen: Character Formation and Civic Training in Soviet Education*. London: Croom Helm, 1987.

Aydıngün, Ayşegül. 'State Symbols and National Identity Construction in Kazakhstan.' In *The Past as Resource in the Turkic Speaking World*, edited by Ildikó Bellér-Hann, 139-58. Würzburg: Ergon, 2008.

Azaryahu, Maoz. 'The Power of Commemorative Street Names.' *Environment and Planning D: Society and Space* 14, no. 3 (June 1996): 311-30.

Baburina, Nina I. *The Soviet Political Poster. 1917-1980: From the USSR Lenin Library Collection*. Translated by Boris Rubalsky. London: Penguin Books, 1988.

Becker, Julia C., Anne Enders-Comberg, Ulrich Wagner, Oliver Christ, and David A. Butz. 'Beware of National Symbols: How Flags Can Threaten Intergroup Relations.' *Social Psychology* 43, no. 1 (2012): 3-6.

Bacon, Edwin, and Mark Sandle, eds. *Brezhnev Reconsidered*. Basingstoke: Palgrave Macmillan Limited, 2002.

Baiburin, Albert, and Alexandra Piir. 'When We Were Happy: Remembering Soviet Holidays.' *Forum for Anthropology and Culture* 5 (2009): 217-53.

Baiburin Al'bert Kashfullovich. *Sovetskii Pasport: Istoriia - struktura - praktiki*. Saint Petersburg: Izdatel'stvo Evropeiskogo universiteta v Sankt-Peterburge, 2017.

Baikova, V. G. *Politicheskoe obrazovanie: Sistema, metodika, metodologiia*. Moscow: Mysl', 1976.

Baliazin, Vladimir Nikolaevich, and Nadezhda Aleksandrovna Soboleva. *Simvoly i nagrady SSSR*. Moscow: OLMA Media Grupp, 2010.

Balina, Marina, and E. A. Dobrenko, eds. *Petrified Utopia: Happiness Soviet Style*. London: Anthem Press, 2009.

Barghoorn, Frederick Charles. *Soviet Russian Nationalism*. New York: Oxford University Press, 1956.

Baron, Nick. 'World Revolution and Cartography.' In *Cartography in the Twentieth Century*, edited by Mark Monmonier, 1766-70. Chicago: University of Chicago Press, 2015.

Barrett, Martyn, and Louis Oppenheimer. 'Findings, Theories and Methods in the Study of Children's National Identifications and National Attitudes.' *European Journal of Developmental Psychology* 8, no. 1 (January 2011): 5-24.

Bassin, Mark, and Catriona Kelly, eds. *Soviet and Post-Soviet Identities*. Cambridge: Cambridge University Press, 2012.

Beeman, William O. 'The Struggle for Identity in Post-Soviet Tajikistan.' *MERIA: Middle East Review of International Affairs* 3, no. 4 (December 1999): 100-105.

Beiner, Ronald. *Civil Religion: A Dialogue in the History of Political Philosophy*. Cambridge: Cambridge University Press, 2011.

Bekus, Nelly. 'Ideological Recycling of the Socialist Legacy: Reading Townscapes of Minsk and Astana.' *Europe-Asia Studies* 69, no. 5 (May 2017): 794-818.

Beliukov, A. M. 'Simvolika krasnogo tsveta v rossiiskoi kul'ture.' In *Aktual'nye voprosy gumanitarnykh nauk: Materialy Vserossiiskoi nauchno-prakticheskoi konferentsii*, edited by R. S. Bikmetov, 43-49. Kemerova: KuzGTU, 2014.

Bell, James. 'Redefining National Identity in Uzbekistan: Symbolic Tensions in Tashkent's Official Public Landscape.' *Ecumene* 6, no. 2 (April 1999): 183-213.

Bellah, Robert N. *Beyond Belief: Essays on Religion in a Post-Traditional World*. Berkeley: University of California Press, 1991.

———. 'Civil Religion in America.' *Daedalus* 96, no. 1 (Winter 1967): 1-21.

Bellah, Robert N., and Phillip E. Hammond. *Varieties of Civil Religion*. San Francisco: Harper and Row, 1980.

Berlin, Brent, and Paul Kay. *Basic Color Terms: Their Universality and Evolution*. Berkeley: University of California Press, 1969.

Berlin, Isaiah, and Henry Hardy. *The Soviet Mind: Russian Culture Under Communism*. Washington, DC: Brookings Institution Press, 2004.

Bertaux, Daniel, Paul Thompson, and Anna Rotkirch. *On Living Through Soviet Russia*. London: Routledge, 2004.

Bertelé, Matteo. 'The Soviet Picture Postcard as a Transmedial Object of Mass Culture and Ideological Practice.' In *Ästhetiken des Sozialismus: Populäre Bildmedien im Späten Sozialismus / Socialist Aesthetics: Visual Cultures of Late Socialism*, edited by Alexandra Köhring and Monica Rüthers, 38-60. Köln: Böhlau Verlag, 2018.

Bezemer, J. W., Alexander Bon, and Robert van Voren. *Nationalism in the USSR: Problems of Nationalities*. Amsterdam: Second World Center, 1989.

Bhabha, Homi K., ed. *Nation and Narration*. London: Routledge, 1990.

Billig, Michael. *Banal Nationalism*. London: Sage, 1995.

———. 'Banal Nationalism and the Imagining of Politics.' In *Everyday Nationhood: Theorising Culture, Identity and Belonging after Banal Nationalism*, edited by Michael Skey and Marco Antonsich, 307-21. London: Palgrave Macmillan UK, 2017.

Billington, James H. *The Icon and the Axe: An Interpretive History of Russian Culture*. New York: Knopf, 1966.

Binns, John. *An Introduction to the Christian Orthodox Churches*. Cambridge: Cambridge University Press, 2002.

Blonsky, Marshall, ed. *On Signs*. Baltimore, MD: Johns Hopkins University Press, 1985.

Boer, Roland. 'Religion and Socialism: A. V. Lunacharsky and the God-Builders.' *Political Theology* 15, no. 2 (March 2014): 188–209.

———. 'Venerating Lenin.' In *Lenin, Religion, and Theology*, 175-206. New York: Palgrave Macmillan US, 2013.

Bokan', Iu. I., V. V. Zaikin, and V. G. Sinitsyn, eds. *Nashi prazdniki (Sovetskie obshchegosudarstvennye, trudovye, voinskie, molodezhnye i semeino-bytovye prazdniki, obriady, rituály)*. Moscow: Izdatel'stvo Politicheskoi literatury, 1977.

Bolotina, S. 'Kak sozdavalsia nash gerb.' *Nauka i zhizn'*, no. 11 (November 1983): 20-24.

Bonnell, Victoria E. *Iconography of Power: Soviet Political Posters Under Lenin and Stalin*. Berkeley: University of California Press, 1997.

―――. 'The Leader's Two Bodies: A Study in the Iconography of the "Vozhd".' *Russian History* 23, no. 1-4 (Spring-Winter 1996): 113-40.

Book Publishing and Libraries in the USSR. Moscow: Press Committee Under the Council of Ministers of the USSR, 1972.

Borisovskii, B. E. 'Pervaia sovetskaia emblema.' *Voprosy istorii*, no. 5 (May 1974): 204-7.

Bown, Matthew Cullerne. *Art Under Stalin*. New York: Holmes & Meier, 1991.

Bown, Matthew Cullerne, and Brandon Taylor, eds. *Art of the Soviets: Painting, Sculpture, and Architecture in a One-Party State, 1917-1992*. Manchester: Manchester University Press, 1993.

Brandenberger, David. *National Bolshevism: Stalinist Mass Culture and the Formation of Modern Russian National Identity, 1931-1956*. Cambridge, MA: Harvard University Press, 2002.

Breakwell, Glynis M., and Evanthia Lyons. *Changing European Identities: Social Psychological Analyses of Social Change*. Oxford: Butterworth-Heinemann, 1996.

Brezhnev, Leonid. 'The 24th Congress of the Communist Party of the Soviet Union: The Report of the C.P.S.U. Central Committee to the 24th Congress of the Communist Party of the Soviet Union. Report by Comrade L. I. Brezhnev, General Secretary of the Central Committee, on March 30, 1971 [Part 2].' *The Current Digest of the Soviet Press* 23, no. 13 (27 April 1971): 1-15.

British Pathé (1896-1978). Accessed 7-8 July 2018. https://www.britishpathe.com; also available on *YouTube* at https://www.youtube.com/britishpathe.

Bronfenbrenner, Urie. *Two Worlds of Childhood: U.S. and U.S.S.R.* New York: Simon and Schuster, 1972.

Brooke, Caroline. 'Changing Identities: The Russian and Soviet National Anthems.' *Slavonica* 13, no. 1 (April 2007): 27-38.

Brooks, Jeffrey. *Thank You, Comrade Stalin!: Soviet Public Culture from Revolution to Cold War*. Princeton: Princeton University Press, 2000.

Brothers, Eric. 'Agit-Prop on Early Soviet Coins.' *CoinWeek* (20 August 2015). http://www.coinweek.com/world-coins/agit-prop-on-early-soviet-coins/.

Brubaker, Rogers. 'Nationalizing States Revisited: Projects and Processes of Nationalization in Post-Soviet States.' *Ethnic and Racial Studies* 34, no. 11 (November 2011): 1785-1814.

Brunn, Stanley D. 'Stamps as Iconography: Celebrating the Independence of New European and Central Asian States.' *GeoJournal* 52, no. 4 (December 2000): 315-23.

―――. 'Stamps as Messengers of Political Transition.' *Geographical Review* 101, no. 1 (January 2011): 19-36.

Bryant, Chris. 'Remains of the Deity.' *New Statesman* 126, no. 4346 (8 August 1997): 17.

Burleigh, Michael. 'National Socialism as a Political Religion.' *Totalitarian Movements and Political Religions* 1, no. 2 (Autumn 2000): 1-26.

Butler, William E. 'Soviet State Symbolism: Flags and Arms of the USSR and Its Constituent Parts, 1917-1971.' *The Flag Bulletin* 11, no. 1 (Winter 1972).

Calhoun, Craig J. *Nationalism*. Minneapolis: University of Minnesota Press, 1997.

―――. 'The Rhetoric of Nationalism.' In *Everyday Nationhood: Theorising Culture, Identity and Belonging after Banal Nationalism*, edited by Michael Skey and Marco Antonsich, 17-30. London: Palgrave Macmillan UK, 2017.

Calhoun, Gloria. 'Saints Into Soviets: Russian Orthodox Symbolism and Soviet Political Posters.' Unpublished master's thesis, Georgia State University, 2014.

Cary, Charles D. 'The Goals of Citizenship Training in American and Soviet Schools.' *Studies in Comparative Communism* 10, no. 3 (Autumn 1977): 281-97.

Cartledge, John. 'Though Cowards Flinch: The Story of the Red Flag as a Symbol of Rebellion.' Paper presented at the Sydney Flag Congress/26th International Congress of Vexillology, Sydney, NSW, Australia, 31 August 2015.

Cerulo, Karen A. 'Identity Construction: New Issues, New Directions.' *Annual Review of Sociology* 23 (August 1997): 385-409.

———. *Identity Designs: The Sights and Sounds of a Nation*. New Brunswick, NJ: Rutgers University Press, 1995.

———. 'Sociopolitical Control and the Structure of National Symbols: An Empirical Analysis of National Anthems.' *Social Forces* 68, no. 1 (September 1989): 76-99.

———. 'Symbols and the World System: National Anthems and Flags.' *Sociological Forum* 8, no. 2 (June 1993): 243-71.

Chabe, Alexander M. 'Star Badges and Red Scarves.' *The Educational Forum* 34, no. 4 (May 1970): 485-93.

Chadaga, Julia Bekman. 'Light in Captivity: Spectacular Glass and Soviet Power in the 1920s and 1930s.' *Slavic Review* 66, no. 1 (Spring 2007): 82-105.

Chamberlain-Creangă, Rebecca. 'The "Transnistrian People": Citizenship and Imaginings of "The State" in an Unrecognized Country.' *Ab Imperio*, no. 4 (2006): 371-99.

Chernikov, Nikolai Dmitrievich, ed. *Nasha krasnaia zvezda*. Moscow: Detskaia literatura, 1987.

Chernov, Vladimir. *Moscow: A Short Guide*. Moscow: Progress Publishers, 1979.

Chernyak, A. S. 'Kremlin Ruby Stars Are 30 Years Old (Development of Ruby Glass).' *Glass and Ceramics* 24, no. 11 (November 1967): 650-51.

Cienki, Alan, and Cornelia Müller. 'Metaphor, Gesture, and Thought.' In *The Cambridge Handbook of Metaphor and Thought*, edited by Raymond W. Gibbs, Jr., 483-501. Cambridge: Cambridge University Press, 2008.

Clawson, Robert W. 'Political Socialization of Children in the USSR.' *Political Science Quarterly* 88, no. 4 (December 1973): 684-712.

'Coins from the Empire of Russia.' *Numista*. Accessed 16 February 2019. https://en.numista.com/catalogue/russia-empire-1.html.

'Coins from Soviet Union (USSR).' *Numista*. Accessed 16 February 2019. https://en.numista.com/catalogue/ancienne_urss-1.html.

Cojocaru, Natalia. 'Nationalism and Identity in Transnistria.' *Innovation: The European Journal of Social Science Research* 19, no. 3-4 (September 2006): 261-72.

Coleman, John A. 'Civil Religion.' *Sociological Analysis* 31, no. 2 (Summer 1970): 67-77.

Collias, Karen A. 'Making Soviet Citizens: Patriotic and Internationalist Education in the Formation of a Soviet State Identity.' In *Soviet Nationality Policies: Ruling Ethnic Groups in the USSR*, edited by Henry R. Huttenbach, 73-93. London: Mansell, 1990.

'The Communist Education of Students.' *Soviet Education* 27, no. 2 (December 1984): 62-110.

Condee, Nancy, ed. *Soviet Hieroglyphics: Visual Culture in Late Twentieth-Century Russia*. Bloomington: Indiana University Press, 1995.

Constitution (Fundamental Law) of the Union of Soviet Socialist Republics, As Amended by the Supreme Soviet of the USSR, on February 25, 1947, on the Recommendations of the Drafting Commission. Washington, DC: Embassy of the Union of the Soviet Socialist Republics, December 1947.

Constitution of the Russian Socialist Federal Soviet Republic: Resolution of the 5th All-Russian Congress of Soviets, Adopted on July 10, 1918. New York: The Nation Press, 1920.

Coomler, David. *The Icon Handbook: A Guide to Understanding Icons and the Liturgy, Symbols and Practices of the Russian Orthodox Church*. Springfield, IL: Templegate Publishers, 1995.

Corley, Felix. *Religion in the Soviet Union: An Archival Reader*. New York: New York University Press, 1996.

C.P.S.U. Central Committee to the 24th Congress of the Communist Party of the Soviet Union. Report by Comrade L. I. Brezhnev, General Secretary of the Central Committee, on March 30, 1971 [Part 2].' *The Current Digest of the Soviet Press* 23, no. 13 (27 April 1971): 1-15.

Crampton, William G. 'Flags as Non-Verbal Symbols in the Management of National Identity.' Unpublished PhD thesis, University of Manchester, 1994.

———. *Flags of the World: A Pictorial History*. New York: Dorset Press, 1990.

Cristi, Marcela. *From Civil to Political Religion: The Intersection of Culture, Religion and Politics*. Waterloo, ON: Wilfrid Laurier University Press, 2001.

Crowfoot, John. 'The Soviet Empire: Flags and Anthems.' *History Today* 41, no. 2 (February 1991): 9-12.

Csepeli, Gyorgy. 'Sense of National Belonging as a Result of Socialisation.' *International Journal of Political Education* 5, no. 4 (December 1982): 377-87.

Cummings, Sally N. 'Inscapes, Landscapes and Greyscapes: The Politics of Signification in Central Asia.' *Europe-Asia Studies* 61, no. 7 (September 2009): 1083-93.

———. 'Leaving Lenin: Elites, Official Ideology and Monuments in the Kyrgyz Republic.' *Nationalities Papers* 41, no. 4 (July 2013): 606-21.

Current Digest of the Soviet Press. 1949-1991. EastView subscription database.

Cushman, Thomas O. 'Ritual and Conformity in Soviet Society.' *Journal of Communist Studies* 4, no. 2 (March 1988): 162-80.

———. 'Ritual and the Sacralization of the Secular: Social Sources of Conformity and Order in Soviet Society.' Unpublished PhD thesis, University of Virginia, 1987.

Davies, A. F. 'The Child's Discovery of Nationality.' *The Australian and New Zealand Journal of Sociology* 4, no. 2 (September 1968): 107-25.

Dawson, Richard E., Kenneth Prewitt, and Karen S. Dawson. *Political Socialization: An Analytic Study*. 2nd ed. Boston: Little, Brown, 1977.

deGraffenried, Julie K. *Sacrificing Childhood: Children and the Soviet State in the Great Patriotic War*. Lawrence: University Press of Kansas, 2014.

Denison, Michael. 'The Art of the Impossible: Political Symbolism, and the Creation of National Identity and Collective Memory in Post-Soviet Turkmenistan.' *Europe-Asia Studies* 61, no. 7 (September 2009): 1167-87.

Denisov, A. I., and M. G. Kirichenko. *Soviet State Law*. Moscow: Foreign Languages Publishing House, 1960.

Derkach, A. A., G. Chubarova, and L. Iashunina. *Kniga vozhatogo*. Moscow: Molodaia Gvardiia, 1982.

Didusenko, Aleksandr Andreevich. *Soviet Children*. Moscow: Progress Publishers, 1965.

Dodds, Klaus. 'An Interview with Professor Michael Billig.' *Political Geography* 54 (April 2016): 73-75.

Domank, Al'bert Stepanovich. *Znaki voinskoi doblesti*. 2nd ed. Moscow: DOSAAF, 1990.

Dreeze, Jonathon R. 'On the Creation of Gods: Lenin's Image in Stalin's Cult of Personality.' Unpublished master's thesis, The Ohio State University, 2013.

Duchesne, Sophie. 'Who's Afraid of Banal Nationalism?' *Nations and Nationalism* 24, no. 4 (October 2018): 841-56.

Duncan, Hugh Dalziel. *Symbols and Social Theory*. New York: Oxford University Press, 1969.

———. *Symbols in Society*. New York: Oxford University Press, 1968.

Dunin-Borkovskii, K. *Al'bom flagov i vympelov Rossiiskoi Sotsialisticheskoi Federativnoi Sovetskoi Respubliki, Soiuznykh Sovetskikh Respublik i inostrannykh gosudarstv: Po materialam Narodnogo Komissariata po inostrannym delam i Shtaba komanduiushchego morskimi sklami respubliki*. Moscow: Izdatel'stvo Narodnogo Komissariat po inostrannym delam RSFSR, 1923.

Dunstan, John. 'Atheistic Education in the USSR.' In *The Making of the Soviet Citizen: Character Formation and Civic Training in Soviet Education*, edited by George Avis, 50-79. London: Croom Helm, 1987.

Durkheim, Émile. *Durkheim on Religion*. Edited by W. S. F. Pickering. Atlanta, GA: Scholars Press, 1994.

———. *The Elementary Forms of Religious Life*. Translated by Carol Cosman. Oxford: Oxford University Press, 2001.

Dushechkina, Elena Vladimirovna. *Russkaia elka: Istoriia, mifologiia, literatura*. Saint Petersburg: Norint, 2002.

Easton, David, and Robert D. Hess. 'The Child's Political World.' *Midwest Journal of Political Science* 6, no. 3 (August 1962): 229-46.

Edele, Mark. *The Soviet Union: A Short History*. Hoboken, NJ: Wiley-Blackwell, 2019.

Edelman, Murray J. *Politics as Symbolic Action: Mass Arousal and Quiescence*. Chicago: Markham Publishing Co., 1971.

———. *The Symbolic Uses of Politics*. Urbana: University of Illinois Press, 1964.

'Educating the Younger Generation in the Spirit of the Norms and Principles of Developed Socialism.' *Soviet Education* 27, no. 5 (March 1985): 39-53.

'The Educational Functions of the Komsomol.' *Soviet Education* 17, no. 4 (February 1975): 3-4.

Elder, Charles D., and Roger W. Cobb. *The Political Uses of Symbols*. New York: Longman, 1983.

Elgenius, Gabriella. 'Expressions of Nationhood: National Symbols and Ceremonies in Contemporary Europe.' Unpublished PhD thesis, The London School of Economics and Political Science, University of London, 2005.

———. *Symbols of Nations and Nationalism: Celebrating Nationhood*. New York: Palgrave Macmillan, 2011.

Embassy of Latvia in Georgia. 'Basic Facts About Latvia', 19 May 2020. https://www.mfa.gov.lv/en/georgia/basic-facts-about-latvia.

Embassy of the Union of the Soviet Socialist Republics in the USA. *Soviet Life* [magazine]. 1965-1991.

Embassy of the Union of the Soviet Socialist Republics in the USA. *The USSR* [magazine]. 1956-1965.

Epstein, Fritz T. '[Review of] *Great Soviet Encyclopedia: A Translation of the Third Edition. Vol. 1*', by Jean Paradise. *Slavic Review* 35, no. 4 (December 1976): 724-27.

Eriksen, Thomas Hylland, and Richard Jenkins. *Flag, Nation and Symbolism in Europe and America*. London: Routledge, 2007.

Evans, Alfred B. 'The Decline of Developed Socialism? Some Trends in Recent Soviet Ideology.' *Soviet Studies* 38, no. 1 (January 1986): 1-23.

———. 'Developed Socialism in Soviet Ideology.' *Soviet Studies* 29, no. 3 (July 1977): 409-28.

Evgen'eva, Anastasiia Petrovna, ed. *Slovar' russkogo iazyka*. 2nd ed., 4 vols. Moscow: Izdatel'stvo 'Russkii iazyk', 1981.

Farnen, Russell Francis, ed. *Nationalism, Ethnicity, and Identity: Cross National and Comparative Perspectives*. New Brunswick, NJ: Transaction Publishers, 1994.

Fedulova, A. 'A Happy Childhood, A Pioneer Childhood.' *Soviet Education* 15, no. 3 (January 1973): 95-99.

Fedulova, A. V., ed. *Vsesoiuznaia pionerskaia organizatsiia imeni V. I. Lenina: Dokumenty i materialy, [1920-1974]*. Moscow: Molodaia gvardiia, 1974.

Feingold, Ellen R. 'The Messages of Money.' *Financial History*, no. 116 (Winter 2016): 20.

Ferro, Mark. 'Simvolika i politika vo vremiia revoliutsii 1917 g.' In *Anatomiia revoliutsii: 1917 god v Rossii: Massy, partii, vlast'*, edited by V. Iu. Cherniaev, 366-71. Saint Petersburg: Glagol, 1994.

Figes, Orlando, and B. I. Kolonitskii. *Interpreting the Russian Revolution: The Language and Symbols of 1917*. New Haven, CT: Yale University Press, 1999.

Filonov, G. N. 'Ideological, Political, and Moral Education.' *Soviet Education* 26, no. 4 (February 1984): 5-19.

Firth, Raymond. *Symbols: Public and Private*. Ithaca, NY: Cornell University Press, 1973.

Flag Institute. William Crampton Library. Kingston upon Hull, UK.

'From the Courtroom: Businessman in Stamp Collecting.' *The Current Digest of the Soviet Press* 14, no. 22 (27 June 1962): 24.

Furin, S. *The World of Young Pioneers*. Moscow: Progress Publishers, 1982.

Gabel, Paul. *And God Created Lenin: Marxism vs. Religion in Russia, 1917-1929*. Amherst, NY: Prometheus Books, 2005.

Galaiko, V. M., ed. *Simvoly rodiny i voinskoi doblesti*. Moscow: Voennoe izdatel'stvo, 1990.

Gamoran, Adam. 'Civil Religion in American Schools.' *Sociological Analysis* 51, no. 3 (Autumn 1990): 235-56.

Gardella, Peter. *American Civil Religion: What Americans Hold Sacred*. Oxford: Oxford University Press, 2014.

Gehrig, Gail. *American Civil Religion: An Assessment*. Storrs, CT: Society for the Scientific Study of Religion, 1981.

———. 'The American Civil Religion Debate: A Source for Theory Construction.' *Journal for the Scientific Study of Religion* 20, no. 1 (March 1981): 51-63.

Geisler, Michael E., ed. *National Symbols, Fractured Identities: Contesting the National Narrative*. Middlebury, VT: Middlebury College Press, 2005.

Gentile, Emilio. 'Fascism, Totalitarianism and Political Religion: Definitions and Critical Reflections on Criticism of an Interpretation.' *Totalitarian Movements and Political Religions* 5, no. 3 (Winter 2004): 326-75.

———. 'Political Religion: A Concept and Its Critics – a Critical Survey.' *Totalitarian Movements and Political Religions* 6, no. 1 (June 2005): 19-32.

———. *Politics as Religion*. Princeton: Princeton University Press, 2006.

Gentile, Emilio, and Robert Mallett. 'The Sacralisation of Politics: Definitions, Interpretations and Reflections on the Question of Secular Religion and Totalitarianism.' *Totalitarian Movements and Political Religions* 1, no. 1 (Summer 2000): 18-55.

Gerhart, Genevra. *The Russian's World: Life and Language*. New York: Harcourt Brace Jovanovich, 1974.

Getty, J. Arch. 'Dead Man Talking: Lenin's Body and Russian Politics', 119th Faculty Research Lecture, University of California, Los Angeles, 19 October 2015. https://www.youtube.com/watch?v=NBpm3CnGT30.

———. *Practicing Stalinism: Bolsheviks, Boyars, and the Persistence of Tradition*. New Haven: Yale University Press, 2013.

Gilbert, Emily, and Eric Helleiner. *Nation-States and Money: The Past, Present and Future of National Currencies*. London: Routledge, 1999.

Gill, Graeme J. 'Changing Symbols: The Renovation of Moscow Place Names.' *The Russian Review* 64, no. 3 (July 2005): 480-503.

———. '"Lenin Lives": Or Does He? Symbols and the Transition from Socialism.' *Europe-Asia Studies* 60, no. 2 (March 2008): 173-96.

———. 'Political Symbolism and the Fall of the USSR.' *Europe-Asia Studies* 65, no. 2 (March 2013): 244-63.

———. 'Political Symbols and Regime Change: The Russian Experience.' *Politics, Religion & Ideology* 19, no. 4 (October 2018): 494-509.

———. 'The Soviet Leader Cult: Reflections on the Structure of Leadership in the Soviet Union.' *British Journal of Political Science* 10, no. 2 (April 1980): 167-86.

———. *Symbolism and Regime Change in Russia*. Cambridge: Cambridge University Press, 2013.

———. *Symbols and Legitimacy in Soviet Politics*. Cambridge: Cambridge University Press, 2011.

Glebkin, Vladimir V. *Ritual v sovetskoi kul'ture*. Moscow: Ianus-K, 1998.

Golyshkin, Vasilii, and V. A. Taborko. *Kniga vozhatogo*. Moscow: Molodaia Gvardiia, 1965.

Goretskii, Vseslav Gavrilovich. *Rodnoe slovo: Uchebnik po chteniiu dlia uchashchikhsia 2 klassa chetyrekhletnei nachal'noi shkoly*. Moscow: Prosveshchenie, 1989.

Goretskii, Vseslav Gavrilovich, Viktor Andreevich Kiriushkin, and Anatolii Filippovich Shanko. *Azbuka*. Moscow: Prosveshchenie, 1991.

———. *Chitaem sami: Posobie dlia uchashchikhsia 1 klassa trekhletnei nachal'noi shkoly*. Moscow: Prosveshchenie, 1989.

Gorter, Jessica, dir. *The Red Soul*. Film on DVD. Brooklyn, NY: Icarus Films, 2017.

Goscilo, Helena, Susan Corbesero, Petre Petrov. *Stalinka: Digital Library of Staliniana*. Pittsburgh: University of Pittsburgh Digital Research Library, 2005. http://digital.library.pitt.edu/collection/stalinka-digital-library-staliniana.

Gosudarstvennye gerby i flagi SSSR, soiuznykh i avtonomnykh respublik. Moscow: Izvestiia sovetov deputatov trudiashchikhsia SSSR, 1972.

Gosudarstvennyi komitet SSSR po statistike. *Itogi Vsesoiuznoi perepisi naseleniia 1989 goda*. Microfiche edition. Volumes 1 and 7. Minneapolis: East View Publications, 1992.

Grant, Jonathan. 'The Socialist Construction of Philately in the Early Soviet Era.' *Comparative Studies in Society and History* 37, no. 3 (July 1995): 476-93.

Gregor, A. James. *Totalitarianism and Political Religion: An Intellectual History*. Stanford, CA: Stanford University Press, 2012.

Griffin, Roger. 'Introduction: God's Counterfeiters? Investigating the Triad of Fascism, Totalitarianism and (Political) Religion.' *Totalitarian Movements and Political Religions* 5, no. 3 (Winter 2004): 291-325.

Grin, Moisei Filippovich, S. V. Kalesnik, and V. F. Pavlenko, eds. *Soviet Union: A Geographical Survey*. Moscow: Progress Publishers, 1976.

Gugushvili, Alexi, and Peter Kabachnik. 'Stalin is Dead, Long Live Stalin? Testing Socialization, Structural, Ideological, Nationalist, and Gender Hypotheses.' *Post-Soviet Affairs* 31, no. 1 (2014): 1-36.

———. 'Stalin on Their Minds: A Comparative Analysis of Public Perceptions of the Soviet Dictator in Russia and Georgia.' *International Journal of Sociology* 49, no. 5-6 (September 2019): 317-41.

Guenter, Scot M. *The American Flag, 1777-1924: Cultural Shifts From Creation to Codification*. Rutherford, NJ: Fairleigh Dickinson University Press, 1990.

———. 'The Cinco de Mayo Flag Flap: Rights, Power, and Identity.' *Raven: A Journal of Vexillology* 19 (2012): 5-26.

———. 'Civil Religion as a Political Tool: Bush, Dukakis, and the Pledge.' *The Flag Bulletin* #128, v. 27, no. 5 (September-October 1988): 161-70.

———. 'The Hippies and the Hardhats: The Struggle for Semiotic Control of the Flag of the United States in the 1960s', *The Flag Bulletin*, #130, v. 28, no. 1-4 (January-August 1989): 131-41.

———. 'Juxtaposing Symbols in Civil Religion: The Lady and the Flag.' *Raven: A Journal of Vexillology* 17 (2010): 1-21.

———. 'Majulah Singapura: National Day and Flag Culture in a Southeast Asian City-State.' *Raven: A Journal of Vexillology* 6 (1999): 9-18.

———. 'Micronesian Flag Cultures: An Exercise in Comparative Vexillology.' *Raven: A Journal of Vexillology* 11 (2004): 61-71.

———. 'This Flag Flew Over the U.S. Capitol.' *The Flag Bulletin* #117, v. 25, no. 4 (July-August 1986): 147-59.

Gurevich, A. A. 'Class Adviser's Working Experience with Class VII Pioneers.' *Soviet Education* 1, no. 8 (June 1959): 44-50.

Hang, Xing. *Encyclopedia of National Anthems*. 2nd ed. 2 vols. Lanham, MD: Scarecrow Press, 2011.

Harper, Samuel N. *Civic Training in Soviet Russia*. Chicago: The University of Chicago Press, 1929.

———. *Making Bolsheviks*. Chicago: The University of Chicago Press, 1931.

Harris, Erika. *Nationalism: Theories and Cases*. Edinburgh: Edinburgh University Press, 2009.

Hasenmueller, Christine. 'Panofsky, Iconography, and Semiotics.' *The Journal of Aesthetics and Art Criticism* 36, no. 3 (Spring 1978): 289-301.

Hayes, Carlton J. H. *Nationalism: A Religion*. New York: Macmillan, 1960.

Hearn, Jonathan. *Rethinking Nationalism: A Critical Introduction*. Houndmills: Palgrave Macmillan, 2006.

Heimer, Željko. *Exploring Vexillology Through Military Unit Flags: With an Analysis of Croatian Armed Forces Flags During and After the 1991-1995 Homeland War*. Zagreb: Hrvatsko grboslovno i zastavoslovno društvo, 2016.

———. *Vexillology as a Social Science*. Danvers, MA: Flag Heritage Foundation, 2017.

Heintz, Monica. 'Republic of Moldova Versus Romania: The Cold War of National Identities.' *Journal of Political Science and International Relations* 2, no. 1 (2005): 71-81.

Heleniak, Timothy. 'The End of an Empire: Migration and the Changing Nationality Composition of the Soviet Successor States.' In *Diasporas and Ethnic Migrants: German, Israel, and Post-Soviet Successor States in Comparative Perspective*, edited by Rainer Münz and Rainer Ohliger, 115-40. London: Frank Cass, 2003.

Helleiner, Eric. 'National Currencies and National Identities.' *American Behavioral Scientist* 41, no. 10 (August 1998): 1409-36.

Hess, Robert D., and Judith Torney. *The Development of Political Attitudes in Children*. Chicago: Aldine Publishing Co., 2007.

Hessman, Robin, dir. *My Perestroika*. Film on DVD. New York: Red Square Productions, 2011.

Hicks, Jeremy. 'A Holy Relic of War: The Soviet Victory Banner as Artefact.' In *Remembering the Second World War*, edited by Patrick Finney, 197-216. London: Taylor and Francis, 2017.

Hirsch, Francine. *Empire of Nations: Ethnographic Knowledge & the Making of the Soviet Union*. Ithaca, N.Y: Cornell University Press, 2005.

Hoyo, Henio. 'Posting Nationalism: Postage Stamps as Carriers of Nationalist Messages.' In *Beyond Imagined Uniqueness: Nationalisms in Contemporary Perspectives*, edited by Joan Burbick and William Glass, 67-92. Cambridge: Cambridge Scholars Publishing, 2010.

Horowitz, Eugene L. 'Some Aspects of the Development of Patriotism in Children.' *Sociometry* 3, no. 4 (October 1940): 329-41.

Hughes, Albert. *Political Socialization of Soviet Youth*. Lewiston, NY: Edwin Mellen Press, 1992.

Hughey, Michael W. *Civil Religion and Moral Order: Theoretical and Historical Dimensions*. Westport, CT: Greenwood Press, 1983.

Hulicka, Karel, and Irene M. Hulicka. *Soviet Institutions, the Individual and Society*. Boston: Christopher Publishing House, 1967.

Huttenbach, Henry R., ed. *Soviet Nationality Policies: Ruling Ethnic Groups in the USSR*. London: Mansell, 1990.

Hvithamar, Annika, Margit Warburg, and Brian Arly Jacobsen. *Holy Nations and Global Identities: Civil Religion, Nationalism, and Globalisation*. Leiden: Brill, 2009.

Ignatieff, Michael. 'Soviet War Memorials.' *History Workshop Journal* 17, no. 1 (Spring 1984): 157-63.

Il'inskii, Vasilii Nikolaevich. *Geral'dika trudovoi slavy*. Moscow: Izdatel'stvo politicheskoi literatury, 1979.

———. *Znachki i ikh kollektsionirovanie: Posobie dlia faleristov*. Moscow: Izdatel'stvo 'Sviaz'', 1977.

Imanakova, E. G. 'Simvoly 9 maia v sovetskoi filokartii: Kul'turologicheskii aspekt.' In *70-letie Velikoi Pobedy: Istoricheskii opyt i problemy sovremennosti. Sbornik nauchnykh statei*, edited by A. V. Speranskii, Chast' 2, pp. 30-37. Ekaterinburg: Institut istorii i arkheologii UrO RAN, 2015.

Isupov, Arkadii Aleksandrovich. *Naselenie SSSR: Po dannym Vsesoiuznoi perepisi naseleniia 1989 g*. Moscow: Finansy i statistika, 1990.

Ivanchenko, Aleksandr Vladimirovich. *Soiuz serpa i molota: Gosudarstvennye simvoly RSFSR*. Moscow: Sovetskaia Rossiia, 1987.

165

Ivanov, I. P. 'The Collective Organizational Activities of the Pioneers.' *Soviet Education* 1, no. 3 (January 1959): 36-41.

Ivanov, Konstantin A. 'Soviet Russian Flags.' Translated by Whitney Smith. *The Flag Bulletin* 6, no. 1-2 (Winter 1966-1967): 42-51.

Izvestiia Digital Archive, 1917-2011. EastView subscription database.

Jackson, R. 'The Development of Political Concepts in Young Children.' *Educational Research* 14, no. 1 (November 1971): 51-55.

Jahoda, Gustav. 'The Development of Children's Ideas About Country and Nationality: Part I: The Conceptual Framework.' *British Journal of Educational Psychology* 33, no. 1 (February 1963): 47-60.

————. 'The Development of Children's Ideas About Country and Nationality: Part II: National Symbols and Themes.' *British Journal of Educational Psychology* 33, no. 2 (June 1963): 143-53.

Järve, Priit. 'Two Waves of Language Laws in the Baltic States: Changes of Rationale?' *Journal of Baltic Studies* 33, no. 1 (Spring 2002): 78-110.

Jenks, Andrew. 'A Metro on the Mount: The Underground as a Church of Soviet Civilization.' *Technology and Culture* 41, no. 4 (October 2000): 697-724.

Jilek, Wolfgang G. 'Nazi and Communist Flags: Semiotic Aspects and Psychophysiological Dynamics of Totalitarian Symbols.' *The Flag Bulletin* #197, v. 40, no. 1 (February 2001): 1-40.

————. 'Semiotic Aspects and Psychophysiological Effects of Totalitarian Symbols: Nazi and Communist Flags.' In *Fahnen Flags Drapeaux: Proceedings of the 15th International Congress of Vexillology, Zurich, 23-27 August 1993*, 117-21. Zurich: Swiss Society of Vexillology, 1999.

Jubulis, Mark A. 'The Persistence of the Baltic Nations Under Soviet Rule: An Ethno-Symbolist Critique of Modernist Perspectives on the Breakup of the USSR.' In *Nationalism in a Global Era: The Persistence of Nations*, edited by Mitchell Young, Eric G. E. Zuelow, and Andreas Sturm, 161-77. London: Routledge, 2007.

Juergensmeyer, Mark, and Wade Clark Roof, eds. *Encyclopedia of Global Religion*. Thousand Oaks, CA: SAGE Publications, 2012.

Kabachnik, Peter. 'The Power of Place, or Powerless Places? Hybrid Attitudes Towards Soviet Symbols in Post-Soviet Georgia.' *Central Asian Survey* 37, no. 2 (June 2018): 265-85.

Kabachnik, Peter, Ana Kirvalidze, and Alexi Gugushvili. *Stalin Today: Contending with the Soviet Past in Georgia*. Tbilisi: Ilia State University, 2016.

Kabush, V. T. *Pionerskie simvoly, ritualy, traditsii*. Minsk: Narodnaia asveta, 1985.

Kairov, I. A. 'Education and Problems of the Young Pioneer Movement.' *Soviet Education* 5, no. 5 (March 1963): 44-47.

Kamentseva, E. I., and A. N. Luppol. 'Kak sozdavalsia sovetskii gerb.' *Voprosy istorii*, no. 12 (December 1962): 194-98.

Kaplan, Lawrence M. Personal Collection of Soviet Banknotes.

Karamanchev, Valentin. *Proletarskaia simvolika*. Moscow: Progress, 1978.

Karpenko, V. 'Nashi slavnye simvoly.' *Vospitanie shkol'nikov*, no. 4 (1986): 59-63.

Kashin, M. 'The School and the Young Pioneer Organization.' *Soviet Education* 6, no. 4 (February 1964): 35-46.

Kassil', Lev Abramovich, ed. *Flazhok: Kniga dlia chteniia vo vtorom klasse*. 4th ed. Moscow: Prosveshchenie, 1972.

Kasvin, G., and A. Savina. 'Young Pioneers in Socialist Countries.' *Soviet Education* 10, no. 4 (February 1968): 18-25.

'Katalog otkrytok.' *Klub Filokartist*. Accessed 21 March 2019. http://www.filokartist.net/catalog/.

Katel, Helen. 'Character Training in School and in Out-of-School Organizations: Activities of the Pioneer and Komsomol Organizations.' *Soviet Education* 11, no. 1 (November 1968): 16-48.

Keating, Michael. 'Nations Without States: The Accommodation of Nationalism in the New State Order.' In *Minority Nationalism and the Changing International Order*, edited by Michael Keating and John McGarry, 19-43. Oxford. Oxford University Press, 2001.

Kelly, Catriona. *Children's World: Growing Up in Russia, 1890-1991*. New Haven, CT: Yale University Press, 2007.

———. *Comrade Pavlik: The Rise and Fall of a Soviet Boy Hero*. London: Granta Books, 2005.

———. 'A Joyful Soviet Childhood: Licensed Happiness for Little Ones.' In *Petrified Utopia: Happiness Soviet Style*, edited by Marina Balina and E. A. Dobrenko, 3-18. London: Anthem Press, 2009.

———. 'The New Soviet Man and Woman.' In *The Oxford Handbook of Modern Russian History*, edited by Simon Dixon. Oxford: Oxford University Press, 2016. https://www.oxfordhandbooks.com/view/10.1093/oxfordhb/ 9780199236701.001.0001/oxfordhb-9780199236701-e-024.

———. '"The School Waltz": The Everyday Life of the Post Stalinist Soviet Classroom.' *Forum for Anthropology and Culture* 1 (2004): 108-58.

Kenez, Peter. *A History of the Soviet Union from the Beginning to Its Legacy*. 3rd ed. New York: Cambridge University Press, 2017.

———. *A History of the Soviet Union from the Beginning to the End*. 2nd ed. New York: Cambridge University Press, 2006.

Khanchin, V. S. 'Differentiating Level in the Work of the Pioneer Organization.' *Soviet Education* 1, no. 1 (November 1958): 13-19.

Khanchin, Vitalii Solomonovich, ed. *Tovarishch: Zapisnaia knizhka pionera na 1961/62 uchebnyi god*. Moscow: Izdatel'stvo Molodaia gvardiia, 1961.

Kharitonov, O. V. *Illiustrirovannoe opisanie obmundirovaniia i znakov razlichiia Krasnoi i Sovetskoi Armii (1918-1945 gg.)*. Leningrad: Artilleriiskii istoricheskii muzei, 1960.

———. *Soviet Military Uniform and Insignia, 1918-1958*. St. Petersburg: Alga-Fund, 1993.

Khodorkivs'kii, I. D., ed. *Soiuz neporushnii*. Kiev: Vidavnitstvo Radians'ka shkola, 1975.

Khodza, Nisson Aleksandrovich. *O Lenine, oktiabriatam*. Leningrad: Gosudarstvennoe izdatel'stvo dctskoi literatury, 1963.

Khripkova, A. G. 'Sociological and Pedagogical Principles of the Interaction of the School, Family, and Community in Shaping Communist Awareness and Behavior in the Younger Generation.' *Soviet Education* 20, no. 9 (July 1978): 5-25.

Kim, Maxim. *The Soviet People: A New Historical Community*. Moscow: Progress Publishers, 1974.

King, Charles. 'Moldovan Identity and the Politics of Pan-Romanianism.' *Slavic Review* 53, no. 2 (Summer 1994): 345-68.

Kirschenbaum, Lisa A. 'Learning to be Soviet: Stalinist Schools and Celebrations in the 1930s.' *History of Education Quarterly* 42, no. 3 (Autumn 2002): 403-13.

———. 'Raising Young Russia: The Family, the State, and the Preschool Child, 1917-1931.' Unpublished PhD thesis, University of California, Berkeley, 1993.

———. *Small Comrades: Revolutionizing Childhood in Soviet Russia, 1917-1932*. New York: RoutledgeFalmer, 2000.

Kiselev, G. F., and N. N. Speransov. *Emblemy mira i truda: Gosudarstvennye gerby i flagi Sovetskogo Soiuza i soiuznykh respublik*. Moscow: Politicheskoi literatury, 1968.

Kiselev, G. F., and V. A. Liubesheva. 'V. I. Lenin i sozdanie gosudarstvennoi pechati i gerba RSFSR.' *Istoriia SSSR*, no. 5 (October 1966): 21-26.

Kishkovsky, Sophia. 'A "7 Up" Series for Russia, With Soviet Roots.' *ArtsBeat (New York Times)* (blog), 4 October 2013. https://artsbeat.blogs.nytimes.com/2013/10/04/a-7-up-series-for-russia-with-soviet-roots/.

Kldiashvili, Giorgi. 'Lustration.' In *Memory of Nations: Democratic Transition Guide [The Georgian Experience]*, 19–27. [Washington, DC]: National Endowment for Democracy, 2018.

Klinghoffer, Arthur Jay. *Red Apocalypse: The Religious Evolution of Soviet Communism*. Lanham, MD: University Press of America, 1996.

Knox, Zoe. *Russian Society and the Orthodox Church: Religion in Russia After Communism*. London: RoutledgeCurzon, 2005.

Koch, Natalie, and Anssi Paasi. 'Banal Nationalism 20 Years On: Re-Thinking, Re-Formulating and Re-Contextualizing the Concept.' *Political Geography* 54 (September 2016): 1-6.

Kokosalakis, Nikos. 'Icons and Non-Verbal Religion in the Orthodox Tradition.' *Social Compass* 42, no. 4 (December 1995): 433-49.

Kolchinsky, Alexander. 'Stalin on Stamps: Design, Propaganda, and Politics.' In *The Winton M. Blount Postal History Symposia: Select Papers, 2010-2011*, edited by Thomas Lera, 45-67. Smithsonian Contributions to History and Technology No. 56. Washington, DC: Smithsonian Institution Scholarly Press, 2012.

Kolstø, Pål. 'National Symbols as Signs of Unity and Division.' *Ethnic and Racial Studies* 29, no. 4 (July 2006): 676-701.

Kolstø, Pål, and Andrei Malgin. 'The Transnistrian Republic: A Case of Politicized Regionalism.' *Nationalities Papers* 26, no. 1 (March 1998): 103-27.

'Komsomol, Young Pioneers, and Other Pupil Organizations in the School.' *Soviet Education* 22, no. 11-12 (September 1980): 67-107.

Konnikova, T. E. 'The Pedagogical Principles Underlying Work with Young Pioneers.' *Soviet Education* 4, no. 11 (September 1962): 57-63.

Kononenko, V. P. 'The Truth About Pavlik Morozov.' *Soviet Education* 32, no. 8 (August 1990): 69-92.

Kornakov, P. K. 'Simvolika i ritualy revoliutsii 1917 g.' In *Anatomiia revoliutsii: 1917 god v Rossii: Massy, partii, vlast'*, edited by V. Iu. Cherniaev, 356-65. Saint Petersburg: Glagol, 1994.

Korolev, Fedar Filippovich. *Education in the U.S.S.R.* London: Soviet News, 1957.

Kostina, Olga. 'The Moscow Metro: "Ode to Joy."' Translated by Albina Ozieva and Jeremy Howard. *Art in Translation* 8, no. 2 (April 2016): 242-58.

Krause, Chester L., Clifford Mishler, and Colin R. Bruce. *Collecting World Coins: A Century of Circulating Issues, 1901-Present*. Iola, WI: Krause Publications, 2001.

Krivko, V. A. *Morskie flagi otechestva*. Moscow: Izdatel'stvo DOSAAF SSSR, 1984.

Krivtsov, V. D. *Sovetskie znaki i zhetony: Katalog dlia kollektsionerov = Soviet Badges and Jetons: Catalogue for Collectors: Price Guide*. Moscow: Avers, 1996.

Kruk, Sergei. 'Semiotics of Visual Iconicity in Leninist "Monumental" Propaganda.' *Visual Communication* 7, no. 1 (February 2008): 27-56.

Krupskaia, Nadezhda Konstantinovna. *Lenin kak propagandist i agitator*. Moscow: Gosudarstvennoe izdatel'stvo politicheskoi literatury, 1956.

———. *O iunykh pionerakh*. Moscow: Izdatel'stvo Akkademii pedagogicheskikh nauk RSFSR, 1957.

———. *Pedagogicheskie sochineniia*. 10 vols. Moscow: Izdatel'stvo Akademii Pedagogicheskikh Hauk, 1957-1962.

———. *A Search in Pedagogics: Discussions of the 1920's and Early 1930s*. Translated by Peter Emerson. Moscow: Progress Publishers, 1990.

Krupskaia, Nadezhda Konstantinovna, and Nikolai Ivanovich Monakhov. *O vozhatom i ego rabote s pionerami*. Moscow: Molodaia Gvardiia, 1961.

Krupskaya, Nadezhda Konstantinovna. *On Education: Selected Articles and Speeches*. Translated by G. P. Ivanov-Mumjiev. Moscow: Foreign Languages Publishing House, 1957.

Kuebart, Friedrich. 'The Political Socialisation of Schoolchildren.' In *Soviet Youth Culture*, edited by Jim Riordan, 103-21. Bloomington: Indiana University Press, 1989.

Kula, Marcin. 'Communism as Religion.' *Totalitarian Movements and Political Religions* 6, no. 3 (December 2005): 371-81.

Kurkovsky, Diana. 'Monumentalizing Wheat: Soviet Dreams of Abundance.' *Gastronomica* 7, no. 1 (Winter 2007): 15-17.

Kuz'min, A. 'Ideological Work and the Communist Upbringing of the Individual.' *Soviet Education* 18, no. 6 (April 1976): 19-38.

Laitin, David D. 'Identity in Formation: The Russian-Speaking Nationally In the Post-Soviet Diaspora.' *European Journal of Sociology / Archives Européennes de Sociologie / Europäisches Archiv Für Soziologie* 36, no. 2 (1995): 281-316.

———. 'National Identities in the Emerging European State.' In *Minority Nationalism and the Changing International Order*, edited by Michael Keating and John McGarry, 84-113. Oxford: Oxford University Press, 2001.

Lane, Christel. *Christian Religion in the Soviet Union: A Sociological Study*. London: G. Allen & Unwin, 1978.

———. 'From Ideology to Political Religion: Recent Development in Soviet Beliefs and Rituals in the "Patriotic Tradition."' In *Symbols of Power: The Esthetics of Political Legitimation in the Soviet Union and Eastern Europe*, edited by Claes Arvidsson and Lars Erik Blomqvist, 87-97. Stockholm: Almqvist & Wiksell International, 1987.

———. *The Rites of Rulers: Ritual in Industrial Society – the Soviet Case*. Cambridge: Cambridge University Press, 1981.

———. 'Ritual and Ceremony in Contemporary Soviet Society.' *The Sociological Review, New Series* 27, no. 2 (May 1979): 253-78.

Lapshin, V. P. *Khudozhestvennaia zhizn' Moskvy i Petrograda v 1917 godu*. Moscow: Sovetskii khudozhnik, 1983.

Lasswell, Harold D. *The Comparative Study of Symbols: An Introduction*. Stanford, CA: Stanford University Press, 1952.

———. *Language of Politics: Studies in Quantitative Semantics*. New York: George W. Stewart, 1949.

Lasswell, Harold D., and Abraham Kaplan. *Power and Society: A Framework for Political Inquiry*. New Haven: Yale University Press, 1950.

Lauer, Josh. 'Money as Mass Communication: U.S. Paper Currency and the Iconography of Nationalism.' *The Communication Review* 11, no. 2 (27 May 2008): 109-32.

Lawson, Edwin D. 'Development of Patriotism in Children — A Second Look.' *The Journal of Psychology* 55 (January 1963): 279-86.

Leach, Edmund Ronald. *Culture and Communication: The Logic by Which Symbols Are Connected*. Cambridge: Cambridge University Press, 1976.

Lebedinskii, V. V. 'The Role of Komsomol and Young Pioneer Organizations in Instilling Ideological Steadfastness, A Sense of Civic Duty, and Conscious Discipline in Schoolchildren.' *Soviet Education* 17, no. 5 (March 1975): 22-48.

Lebina, N. B. *Entsiklopediia banal'nostei: Sovetskaia povsednevnost'—kontury, simvoly, znaki*. Saint Petersburg: Dmitrii Bulanin, 2008.

Lenin, Vladimir Il'ich. *Collected Works*. 46 vols. Moscow: Progress Publishers, 1960-1970.

———. *Marxism & Nationalism*. Chippendale, N.S.W.: Resistance Books, 2002.

———. *Polnoe Sobranie Sochinenii*. 5th ed. 55 vols. Moscow: Izdatel'stvo politicheskoi literatury, 1958-67.

———. *Selected Works*. 12 vols. New York: International Publishers, 1943.

———. *What Is to Be Done?: Burning Questions of Our Movement*. New York: International Publishers, 1969.

Leont'eva, Svetlana G. 'Pioner: Vsem primer.' *Otechest'vennye zapiski*, no. 3 (18) (2004): 249-59.

Leont'eva, Svetlana G. 'Zhizneopisanie pionera-geroia: Tekstovaia traditsiia i ritual'nyi kontekst.' In *Sovremennaia rossiiskaia mifologiia*, edited by M. V. Akhmetova, 89-123. Moscow: Rossiiskii gosudartsvennyi gumanitarnyi universitet, 2005.

Lepeshinskii, L. 'Aktivno uchastvovat' v kommunisticheskom vospitanii trudiashchikhsia!' *Sovetskii kollektsioner*, no. 1 (1963): 7-12.

Leshchenko, Natalia. 'A Fine Instrument: Two Nation-Building Strategies in Post-Soviet Belarus.' *Nations and Nationalism* 10, no. 3 (2004): 333-52.

————. 'The National Ideology and the Basis of the Lukashenka Regime in Belarus.' *Europe-Asia Studies* 60, no. 8 (October 2008): 1419-33.

Levin, Deana. *Children in Soviet Russia*. London: Faber and Faber, 1942.

————. *Leisure and Pleasure of Soviet Children*. London: MacGibbon and Kee, 1966.

Lewin, Eyal. *Comparative Perspectives on Civil Religion, Nationalism, and Political Influence*. Hershey, PA: Information Science Reference, 2017.

Liashenko, Mikhail Ur'evich. *Tvoe krasnokryloe znamia*. Moscow: Detskaia literatura, 1978.

Likhitskiy, I. I. *Art of Russian Metal Miniature: Catalogue of Badges, 1917-1991*. Lvov: Udacha, 1995.

'List of Commemorative Coins of the Soviet Union.' *Wikipedia*, 19 June 2018. https://en.wikipedia.org/w/index.php?title=List_of_commemorative_coins_of_the_Soviet_Union&oldid=846625867.

Litvinov, Victor, and Alexander Yegorov. *The Posters of Glasnost and Perestroika*. Translated by John Crowfoot. London: Penguin Books, 1989.

Litvin, Alter L. *Writing History in Twentieth-Century Russia: A View from Within*. Houndmills: Palgrave, 2001.

Losev, Aleksei Fedorovich. *Problema simvola i realisticheskoe iskusstvo*. Moscow: Iskusstvo, 1976.

Lowe, Brian M. 'Soviet and American Civil Religion: A Comparison.' *Journal of Interdisciplinary Studies* 13, no. 1-2 (2001): 73-96.

'Lyrics for Soviet Anthem Revised, So People No Longer Have to Hum.' *New York Times* (1 September 1977): 2.

MacIntyre, Jean. 'Political Socialization of Youth in the Soviet Union: Its Theory, Use, and Results.' Unpublished master's thesis, Naval Postgraduate School, 1993.

Maiakovskii, Vladimir. *Sobranie sochinenii v dvenadtsati tomakh*. Moscow: Pravda, 1978.

Maier, Hans. '"Political Religion": The Potentials and Limitations of a Concept.' In *Totalitarian Movements and Political Religions, Volume II: Concepts for the Comparison of Dictatorships*, 272-82. London: Routledge, 2007.

————. 'Political Religions and Their Images: Soviet Communism, Italian Fascism and German National Socialism.' *Totalitarian Movements and Political Religions* 7, no. 3 (September 2006): 267-81.

Maier, Hans, and Michael Schäfer. *Totalitarianism and Political Religions, Volume II: Concepts for the Comparison of Dictatorships*. Translated by Jodi Bruhn. London: Routledge, 2012.

Makoveev, Mikh. *O znameni, kotoromu prisiagaem*. Moscow: Voennoe izdatel'stvo Ministerstva oborony SSSR, 1974.

Maksiashev, P. F. 'Kogda vpervye v Rossii bylo podniato krasnoe znamia.' *Voprosy istorii*, no. 3 (March 1965): 206-7.

Maksimenko, G. D. 'The Patriotic Upbringing of Youth Under the Conditions of Developed Socialism.' *Soviet Education* 18, no. 8 (June 1976): 57-58.

Malinkin, A. N. *Simvolika ordenov SSSR: Issledovanie po sotsiologii nagrady*. Moscow: Novoe tysiacheletie, 2005.

Mamaev, Konstantin Konstantinovich. *Flagi rasskazyvaiut*. Leningrad: Avrora, 1972.

Marshall, Tim. *A Flag Worth Dying For: The Power and Politics of National Symbols*. New York: Scribner, 2017.

Martoloha, I. *Na dopomohu kul'turno-osvitnim pratsivnykam ta samodiial'nym khudozhnykam v oformlenni naochnoï agitatsiï*. n.p.: Kirovohrads'ke oblasne upravlinnia kul'tury oblasnii budinok narodnoï tvorchosti, 1959.

Marx, Karl, and Friedrich Engels. *Manifest Kommunisticheskoi partii*. Moscow: Izdatel'stvo politicheskoi literatury, 1980.

———. *Manifesto of the Communist Party*. New York: International Publishers, 1948.

———. *On Religion*. New York: Schocken Books, 1964.

Maslinskaya, Svetlana. 'A Child Hero: Heroic Biographies in Children's Literature.' Lecture presented at the University of California, Santa Barbara, Santa Barbara, CA, 27 April 2017.

Matiushkin, N. I. *Sovetskii patriotizm: Moguchaia dvizhushchaia sila sotsialisticheskogo obshchestva*. Moscow: Politizdat, 1952.

Matjunin, Sergei. 'The New State Flags as the Iconographic Symbols of the Post-Soviet Space.' *GeoJournal* 52, no. 4 (December 2000): 311-13.

Matveeva, T., and Z. Tumanova. *Kniga vozhatogo*. Moscow: Izdatel'stvo TSK VLKSM 'Molodaia gvardiia', 1954.

McDowell, Jennifer. 'Soviet Civil Ceremonies.' *Journal for the Scientific Study of Religion* 13, no. 3 (September 1974): 265-79.

Mchedlov, M. 'Formation of the Communist World View - The Main Element in the Education of the New Man.' *Soviet Education* 18, no. 6 (April 1976): 74-89.

Merriam, Charles Edward. *Political Power*. New York: Collier Books, 1964.

Meurs, Wim van. 'Social Citizenship and Non-Migration: The Immobility of the Russian Diaspora in the Baltics.' In *Diasporas and Ethnic Migrants: German, Israel, and Post-Soviet Successor States in Comparative Perspective*, edited by Rainer Münz and Rainer Ohliger, 174-90. London: Frank Cass, 2003.

Mikhalkov, Sergei Vladimirovich, and N. Kudriavtseva. *Karusel'*. Moscow: Malysh, 1986.

Miller, Jessie L., and James G. Miller. 'Behavioral Scientists Visit the Soviet Union.' *Behavioral Science* 7, no. 3 (July 1962): 343-377.

Ministerstvo oborony SSSR. *Voenno-morskie flagi SSSR*. Moscow: Kartfabrika VMF, 1964.

Miroshnichenko, Sergei, dir. *Semiletnie. Rozhdennye v SSSR / Age 7 in the USSR*. Film on DVD. Newton, NJ: Shanachie Entertainment, 1993.

Mitiaev, Anatolii Vasil'evich, and Iurii Koieiko. *Segodnia prazdnik: Rasskazy*. Moscow: Detskaia literatura, 1981.

Morrison, Thea. 'The Banning of Soviet Symbols in Georgia.' *Georgia Today*, 10 May 2018. http://georgiatoday.ge/news/10215/The-Banning-of-Soviet-Symbols-in-Georgia.

Morton, Miriam. *Growing Up in the Soviet Union: From the Cradle to Coming of Age*. Moscow: Progress Publishers, 1982.

Moskoff, William. 'Soviet Postal Material and State Propaganda, 1928-1945.' Paper presented at The Winton M. Blount Postal History Symposium, Smithsonian National Postal Museum, Washington, DC, 30 September - 1 October, 2010. https://postalmuseum.si.edu/research/pdfs/Moskoff-Soviet_Postal_Material.pdf.

Mukhina, Vera Ignatevna. *A Sculptor's Thoughts*. Moscow: Foreign Languages Publishing House, 1952.

Muratov, Iu. I. 'The Alliance of the School and the Komsomol in the Education of Young Builders of Communism.' *Soviet Education* 17, no. 5 (March 1975): 4-21.

———. 'The School and the Komsomol.' *Soviet Education* 26, no. 4 (February 1984): 83-104.

Murray, John. *Politics and Place-Names: Changing Names in the Late Soviet Period*. Birmingham Slavonic Monographs, No. 32. Birmingham: Department of Russian, University of Birmingham, 2000.

Murzin, A. 'Krasnyi flag otchizny.' *Vospitanie shkol'nikov*, no. 1 (1978): 14-15.

Mysova, L. 'Ispol'zovanie gosudarstvennoi simvolika v vospitatel'noi rabote.' *Vospitanie shkol'nikov*, no. 6 (1986): 13-16.

Nenarokov, Al'bert Pavlovich., and Aleksandr Vasil'evich Proskurin. *How the Soviet Union Solved the Nationalities Question*. Moscow: Novosti Press Agency Publishing House, 1983.

Neumann, Matthias. 'Children Diplomacy During the Late Cold War: Samantha Smith's Visit of the "Evil Empire."' *History* 104, no. 360 (2019): 275-308.

New York Times. Articles and blog posts. ProQuest subscription database.

Nexis Uni. LexisNexis subscription database.

Nikolaev, V. 'Tvoi pionerskii znachok.' *Iunyi tekhnik*, no. 5 (May 1972): 18-19, 76.

Nimirov, N. G., ed. *Boevoe krasnoe znamia*. Moscow: Tsentral'nyi muzei Sovetskoi Armii, 1964.

O'Connor, Timothy E. 'Lunacharskii's Vision of the New Soviet Citizen.' *The Historian* 53, no. 3 (Spring 1991): 443-54.

O'Dell, Felicity. 'Forming Socialist Attitudes Towards Work Among Soviet Schoolchildren.' In *The Making of the Soviet Citizen: Character Formation and Civic Training in Soviet Education*, edited by George Avis, 80-106. London: Croom Helm, 1987.

O'Dell, Felicity Ann. *Socialisation Through Children's Literature: The Soviet Example*. Cambridge: Cambridge University Press, 1978.

OED Online. Oxford: Oxford University Press, n.d. http://www.oed.com.

Olcott, Martha Brill, Lubomyr Hajda, and Anthony Olcott. *The Soviet Multinational State: Readings and Documents*. Armonk, NY: M.E. Sharpe, 1990.

Ogonëk Digital Archive, 1923-2019. EastView subscription database.

Ogorodnikov, I. T. 'Komsomol, Young Pioneers, and Other Pupil Organizations in the School.' *Soviet Education* 22, no. 11-12 (October 1980): 67-107.

'Oktiabriatskaia zvezdochka.' *Vozhatyi*, 1958, 45.

Orleanskaia, S. V. *Nashe imia – oktiabriata: Sbornik rasskazov, stikhov, stsenok, pesen, igr, zagadok, skorogovorok dlia oktiabriat*. Moscow: Detgiz, 1959.

Orlova, E. *Vnimanie, otriad! Sputnik otriadnogo vozhatogo mladshikh pionerov*. Moscow: Molodaia gvardiia, 1969.

Orr, Graeme. 'A Fetished Gift: The Legal Status of Flags.' *Griffith Law Review* 19, no. 3 (December 2010): 504-26.

Osipova, Nelli Khristoforovna. *Dve zvezdochki*. n.p.: Izdatel'stvo Malysh, 1974.

Palmer, Scott W. 'How Memory Was Made: The Construction of the Memorial to the Heroes of the Battle of Stalingrad.' *The Russian Review* 68, no. 3 (July 2009): 373-407.

Panofsky, Erwin. 'Iconography and Iconology: An Introduction to the Study of Renaissance Art.' In *Meaning in the Visual Arts: Papers in and on Art History*, 26-54. Garden City, NY: Doubleday, 1955.

Panova, N. *Oktiabriata*. Moscow: Molodaia gvardiia, 1959.

Papadopoulos, Georgios. 'Currency and the Collective Representations of Authority, Nationality, and Value.' *Journal of Cultural Economy* 8, no. 4 (2015): 521-34.

Pavlov, V. M., V. Chudakov, A. Terziev, N. Rakhmanov, and R. Papik'ian. *Moskovskoe metro = Moscow Metro: [fotoal'bom]*. 2nd ed. Moscow: Moskovskii rabochii, 1980.

Pchelov, Evgenii Vladimirovich. *Gosudarstvennye simvoly Rossii: Gerb, flag, gimn: Uchebnoe posobie dlia 5-9 klassov*. 2nd ed. Moscow: Russkoe slovo, 2002.

Pearson, Raymond. *National Minorities in Eastern Europe, 1848-1945*. New York: St. Martin's Press, 1983.

Penrose, Jan. 'Designing the Nation. Banknotes, Banal Nationalism and Alternative Conceptions of the State.' *Political Geography* 30, no. 8 (November 2011): 429-40.

Perkins, Bernadette. 'Civil Religion in Russia: Fifteenth Century to the Present.' Unpublished master's thesis, Baylor University, 1997.

Peterson, Charles B. 'The Nature of Soviet Place-Names.' *Names: Journal of the American Name Society* 25, no. 1 (March 1977): 15-24.

Petrone, Karen. *Life Has Become More Joyous, Comrades: Celebrations in the Time of Stalin*. Bloomington: Indiana University Press, 2000.

Petrone, Karen, and Kenneth Slepyan. *The Soviet Union and Russia, 1939-2015: A History in Documents*. New York: Oxford University Press, 2017.

Petrova, E. N., and Iozef Kiblitskii. *Krasnyi tsvet v russkom iskusstve*. Saint Petersburg: Gosudarstvennyi russkii muzci, 1997.

'The Philatelist's Corner: New Money, New Stamps.' *The Current Digest of the Soviet Press* 12, no. 49 (4 January 1961): 26-27.

Phillips, David F. Personal Collection of Soviet Postal Covers.

Pisch, Anita. *The Personality Cult of Stalin in Soviet Posters, 1929-1953: Archetypes, Inventions & Fabrications*. Acton, ACT: Australian National University Press, 2016.

Platoff, Anne M. 'Of Tablecloths and Soviet Relics: A Study of the Banner of Victory (*Znamia Pobedy*).' *Raven: A Journal of Vexillology* 20 (January 2013): 55-83.

———. Personal Collection of Soviet Coins and Postage Stamps.

———. Personal Collection of Soviet Flags [official and unofficial].

———. Personal Collection of Soviet *znachki* (metal badges).

———. 'Soviet Children's Flags.' *Raven: A Journal of Vexillology* 17 (November 2010): 63-84.

Plekhanov, Georgii Valentinovich. 'O zadachakh sotsialistov v bor'be s golodom v Rossii (Pis'ma k molodym tovarishcham). Pis'mo tret'e. Nashi zadachi.' In *Sochineniia*, edited by D. B. Riazanov, 3:386–420. Moscow: Gosudartstvennoe izdatel'stvo, 1923.

'Pobeda nad znamenem.' *Ogonëk* no. 19, (7-13 May 2007): 8.

Podrez, V. 'All the Colors of the Pioneer Rainbow.' *Soviet Education* 15, no. 3 (January 1973): 47-55.

Pokhlebkin, V. V. 'Krasnaia piatikonechnaia zvezda.' *Voprosy istorii*, no. 11 (November 1967): 212-14.

Ponikarova, N. M. *Znachki dvadtsatykh-sorokovykh godov iz fondov Gosudarstvennogo muzeia oborony Moskvy*. Moscow: Gosudarstvennyi muzei oborony Moskvy, 1995.

Poroikov, Iu. 'Bearing Lenin's Name.' *Soviet Education* 15, no. 3 (January 1973): 10 13.

Potseluev, Vladimir A. *Gerby Soiuza SSR: Iz istorii razrabotki*. Moscow: Izdatel'stvo politicheskoi literatury, 1987.

Prokhorov, Aleksandr Mikhailovich, ed. *Bol'shaia sovetskaia entsiklopediia*. 3rd ed. 30 vols. Moscow. Izdatel'stvo 'Sovetskaia entsiklopediia', 1970-78.

———. *Great Soviet Encyclopedia: A Translation of the Third Edition (Bol'shaia Sovetskaia Entsiklopediia)*. 31 vols. New York: Macmillan, 1973-1983.

Pravda Digital Archive, 1912-2009. EastView subscription database.

Pronin, Alexander, and Barbara Pronin. *Russian Folk Arts*. South Brunswick, NJ: A. S. Barnes and Company, 1975.

Rajamaa, Hermann. *The Moulding of Soviet Citizens: A Glance at Soviet Educational Theory and Practice*. London: Boreas Publishing Co., 1948.

Ramet, Sabrina P., ed. *Religious Policy in the Soviet Union*. Cambridge: Cambridge University Press, 1993.

Redl, Helen B., ed. and trans. *Soviet Educators on Soviet Education*. New York: Free Press of Glencoe, 1964.

Ree, Erik van. 'Stalinist Ritual and Belief System: Reflections on "Political Religion."' *Politics, Religion & Ideology* 17, no. 2-3 (July 2016): 143-61.

Reid, Donald M. 'The Symbolism of Postage Stamps: A Source for the Historian.' *Journal of Contemporary History* 19, no. 2 (April 1984): 223-49.

Richey, Russell E., and Donald G. Jones. *American Civil Religion*. New York: Harper and Row, 1974.

Riegel, Klaus-Georg. 'Marxism-Leninism as a Political Religion.' *Totalitarian Movements and Political Religions* 6, no. 1 (June 2005): 97-126.

Riegel, Klaus-Georg. 'Marxism-Leninism as Political Religion.' In *Totalitarian Movements and Political Religions, Volume II: Concepts for the Comparison of Dictatorships*, edited by Hans Maier and Michael E. Geisler, 61-112. New York: Routledge, 2007.

Riordan, James. *Soviet Youth Culture*. Bloomington: Indiana University Press, 1989.

Riordan, Jim. '"Be Prepared": Russian Boy Scouts and Soviet Pioneers.' *Stadion: Internationale Zeitschrift für Geschichte des Sports/International Journal of the History of Sports* 11, no. 1 (January 1985): 93-106.

———. 'The Komsomol.' In *Soviet Youth Culture*, edited by Jim Riordan, 16-44. Bloomington: Indiana University Press, 1989.

———. 'The Role of Youth Organizations in Communist Upbringing in the Soviet School.' In *The Making of the Soviet Citizen: Character Formation and Civic Training in Soviet Education*, edited by George Avis, 136-160. London: Croom Helm, 1987.

———. 'The Russian Boy Scouts.' *History Today* 38, no. 10 (October 1988): 48-52.

Roberts, David D. '"Political Religion" and the Totalitarian Departures of Inter-War Europe: On the Uses and Disadvantages of an Analytical Category.' *Contemporary European History* 18, no. 4 (November 2009): 381-414.

Roshchin, Lev V. *Nashi voinskie simvoly*. Moscow: Izdatel'stvo DOSAAF SSSR, 1989.

Rousseau, Jean-Jacques. 'On Civil Religion.' In *On the Social Contract with Geneva Manuscript and Political Economy*, edited by Roger D. Masters, translated by Judith R. Masters, 124-33. New York: St. Martin's Press, 1978.

Rowley, Alison. 'Miniature Propaganda: Self-Definition and Soviet Postage Stamps, 1917-41.' *Slavonica* 8, no. 2 (November 2002): 135-57.

Rubinchik, A. L. *Zhivopis' sotsrealizma v sovetskikh otkrytkakh / Socialist Realism Paintings in Soviet Postcards*. Translated by A. B. Klionsky. Moscow: Izdatel'stvo OOO 'Magma', 2008.

Rudling, Per Anders. 'Belarus in the Lukashenka Era: National Identity and Relations with Russia.' In *Europe's Last Frontier? Belarus, Moldova, and Ukraine between Russia and the European Union*, edited by Oliver Schmidtke and Serhy Yekelchyk, 55-77. New York: Palgrave Macmillan US, 2008.

Rudnev, V. A. *Prazdniki, obriady, ritualy v trudovom kollektive*. Moscow: Profizdat, 1984.

———. *Sovetskie prazdniki, obriady, ritualy*. Leningrad: Lenizdat, 1979.

Safronov, V. M. *Ty — grazhdanin Sovetskogo Soiuza*. Moscow: Iuridicheskaia literatura, 1978.

Sahm, Astrid. 'Political Culture and National Symbols: Their Impact on the Belarusian Nation-Building Process.' *Nationalities Papers* 27, no. 4 (December 1999): 649-60.

Salnikova, Alla. 'Not Yuletide? Fir Tree Ornaments as an Integral Part of Soviet Socialization Practices (1920s-1960s).' *History of Education & Children's Literature* 5, no. 1 (2010): 355-74.

Sandle, Mark. 'Brezhnev and Developed Socialism: The Ideology of Zastoi?' In *Brezhnev Reconsidered*, edited by Edwin Bacon and Mark Sandle, 165-87. Basingstoke: Palgrave Macmillan Limited, 2002.

Saparov, Arseny. 'The Alteration of Place Names and Construction of National Identity in Soviet Armenia.' *Cahiers du Monde russe* 44, no. 1 (January-March 2003): 179-198.

Sarafannikova, G. P. 'Komsomol and Pioneer Organization.' *Soviet Education* 1, no. 5 (March 1959): 39-42.

Savenkova, E. V. 'Kult' pionerov-geroev: Zhertvennyi entuziazm v zhanre "dlia srednego shkol'nogo vozrasta."' *Vestnik Samarskoi gumanitarnoi akademii. Seriia 'Filosofiia. Filologiia.'*, no. 1 (17) (2015): 43-53.

Schlesinger, Ina. 'The Pioneer Organization: The Evolution of Citizenship Education in the Soviet Union.' Unpublished PhD thesis, Columbia University, 1967.

Schumpeter, Joseph A. *Capitalism, Socialism, and Democracy*. New York: Harper & Brothers, 1942.

Sebba, Mark. 'The Visual Construction of Language Hierarchy: The Case of Banknotes, Coins and Stamps.' *Journal of Language and Politics* 12, no. 1 (January 2013): 101-25.

Sebeok, Thomas A. *Signs: An Introduction to Semiotics*. 2nd ed. Toronto: University of Toronto Press, 2001.

Semenov, V. S. 'The Theory of Developed Socialism and Its Growth into Communism.' *Soviet Studies in Philosophy* 19, no. 4 (Spring 1981): 3-32.

Sen, Amartya. *Identity and Violence: The Illusion of Destiny*. New York: W. W. Norton & Co, 2007.

Senderovich, Sasha. 'Goodbye, Lenin?' *New York Times Online* (blog), 9 December 2013. ProQuest NYT database.

Serov, Boris Nikolaevich. *Pourochnye razrabotki po kursu 'Gosudarstvennaia simvolika': Gimn. gerb. flag*. Moscow: BAKO, 2005.

Shanskii, Nikolai Maksimovich. *Russian Word Formation*. Oxford: Pergamon Press, 1968.

Shcvtsov, V. S. *Grazhdanstvo v sovetskom soiuznom gosudarstve*. Moscow: Iuridicheskaia literatura, 1969.

Shmakov, S. A. 'To Inspire Children (A Pioneer Leader's Notebook).' In *Soviet Educators on Soviet Education*, edited by Helen B. Redl, 245-52. New York: Free Press of Glencoe, 1964.

Signev, A. 'Kak sozdavalsia gosudarstvennyi flag nashei rodiny.' *Voprosy istorii*, no. 11 (November 1964): 211-15.

Silitski, Vitali. 'Still Soviet?: Why Dictatorship Persists in Belarus.' *Harvard International Review* 28, no. 1 (Spring 2006): 46-53.

Skey, Michael. 'The National in Everyday Life: A Critical Engagement with Michael Billig's Thesis of *Banal Nationalism*.' *The Sociological Review* 57, no. 2 (May 2009): 331-46.

Skey, Michael, and Marco Antonsich, eds. *Everyday Nationhood: Theorising Culture, Identity and Belonging after Banal Nationalism*. London: Palgrave Macmillan, 2017.

Skvirsky, David, trans. *Publishing in the Soviet Union*. Moscow: Progress Publishers, 1967.

Smirnov, Г. V. 'Always Prepared!' *Soviet Education* 15, no. 2 (December 1972): 6-71.

Smirnova, Aleksandra S. *Oktiabriata – budushchie pionery: Rekomendatel'nyi ukazatel' literatury dlia vozhatykh oktiabriatskikh grupp i zvezdochek*. 2nd ed. Leningrad: Ministerstvo kul'tury RSFSR, 1960.

Smith, Anthony D. *The Ethnic Origins of Nations*. Oxford: Basil Blackwell, 1987.

———. *National Identity*. Reno: University of Nevada Press, 1991.

Smith, Hedrick. 'Pin Hobby, Soviet Fad, Is Criticized.' *New York Times*. (22 September 1974): 6.

———. 'Religion Still Deeply Embedded in Soviet.' *New York Times*, (14 April 1974): 2, 26.

———. *The Russians*. New York: Quadrangle/New York Times Book Co., 1976.

Smith, John E. *Quasi-Religions: Humanism, Marxism, and Nationalism*. New York: St. Martin's Press, 1994.

Smith, Samantha. *Journey to the Soviet Union*. Boston: Little, Brown, 1985.

Smith, Whitney. 'Arab Flags.' *The Arab World* 5, no. 10 (October 1959): 12-13.

———. *The Bibliography of Flags of Foreign Nations*. Boston: G. K. Hall, 1965.

———. 'Definition of the National Flag.' *The Flag Bulletin* #113, v. 24, no. 5 (October 1985): 152-55.

———. Dr. Whitney Smith Flag Research Center Collection, c. 1700's-2013 (bulk 1957-2011). Dolph Briscoe Center for American History, The University of Texas at Austin.

———. *The Flag Book of the United States*. New York: William Morrow & Company, Inc., 1970.

———. *Flags and Arms Across the World*. New York: McGraw-Hill, 1980.

———. *Flags Through the Ages and Across the World*. New York: McGraw-Hill, 1975.

———. 'Principles of Vexillology.' In *The 23rd International Congress of Vexillology: Official Proceedings*, CD-ROM: Paper 0717.5. Tokyo: Japanese Vexillological Association, 2009.

———. 'Prolegomena to the Study of Political Symbolism.' Unpublished PhD thesis, Boston University, 1968.

———. 'Soviet State Symbolism.' In *Soviet State Symbolism: Flags and Arms of the USSR and Its Constituent Parts, 1917-1971*, 26-42. *The Flag Bulletin*, 11 no. 1. Winchester, MA: Flag Research Center, Winter 1972.

Smolkin, Victoria. *A Sacred Space Is Never Empty: A History of Soviet Atheism*. Princeton: Princeton University Press, 2018.

Soboleva, N. A. 'K voprosu o simvolike Rossii v pervoi chetverti XX stoletiia: Novye podkhody k issledovaniiu.' In *Rossiia v XIX-XX vekakh: Materialy II nauchnykh chtenii pamiati professora Valeriia Ivanovicha Bovykina, Moskva, MGU im. M. V. Lomonosova, 22 ianvaria 2002 g*, edited by V. I. Bovykin, A. G. Golikov, and A. P. Korelin, 337-57. Moscow: ROSSPEN, 2002.

———. *Ocherki istorii rossiiskoi simvoliki: Ot tamgi do simvolov gosudarstvennogo suvereniteta*. Moscow: Iazyki slavianskikh kul'tur, 2006.

———. *Rossiiskaia gosudarstvennaia simvolika: Istoriia i sovremennost'*. Moscow: Gumanitarnyi izdatel'skii tsentr VLADOS, 2002.

Soboleva, Nadezhda Aleksandrovna. 'The Composition of State Anthems of the Russian Empire and the Soviet Union. *Russian Studies in History* 47, no. 2 (Fall 2008): 31-58.

———. 'From the History of Soviet Political Symbolism.' *Russian Studies in History* 47, no. 2 (Fall 2008): 59-91.

———. 'Iz istorii otechestvennykh gosudarstvennykh gimnov.' *Otechestvennaia istoriia*, no. 1 (February 2005): 3-21.

———. 'Iz istorii sovetskoi politicheskoi simvoliki.' *Otechestvennaia istoriia*, no. 2 (April 2006): 89-109.

Socialism on Film: The Cold War and International Propaganda (1918-1988). Adam Matthew subscription database.

Sokolov, V. A. 'The Evolution of the State Symbols of the Byelorussian S.S.R.' *The Flag Bulletin* #126, v. 27, no. 3 (June 1988): 108-17.

Sokolov, Vladislav Aleksandrovich. *Flagi Rossiiskoi imperii i SSSR v dokumentakh*. Moscow: MGIU, 2001.

Soloveichik, Simon. *Soviet Children at School*. Moscow: Novosti Press Agency Publishing House, 1976.

Solov'ev, V. Iu. *Pochtovye marki Rossii i SSSR (1857-1991 gg.): Spetsializirovannyi katalog-spravochnik*. Moscow: Izdatel'stvo po atomnoi nauke i tekhnike IzdAT, 1998.

Sovetskii kollektsioner 1-28 (1963-1991). https://sovmint.ru/library/zhurnaly/zhurnal-sovetskij-kollekcioner-1963-1992/.

Sovetskii Soiuz. *Konstitutsiia (Osnovnoi zakon) Soiuza Sovetskikh Sotsialisticheskikh Respublik: Priniata na vneocherednoi sed'moi sessii Verkhovnogo Soveta SSSR deviatogo sozyva 7 oktiabria 1977 goda*. Moscow: Izdatel'stvo 'Iuridicheskaia literatura', 1979.

Sovetskii Soiuz. Tsentral'noe statisticheskoe upravlenie. *Chislennost' i sostav naseleniia SSSR: Po dannym Vsesoiuznoi perepisi naseleniia 1979 goda*. Moscow: Finansy i statistika, 1984.

Soviet Education 1-33 (1958-1991). Translations of articles from Soviet education journals.

Soviet Era Books for Children and Youth. Princeton University Digital Library. http://pudl.princeton.edu/collections/pudl0127.

Soviet Union. *The Soviet Socialist Constitution*. Moscow: Russia To-day Society, 1941.

Stalin, Joseph. *Marxism and the National and Colonial Question: A Collection of Articles and Speeches*. London: Lawrence & Wishart, 1940.

State Statistics Committee of Ukraine. 'All-Ukrainian Population Census '2001: Linguistic Composition of the Population (English Edition).' Accessed 3 September 2020. http://2001.ukrcensus.gov.ua/eng/results/general/language/.

Statt, David. 'Flag Choices of Elite American and Canadian Children.' *Psychological Reports* 32, no. 1 (February 1973): 85-86.

Stauffer, Robert E. 'Bellah's Civil Religion.' *Journal for the Scientific Study of Religion* 14, no. 4 (December 1975): 390-95.

Stepanenko, V. 'Gerb Sovetskogo Soiuza.' *Vospitanie shkol'nikov*, no. 1 (1978): 16-17.

Stites, Richard. 'The Origins of Soviet Ritual Style: Symbol and Festival in the Russian Revolution.' In *Symbols of Power: The Esthetics of Political Legitimation in the Soviet Union and Eastern Europe*, 23-42. Stockholm: Almqvist & Wiksell International, 1987.

———. 'The Role of Ritual and Symbols.' In *Critical Companion to the Russian Revolution, 1914-1921*, edited by Edward Acton, V. Iu. Cherniaev, and William G. Rosenberg, 565-71. Bloomington: Indiana University Press, 1997.

Stites, Richard, and Michael E. Geisler. 'Russian Symbols – Nation, People, and Ideas.' In *National Symbols, Fractured Identities: Contesting the National Narrative*, edited by Michael E. Geisler, 101-17. Middlebury, VT: Middlebury College Press, 2005.

Strayer, Robert W. *Why Did the Soviet Union Collapse?: Understanding Historical Change*. Armonk, NY: M. E. Sharpe, 1998.

Sulemov, Vladimir Aleksandrovich. *Istoriia VLKSM i Vsesoiuznoi pionerskoi organizatsii imeni V. I. Lenina*. Moscow: Prosveshchenie, 1983.

Sun-tsu. *The Art of Warfare: The First English Translation Incorporating the Recently Discovered Yin-ch'üeh-shan Texts*. Translated by Roger T. Ames. New York: Ballantine Books, 1993.

Suny, Ronald Grigor. 'The Contradictions of Identity: Being Soviet and National in the USSR and After.' In *Soviet and Post-Soviet Identities*, edited by Mark Bassin and Catriona Kelly, 17-36. Cambridge: Cambridge University Press, 2012.

———. *Looking Toward Ararat: Armenia in Modern History*. Bloomington: Indiana University Press, 1993.

———. 'Reading Russia and the Soviet Union in the Twentieth Century: How the "West" Wrote Its History of the USSR.' In *The Cambridge History of Russia*, edited by Ronald Grigor Suny, Volume 3, The Twentieth Century, 5-64. Cambridge: Cambridge University Press, 2006.

———. *The Revenge of the Past: Nationalism, Revolution, and the Collapse of the Soviet Union*. Stanford, CA: Stanford University Press, 1993.

Suny, Ronald Grigor, ed. *The Cambridge History of Russia*. Vol. 3, The Twentieth Century. Cambridge: Cambridge University Press, 2006.

Şveţ, Ala. 'Staging the Transnistrian Identity Within the Heritage of Soviet Holidays.' *History and Anthropology* 24, no. 1 (March 2013): 98-116.

Taborsky, Edward. 'The Destalinized Stalinism.' *Southwestern Social Science Quarterly* 37, no. 4 (March 1957): 311-29.

Ter-Ghazaryan, Diana K. '"Civilizing the City Center": Symbolic Spaces and Narratives of the Nation in Yerevan's Post-Soviet Landscape.' *Nationalities Papers* 41, no. 4 (July 2013): 570-89.

———. 'Re-Imagining Yerevan in the Post-Soviet Era: Urban Symbolism and Narratives of the Nation in the Landscape of Armenia's Capital.' Unpublished PhD thesis, Florida International University, 2010.

Thomas, Dean. 'Flags and Emblems of the Democratic People's Republic of Korea: Vexillidolatry in Its Purest Form.' *Raven: A Journal of Vexillology* 21 (2014): 95-115.

Thrower, James. *Marxism-Leninism as a Political Religion: God's Commissar*. Lewiston, NY: Edwin Mellen Press, 1992.

Tiazhel'nikov, E. 'Bring Up Young Leninists.' *Soviet Education* 15, no. 3 (January 1973): 23-46.

———. 'Socialist Competition and the Indoctrination of Youth.' *Soviet Education* 17, no. 4 (February 1975): 70-91.

Titarenko, S. *Patriotism and Internationalism*. London: Soviet News, 1950.

Tokarev, A. A. 'Otritsanie, vstraivanie, postepennoe zabvenie: Gosudarstvennye strategii po otnosheniiu k sovetskomu naslediiu v Gruzii, Armenii i Azerbaidzhane.' *Vestnik. MGIMO-Universiteta* 5, no. 56 (September 2017): 60-80.

Tokluoglu, Ceylan. 'Definitions of National Identity, Nationalism and Ethnicity in Post-Soviet Azerbaijan in the 1990s.' *Ethnic and Racial Studies* 28, no. 4 (July 2005): 722-58.

Topolin, Mikhail Aleksandrovich. *Kremlevskie zvezdy*. Moscow: Moskovskii rabochii, 1980.

'Toward the Bright Future of Communism': Soviet Propaganda Posters from Brezhnev to Gorbachev [Exhibit Guide]. [Clinton, N.Y.]: Emerson Gallery, Hamilton College, 1995.

Trembicky, Walter. *Flags of Non-Russian Peoples Under Soviet Rule.* Published as *The Flag Bulletin* 8 no. 3. Lexington, MA: Flag Research Center, 1969.

Troebst, Stefan. '"We Are Transnistrians!" Post-Soviet Identity Management in the Dniester Valley.' *Ab Imperio*, no. 1 (2003): 437-66.

Tuchtenhagen, Ralph. 'The Problem of Identities in the Baltic Countries.' In *The Fall of an Empire, the Birth of a Nation: National Identities in Russia*, edited by Chris J. Chulos and Timo Piirainen, 141-60. Aldershot, England: Ashgate, 2000.

Tumarkin, Nina 'The Great Patriotic War as Myth and Memory.' *European Review* 11, no. 4 (October 2003): 595-611.

————. *Lenin Lives!: The Lenin Cult in Soviet Russia.* Cambridge, MA: Harvard University Press, 1983.

————. 'Myth and Memory in Soviet Society.' *Society* 24, no. 6 (October 1987): 69-72.

————. 'Political Ritual and the Cult of Lenin.' *Human Rights Quarterly* 5, no. 2 (May 1983): 203-6.

————. 'Religion, Bolshevism, and the Origins of the Lenin Cult.' *The Russian Review* 40, no. 1 (January 1981): 35-46.

Tuminez, Astrid S. 'Nationalism, Ethnic Pressures, and the Breakup of the Soviet Union.' *Journal of Cold War Studies* 5, no. 4 (Fall 2003): 81-136.

Union of Soviet Socialist Republics. Glavnoe upravlenie geodezii i kartografii. 'Karta narodov SSSR.' Moscow: Glavnoe upravlenie geodezii i kartografii, Ministerstva geologii i okhrany nedr SSSR, 1962.

Union of Soviet Socialist Republics. 'Karta narodov SSSR uchebnaia karta.' Moscow: GUGK, 1966.

United States. Central Intelligence Agency. 'Soviet Union Nationalities.' Map # 505173 6-82. Washington, D.C.: Central Intelligence Agency, 1982.

University of Nottingham. 'Propaganda and Ideology in Everyday Life - Online Course.' *FutureLearn*. Accessed July 2017. https://www.futurelearn.com/courses/propaganda/.

User 'iaruna', 'Good Bye Lenin!: Desovietyzatsiia Ukraïny. Kinets' 2013 - pochatok 2014 rokiv', interactive map, *Carto*, https://iaryna.carto.com/viz/b42d0d78-9b3b-11e3-9701-0ed66c7bc7f3/public_map.

Uspenskii, Lev Vasil'evich. *Pochemu ne inache?: Etomologicheskii slovarik shkol'nika.* Moscow: Izdatel'stvo Detskaia literatura, 1967.

Vainshtein, E. 'Pervyi pionerskii znachok.' *Sovetskii Kollektsioner*, 1964.

Various Artists. Collection of Soviet Postcards. Collected by Anne M. Platoff.

Vavilov, S. I., and B. A. Vvedenskii, eds. *Bol'shaia sovetskaia entsiklopediia.* Moscow: Gosudarstvennoe nauchnoe izdatel'stvo 'Bol'shaia sovetskaia entsiklopediia', 1949.

Velikanova, Olga. *Making of an Idol: On Uses of Lenin.* Göttingen: Muster-Schmidt, 1996.

'Victory Day: Soviet Liberators or Occupiers?', *Voice of America* (13 May 2011), http://blogs.voanews.com/russia-watch/2011/05/13/victory-day-soviet-liberators-or-occupiers/, accessed 29 August 2012.

Vihalemm, Triin, and Anu Masso. '(Re)Construction of Collective Identities after the Dissolution of the Soviet Union: The Case of Estonia.' *Nationalities Papers* 35, no. 1 (March 2007): 71-91.

Vishneva-Sarafanova, N. *The Privileged Generation: Children in the Soviet Union.* Moscow: Progress Publishers, 1984.

Vitkus, Zigmas. 'The Armenian Genocide - Not Forgotten.' *Armenpress News Agency (Yerevan, Armenia)*, 9 May 2020, *Access World News* database edition.

Votey, Scott E. 'Political Attitudes Reflected in Soviet Elementary Textbooks.' *Social Education* 42 (March 1978): 228-30.

Wagner, David G. 'Flag Usage in the Soviet Union.' *The Flag Bulletin* #122, v. 26, no. 5 (October 1987): 238-44.

178

Walker, Gregory P. M. *Soviet Book Publishing Policy*. Cambridge: Cambridge University Press, 1978.

Wall Street Journal (Online). ProQuest subscription database.

Wallace, Ruth A. 'Emile Durkheim and the Civil Religion Concept.' *Review of Religious Research* 18, no. 3 (Spring 1977): 287-90.

———. 'The Secular Ethic and The Spirit of Patriotism.' *Sociological Analysis* 34, no. 1 (Spring 1973): 3-11.

Weaver, Kitty D. *Lenin's Grandchildren: Preschool Education in the Soviet Union*. New York: Simon and Schuster, 1971.

Weber, David A. 'Changing Sacredness and Historical Memory of Moscow's Red Square.' *Studies in Slavic Cultures* 8 (August 2009): 43-64.

Weinstein, Eugene A. 'Development of the Concept of Flag and the Sense of National Identity.' *Child Development* 28, no. 2 (June 1957): 167-74.

Weitman, Sasha R. 'National Flags: A Sociological Overview.' *Semiotica* 8, no. 4 (January 1973): 328-67.

Wende Museum of the Cold War. Collection of Soviet Artifacts. Culver City, CA.

West, Ellis M. 'A Proposed Neutral Definition of Civil Religion.' *Journal of Church and State* 22, no. 1 (Winter 1980): 23-40.

White, Stephen. *The Bolshevik Poster*. New Haven: Yale University Press, 1988.

Wilson, Sarah. 'The Soviet Pavilion in Paris.' In *Art of the Soviets: Painting, Sculpture, and Architecture in a One-Party State, 1917-1992*, edited by Matthew Cullerne Bown and Brandon Taylor, 106-20. Manchester: Manchester University Press, 1993.

Wimberley, Ronald C. 'Testing the Civil Religion Hypothesis.' *Sociological Analysis* 37, no. 4 (Winter 1976): 341-52.

Wimberley, Ronald C., Donald A. Clelland, Thomas C. Hood, and C. M. Lipsey. 'The Civil Religious Dimension: Is It There?' *Social Forces* 54, no. 4 (June 1976): 890-900.

Yanker, Gary. 'The Political Poster: A Worldwide Phenomenon.' *World Affairs* 133, no. 3 (December 1970): 215-23.

Yelchin, Eugene. *Breaking Stalin's Nose*. New York: Henry Holt, 2011.

Yurchak, Alexei. 'Bodies of Lenin: The Hidden Science of Communist Sovereignty.' *Representations* 129, no. 1 (February 2015): 116-57.

——— 'Form Versus Matter: Miraculous Relics and Lenin's Scientific Body.' In *Death and Mortality: From Individual to Communal Perspectives*, edited by Outi Hakola, Sara Heinämaa, and Sami Pihlström, 61-81. Helsinki: Helsinki Collegium for Advanced Studies, 2015.

Zagorskii, V. B. *Bumazhnye denezhnye znaki Rossii: Gosudarstvennye vypuski s 1769 goda: Katalog = Paper Money of Russia: State Issues From 1769: Catalogue*. Saint Petersburg: Standart-Kollektsiia, 2010.

———. *Pochtovye kartochki SSSR 1938-1953: Spravochnik tsen*. Saint Petersburg: Standart-Kollektsiia, 2006.

Zagorsky, V. B., ed. *Postage Stamp Catalogue: Russia 1857-1917, RSFSR 1918-1923, USSR 1923-1991*. Hallandale, FL: Zagorsky, Inc., 2013.

Zajda, Joseph. 'The Moral Curriculum in the Soviet School.' *Comparative Education* 24, no. 3 (1988): 389-404.

Zbarskii, I. B., Samuel Hutchinson, and Barbara Bray. *Lenin's Embalmers*. London: Harvill, 1998.

Zei, Vida. 'Stamps and the Politics of National Representation.' *Javnost – The Public* 4, no. 1 (1997): 65-84.

Zeldin, Mary-Barbara. 'The Religious Nature of Russian Marxism.' *Journal for the Scientific Study of Religion* 8, no. 1 (Spring 1969): 100-111.

Zhukov, I. A., Iu. V. Pogodaev, and A. I. Cherepov. *Znaki i znachki Komsomola: Ocnovnye znaki komsomola (KIM, RLKSM, RKSM i VLKSM): (1920-1991 gg.)*. Moscow: Izdatel'stvo 'Lukomor'e', 2014.

Zikmund, Joseph, II. 'National Anthems as Political Symbols.' *Australian Journal of Politics and History* 15, no. 3 (December 1969): 73-80.

Znamensky, Pierre, and Guy Gallice. *Sous les plis du drapeau rouge*. Rodez: Rouergue, 2010.

Znamierowski, Alfred. *The World Encyclopedia of Flags: The Definitive Guide to International Flags, Banners, Standards and Ensigns*. London: Lorenz, 1999.

Zuev, Iurii Petrovich, and Natal'ia Viacheslavovna Truseneva. *Rol' sotsialisticheskoi obriadnosti v formirovanii nravstvennogo oblika sovetskogo cheloveka*. Moscow: Znanie, 1978.

About the Author

Anne M. (Annie) Platoff was born in Topeka, Kansas in 1962, weeks before the Cuban Missile Crisis. She was politically socialized in American Civil Religion through the Topeka Public Schools and her membership in the Girl Scouts of the USA. She holds a BA in political science and history from Kansas State University, an MS in Library Science from the University of North Texas, an MA in historical studies from the University of Houston – Clear Lake, a graduate certificate in museum studies from Arizona State University, and a PhD in history from the University of Leicester. Annie is currently employed as a Research and Engagement Librarian at the University of California, Santa Barbara specializing in science, engineering, and Slavic studies.

Photo by H. Rafael Chacon

As a vexillologist Annie has published on topics including *vodou* flags, the lunar flag assembly, symbols on NASA mission patches, the Soviet Victory Banner (*Znamia Pobody*), and the bear as a symbol of Russia. She is a two-time recipient of the Captain Driver Award for the best paper presented to the North American Vexillological Association (NAVA). Annie received the Vexillon Award from the Fédération internationale des associations vexillologiques (FIAV) for her book, *Russian Regional Flags*, and FIAV's Whitney Smith Award for her presentation of a co-authored paper at the Sydney Flag Congress (ICV 26). She has also been recognized as a Fellow of FIAV, a Fellow of the Vexillological Association of the State of Texas, and a Fellow of the Flag Research Center. Annie manages NAVA's Digital Library, has served as a member of the NAVA Executive Board, and is a Trustee of the Flag Heritage Foundation.

Selected Works by the Author:

Anne M. Platoff. '*Drapo Vodou*: Sacred Standards of Haitian Vodou,' *Flag Research Quarterly*, no. 7 / vol. 2. #3-4 (August 2015), pp. 1, 3-23. https://escholarship.org/uc/item/5mc5w4g2

Annie Platoff. *Eyes on the Red Planet: A History of Manned Mars Mission Planning, 1952-1970*. NASA CR-2001-208928. Houston: NASA Johnson Space Center, July 2001. https://escholarship.org/uc/item/0dx7866r

Anne M. Platoff. 'Flags as Flair: The Iconography of Space Shuttle Mission Patches. Part 1: The Origin of Mission Patches, and Patches of the Pre-shuttle Era,' *Flag Research Quarterly*, no. 4 (December 2013), pp. 1, 3-8. https://escholarship.org/uc/item/6db004hr

Anne M. Platoff. 'Flags as Flair: The Iconography of Space Shuttle Mission Patches. Part 2: Patches in the Space Shuttle Era,' *Flag Research Quarterly*, no. 6 (June 2014), pp. 1, 3-14. https://escholarship.org/uc/item/6db004hr

Anne M. Platoff. *Flags in Space: NASA Symbols and Flags in the U.S. Manned Space Program.* Monograph published as volume 46, # 5-6 of *The Flag Bulletin: The International Journal of Vexillology* (Sept.-Dec. 2007), published in December 2010. https://escholarship.org/uc/item/1tt282fs

Anne M. Platoff. 'The 'Forward Russia' Flag: Examining the Changing Use of the Bear as a Symbol of Russia,' *Raven: A Journal of Vexillology*, 19 (2012), pp. 99-126. https://escholarship.org/uc/item/5xz8x2zc

Anne M. Platoff. [Memoir About Whitney Smith]. *The Flag Bulletin: The International Journal of Vexillology* (July 2008-October 2011), pp. 108-113.

Anne M. Platoff. 'Of Tablecloths and Soviet Relics: A Study of the Banner of Victory (*Znamia Pobedy*),' *Raven: A Journal of Vexillology*, 20 (2013), pp. 55-84. https://escholarship.org/uc/item/2db980gg

Anne M. Platoff. 'The Pike-Pawnee Flag Incident: Reexamining a Vexillological Legend,' *Raven: A Journal of Vexillology*, 6 (1999), pp. 1-8. https://escholarship.org/uc/item/58c1k52h

Anne M. Platoff. 'Political and Technical Aspects of Placing a Flag on the Moon,' *Quest: The History of Spaceflight Quarterly*, 16 #2 (2009), p. 34-38.

Anne M. Platoff. *Russian Regional Flags: The Flags of the Subjects of the Russian Federation.* n.p.: North American Vexillological Association, 2009. ISBN: 978-0-9747728-2-0. Book published as volume 16 of *Raven: A Journal of Vexillology.* https://escholarship.org/uc/item/8c36x1g5

Anne M. Platoff. 'A Shuttle Full of Flags: Use of Flags in the Space Shuttle Program.' In *Proceedings of the 25th International Congress of Vexillology* (n.p.: Nederlandse Vereniging voor Vlaggenkunde and Stichting Vlaggenparade Rotterdam, 2016), pp. 6/1-6/26. https://escholarship.org/uc/item/3jr7w2mc

Anne M. Platoff. 'Six Flags Over Luna: The Role of Flags in Moon Landing Conspiracy Theories.' In *Proceedings of the 24th International Congress of Vexillology* (n.p.: North American Vexillological Association, 2011), pp. 820-881. https://escholarship.org/uc/item/5h31r40r

Anne M. Platoff. '*Soiuz* and Symbolic Union: Representations of Unity in Soviet State Symbols.' *Flagmaster* no. 160 (Summer 2020), pp. 36-45. https://escholarship.org/uc/item/5rd7039g

Anne M. Platoff. '*Soiuz* and Symbolic Union: Representations of Unity in Soviet Symbolism.' *Raven: A Journal of Vexillology*, vol. 27 (2020), pp. 23-97. https://escholarship.org/uc/item/6mk5f6c8

Anne M. Platoff. 'Soviet Children's Flags,' *Raven: A Journal of Vexillology*, 17 (2010), pp. 63-84. https://escholarship.org/uc/item/1fv263z8

Anne M. Platoff. 'Where No Flag Has Gone Before: Political and Technical Aspects of Placing a Flag on the Moon,' *Raven: A Journal of Vexillology*, 1 (1994), pp. 3-10. https://nava.org/digital-library/raven/Raven_v01_1994_p003-016.pdf

Anne M. Platoff. 'Where No Flag Has Gone Before,' *Final Frontier*, 7 (July/August 1994): 74-75. Reprinted in *JSC Space News Roundup*, 33 (July 22, 1994), p. 3. https://historycollection.jsc.nasa.gov/JSCHistoryPortal/history/roundups/issues/94-07-22.pdf#page=3

Anne M. Platoff. 'Where No Flag Has Gone Before: Political and Technical Aspects of Placing a Flag on the Moon.' NASA CR-188251. Houston: NASA Johnson Space Center, 1992. http://escholarship.org/uc/item/93t5x9dq; https://ntrs.nasa.gov/citations/19940008327

Anne M. Platoff. 'The World Flag of the Girl Guides and Girl Scouts,' *NAVA News*, 22 #5 (September/October 1989), p. 3. https://nava.org/digital-library/NAVANews_1989_v22no5.pdf#page=3

Anne M. Platoff. 'Zastave u Svemiru: Zastave programa Space Shuttle / Flags in Space: Flags of the Space Shuttle Program,' *Grb i Zastava*, 5 #10 (November 2011), pp. 5-7. https://escholarship.org/uc/item/9dz007nw

The Flag Heritage Foundation Monograph and Translation Series

Earlier volumes in the Series were edited by David F. Phillips. After his passing, the continuing publication of the series is a tribute to his service to the Foundation and his scholarship in the fields of heraldry and vexillology.

1: *The Estonian Flag*, by Karl Aun (2009)

2: *Emblems of the Indian States*, by David F. Phillips (2011)

3: *The Haitian Flag of Independence*, by Odette Roy Fombrun (2013)

4: *The Double Eagle*, by David F. Phillips (2014)

5: *Flags and Emblems of Colombia*, by Pedro Julio Dousdebés (2016)

6: *Vexillology as a Social Science*, by Željko Heimer (2017)

7. *Japanese Heraldry and Heraldic Flags*, by David F. Phillips, Emmanuel Valerio, and Nozomi Kariyasu (2018)

8: *The Sun and the Lion as Symbols of the Republic of Macedonia*, by Jovan Jonovski (2020)

9. *Symbols in Service to the State: Flags and Other Symbols in Soviet Civil Religion*, by Anne M. Platoff (2021)

Colophon

This book was composed and laid out using Microsoft Word. It was printed with soy-based inks on a 60 pound offset paper (12 point C2S paper for the covers) by Suburban Press of Hayward, California, on a 4-colour 40" Perfector Man Roland Rekord press for the main text and a 6-colour 40" Man Roland 600 press with AQ coater for the covers and colour plates. The principal font is Times New Roman: 12 point for body text, 11 point for block quotes, and 10 point for endnotes and the bibliography. Image captions are also set in Times New Roman, 10 point. The first printing was 1600 copies.

Map of the Union of Soviet Socialist Republics

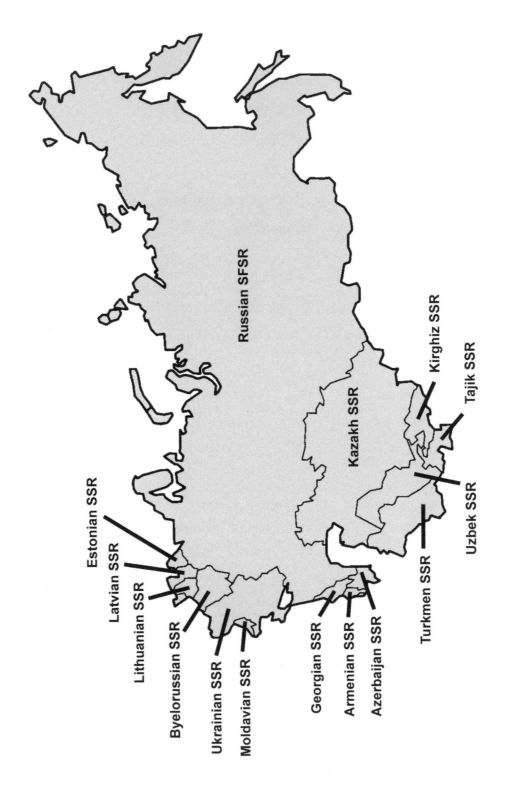

EVOLUTION OF THE BADGE OF THE RED ARMY

Left: Badge of the Workers' and Peasants' Red Army with the red star, hammer, and plough (ca. 1918-1922). **Centre:** Badge of the Workers' and Peasants' Red Army as established by RRMC[1] Order No. 753 (13 April 1922). **Right:** Badge of the Workers' and Peasants' Red Army as established by RRMC Order No. 1691(11 July 1922). *See discussion of figures 2.4-2.6, page 25.*

EARLY EMBLEMS OF THE
RUSSIAN SOVIET FEDERATIVE SOCIALIST REPUBLIC

Left: Seal of the Russian Soviet Federative Socialist Republic (RSFSR) (1918-1920). **Right:** Coat of arms of the RFSFR (1920-1956). *See discussion of figures 2.1-2.2, page 23.*

---

[1] RRMC is an abbreviation for Republic's Revolutionary Military Council. In Russian this would be *Revoliutsionnyi Voennyi Sovet Respubliki (RVSR).*

STATE EMBLEMS OF THE SOVIET REPUBLICS

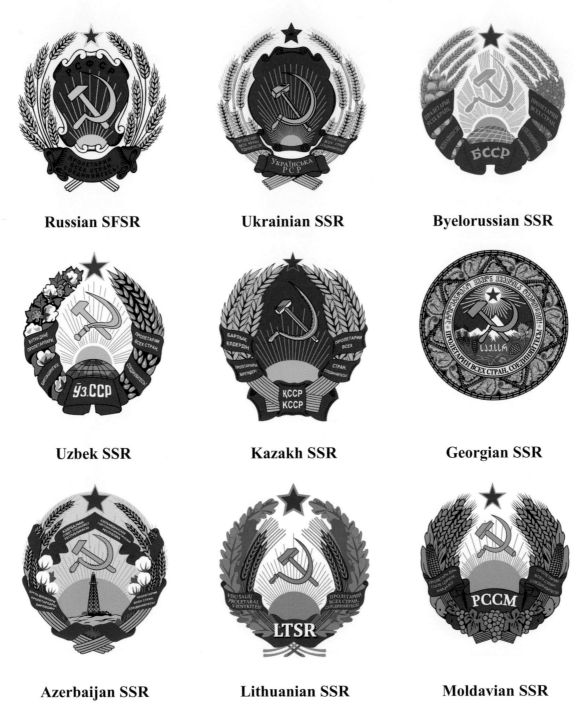

Russian SFSR   **Ukrainian SSR**   **Byelorussian SSR**

Uzbek SSR   **Kazakh SSR**   **Georgian SSR**

Azerbaijan SSR   **Lithuanian SSR**   **Moldavian SSR**

State Arms of the Soviet Republics in Soviet order of precedence ('Constitutional order'). *See discussion of figures A1-A9, page 122.*

STATE EMBLEMS OF THE SOVIET REPUBLICS (CONTINUED)

Latvian SSR   **Kirghiz SSR**   **Tajik SSR**

Armenian SSR   **Turkmen SSR**   **Estonian SSR**

State Arms of the Soviet Republics in Soviet order of precedence (continued). *See discussion of figures A10-A15, pages 122-123.*

EARLY DESIGNS FOR SOVIET REPUBLIC FLAGS

Flags of the Ukrainian Soviet Socialist Republic based upon the red banner of the revolution and the Soviet national flag. *Left:* Flag used 1919-1929, *Right:* Flag used 1937-1950. *See discussion of figures A16-A17, page 123. See also, final versions of all 15 republic flags on inside back cover.*

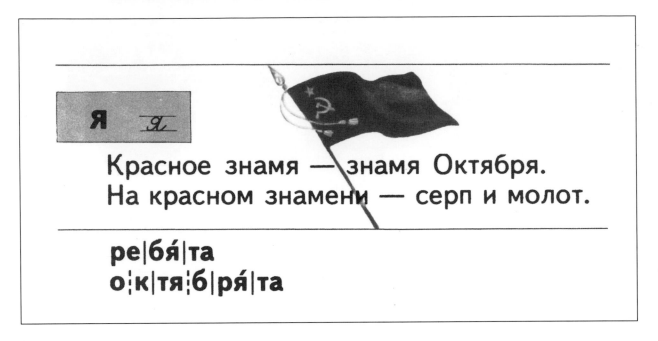

Explanation of the Soviet flag from a children's alphabet book. Text reads 'The red banner is the banner of October. On the red banner is the sickle and hammer'. Beneath the text are the words for 'children' and 'Little Octobrists'. *See discussion of figure 3.3, page 52.*

A group of fifteen children celebrate the 'unbreakable union of freeborn republics'. *See discussion of figure 3.5, page 53.*

MEMBERSHIP BADGES OF THE LITTLE OCTOBRIST ORGANIZATION

Three variations of the Little Octobrist badge combining the red star and an image of Lenin as a young child. The plastic badge at *left* is from the late 1950s. Dates for the other two specimens are unknown. *See discussion of figures 3.6-3.8, page 55.*

FLAG OF THE LITTLE OCTOBRIST ORGANIZATION

Flag of the Little Octobrists from 1986. *See discussion of figure 3.9, page 56.*

MEMBERSHIP BADGES OF THE YOUNG PIONEER ORGANIZATION

Top Row: Emblems of the Young Pioneers from the 1920s. ***Left:*** Badge used from 1923-1927 reading 'Be Prepared'. ***Right:*** Tie clip with motto 'Always Prepared' (1929-ca. 1942). ***Centre Row:*** Young Pioneer emblem used during the Second World War. ***Bottom Row: Left:*** Badge, circa 1946-1962. ***Right:*** Emblem used 1962-1991. *See discussion of figures 3.10-3.14, page 59.*

BANNERS AND FLAGS OF THE YOUNG PIONEER ORGANIZATION

Left: Banner of the school-level Pioneer troop showing the emblem in use from 1962-1991. ***Right:*** The flag of a Young Pioneer detachment from the same period. *See discussion of figures 3.15-3.16, page 60.*

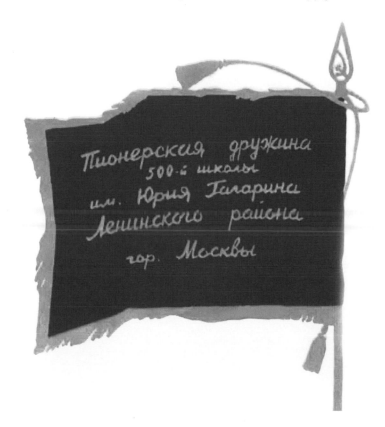

Reverse side of a Pioneer banner showing the honorary name of the detachment. The text reads 'Pioneer detachment, school 500, in the name of Iurii Gagarin, Lenin Region, City of Moscow. *See discussion of figure 3.17, page 60.*

SOVIET CHILDREN DEMONSTRATING PATRIOTISM WITH FLAGS

Three postcards for May Day showing children with red flags. *See discussion of figures 3.19-3.21, page 66.*

Litte holiday flag (toy flag) designed for Soviet children. The design features the Soviet state emblem and the abbreviation 'SSSR' (USSR) in Russian. *See discussion of figure 3.31, page 68.*

PROPAGANDA POSTERS INCORPORATING SOVIET SYMBOLS

Three Soviet propaganda posters showing different ways in which symbols were used on this mode of communication. *See discussion of figures 4.26-4.28, page 90.*

DECORATIVE ELEMENTS FROM MOSCOW METRO STATIONS

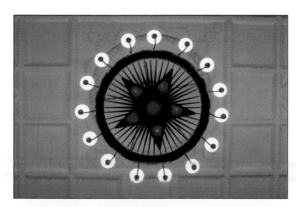

Examples of the use of Soviet symbols in the ornamentation of Moscow Metro stations. *See discussion of figures 4.12-4.15, page 85.*

POSTAGE STAMPS WITH LENIN IMAGERY

Three stamps using images of Lenin to portray the concept of legitimacy. *Left:* Stamp showing Lenin as the intellectual heir of Marx. *Centre:* Postage stamp showing the progression of Communist ideology from Marx and Engels, to Lenin, and then to Stalin. *Right:* Stamp portraying the Communist Party of the Soviet Union as continuing the work of Lenin. *See discussion of figures 4.35-4.37, page 92.*

COMMEMORATIVE STAMPS WITH SOVIET SYMBOLS

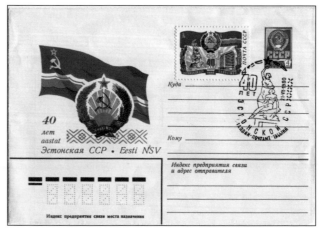

Top Left: Stamp for the New Year (1982). *Top Centre:* Souvenir sheet for May Day (1989). *Top Right:* Stamp showing the Soviet flag and the dome of the Kremlin Senate (1980). *Bottom Left:* Lenin stamp on a souvenir sheet showing a unity flag display (1982). *Bottom Right:* Postal Cover commemorating 40 Years of the Estonian SSR (1980). *See discussion of figures 4.38-4.39, page 93; figures 4.41-4.42, page 94; and figure 4.44, page 94.*

ZNACHKI (BADGES) USING FLAGS AND ARMS TO PORTRAY UNITY

Znachki (metal badges) for Soviet anniversaries incorporating unity flag displays (1972 and 1982). Highly simplified flags of the republics are arranged in 1977 Constitutional order from the top down. ***Left:*** Flags are tiled left to right, in four rows against the background of the Soviet national flag. ***Right***: Flags are in order from left to right, starting at the top and arranged around the Soviet national emblem. The red banner of revolution bearing the letters *SSSR* tops off the display. *See discussion of figures 4.47-4.48, page 96.*

ZNACHKI (BADGES) FROM UNITY SETS FOR COLLECTORS

Znachki from five different unity sets. ***Top to Bottom, Left to Right:*** Ukrainian SSR, Armenian SSR, Georgian SSR, Latvian SSR, and Turkmen SSR (various dates). *See discussion of figures 4.49-4.53, page 97.*

HOLIDAY POSTCARDS INCORPORATING SOVIET SYMBOLS

Three holiday postcards with military themes. **Left:** 'Glory to the Soviet Armed Forces!'. **Centre:** 'Glory to the armed forces of the USSR!' **Right:** 'Glory to the armed forces of the USSR!' *See discussion of figures 4.54-4.56, page 98.*

Two cards for May Day celebrating labour. **Left:** 'With the holiday 1 May!'; text in the background says 'peace', 'labour', 'May', and 'socialism' in various languages. **Right:** '1 May'. *See discussion of figures 4.57-4.58, page 99.*

Two May Day postcards using the 3-races theme to illustrate internationism. **Left:** Text reads 'Long live 1 May!' in Latvian. **Right:** Banners read 'Peace, May, Labour'. Text below reads '1 May – Day of the International Solidarity of the Workers!'. *See discussion of figures 4.59-4.60, page 99.*

Two cards for Great October. *Left:* 'Glory to Great October'. *Right:* The hammer and sickle are formed from text reading '1917 October'. The greeting below reads 'With the holiday!' *See discussion of figures 4.61-4.62, page 100.*

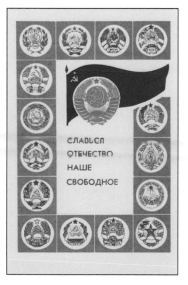

Postcards with unity displays of Soviet and republic symbols. *Left:* Card for May Day, reading 'Peace, Labour, May'. *Centre:* Card for International Women's Day with text '8 March' and 'Glory to Soviet women'. *Right:* 'Be glorious, our free fatherland', a phrase from the national anthem. *See discussion of figures 4.63-4.65, page 100.*

HOLIDAY POSTCARDS INCORPORATING SOVIET SYMBOLS

Two Soviet holiday postcards using displays of republic flags to illustrate Soviet unity. **Left:** Card for May Day reading '1 May' and 'With the holiday!' **Right:** Card for the anniversary of the October Revolution reading 'With the holiday Great October!' *See discussion of figures 4.74-4.75, page 104.*

New Year's postcards with Soviet symbols, reading 'With the New Year!'. **Left:** Text at the top of the card reads 'Glory to the Union of Soviet Republics'. **Right:** Vera Mukhina's 'Worker and Kolkhoz Woman' are superimposed over the clock face of the Kremlin's Saviour Tower. *See discussion of figure 4.72, page 103; figures 4.67-4.68, page 101.*

SOVIET SYMBOLS AND THE NEW YEAR

Soviet symbols on New Year's ornaments. The red star tree topper resembles a Kremlin star, as seen on a card with *Ded Morozh* on Red Square. *See discussion of figures 4.69-4.71 and 4.73, pages 102-3.*

POST-SOVIET SYMBOLS IN CENTRAL ASIA REPUBLICS

National emblems of independent Tajikistan (***left***) and Uzbekistan (***right***), influenced by the socialist style of heraldry. Both coats of arms retain sun imagery and Soviet-style agricultural wreaths, replacing the red colour of the ribbon with stripes from their flags of independence. A new distinctly Uzbek star, bearing Islamic symbols, has replaced the red star crest. *See discussion of figures 5.1-5.2, page 109.*

SYMBOLS OF THE PRIDNESTROVIAN MOLDAVIAN REPUBLIC

Greater arms (*left*) and lesser arms (*right*) of the Pridnestrovian Moldavian Republic (Transnistria), derived from the arms of the Moldavian Soviet Socialist Republic. *See discussion of figures 5.4-5.5, page 112.*

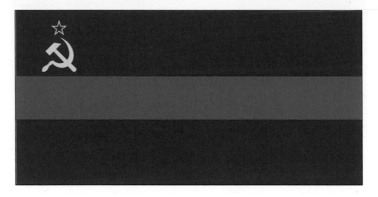

Flag of the breakaway Pridnestrovian Moldavian Republic (Transnistria), replicating the flag of Soviet Moldavia. *See discussion of figure 5.3, page 112.*

SOVIET-INFLUENCED SYMBOLS OF THE REPUBLIC OF BELARUS

Soviet-inspired state symbols of Belarus adopted after the 1995 referendum. *See discussion of figures 5.7-5.8, page 116.*